LIVY: BOO

G000123261

LIVY

BOOK XXX

Edited by

H.E. Butler

and

H.H. Scullard

Bristol Classical Press

This impression 2005
This edition published in 2004 by
Bristol Classical Press
an imprint of
Gerald Duckworth & Co. Ltd.
90-93 Cowcross Street, London EC1M 6BF
Tel: 020 7490 7300
Fax: 020 7490 0080
inquiries@duckworth-publishers.co.uk
www.ducknet.co.uk

First published by Methuen in 1939

A catalogue record for this book is available
from the British Library

ISBN 1-85399-679-3

Printed and bound in Great Britain by
Antony Rowe Ltd, Eastbourne

PREFACE

THE Thirtieth Book of Livy presents few textual difficulties, and it has not seemed worth while to include any account of the manuscript tradition. The text here printed contains no novelties, though not based on any one published text.

The thanks of the editors are due to the Clarendon Press for permission to include a few pages dealing with Livy's life and work, which originally appeared in the Introduction to " The Close of the Second Punic War " (edited by H. E. Butler). For further details about the history of the period covered by this book of Livy, reference may be made here once and for all to " Scipio Africanus in the Second Punic War " by H. H. Scullard and to the literature there cited.

H. E. BUTLER
H. H. SCULLARD

January, 1939

v

CONTENTS

MAPS AND PLANS

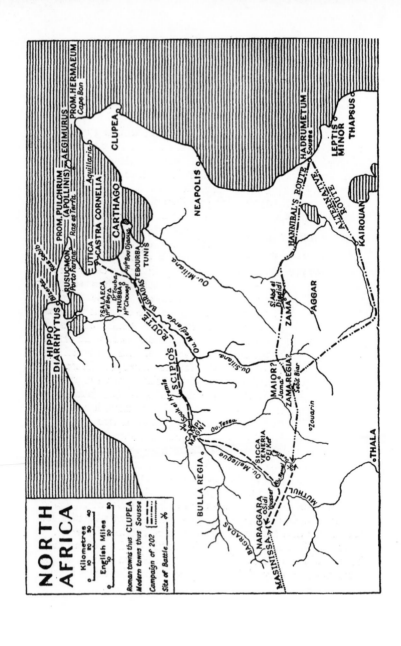

NORTH AFRICA

Kilometres
0 10 20 30 40

English Miles
0 10 20 30

Roman towns thus CLUPEA
Modern towns thus Sousse

Campaign of 202
Site of Battle ⚔

PROM.HERMAEUM
Cape Bon

PROM.PULCHRUM
(APOLLINIS) AEGIMURUS
Ras es Tarfa. Aquillaria.b

CLUPEA

HIPPO
DIARRHYTUS
Bizerta
RUSUCMON
Porto Farina.
UTICA
CASTRA CORNELIA
CARTHAGO
TUNIS

NEAPOLIS

LEPTIS
MINOR
Sousse
HADRUMETUM

THAPSUS

?SALAECA
H^te el Bey. Dr.Touba,
THUBBA Dr.Touba,
H^te Chouigui H^te Bou Djaoua

TEBOURBA
BAGRADAS ROUTE

SCIPIO'S ROUTE

Ou.Miliana.

Ou.Siliana.

S.i Abd el Djedidi
ZAMA
AGGAR

HANNIBAL'S ROUTE
ALTERNATIVE ROUTE

KAIROUAN

CAMP?
Souk el Kramis
Ou.Tessa

MAIOR?
Jama
ZAMA-REGIA?
Sebia Biar
?Zouarin

Ou.Milianda

Ou.Mellegue

BULLA REGIA

SICCA
VENERIA
Ou.Kef

MUTHUL

THALA

NARAGGARA
Sidi Youssef

MASINISSA

BAGRADAS

INTRODUCTION

1. ROME AND CARTHAGE

WORLD Dominion was the prize set before the victor at the battle of Zama, which forms the culminating episode of this book. The fact that the victory fell to Rome has had a profound effect on the later history of Western Europe. Carthage had little to give the world, Rome had much. Through their predilection for law and order and their powers of organization and administration, the Romans built up a political framework which ultimately included nearly the whole civilized world. The dream of Alexander the Great of introducing a unity into world history was achieved by Rome. With unity came peace and the rule of law, so that with the frontiers securely guarded for centuries, the inhabitants of the Roman Empire could develop a common Graeco–Roman civilization. True, the barbarians from the North at length broke through the frontiers, and Rome herself went down before the invaders, but not before she had achieved her great work of Romanizing Western Europe. Here the Latin language and Roman civilization were too deeply rooted to be obliterated by the tides of the barbarian invasions: rather they determined the direction of the future history of these lands, a direction which has been followed until to-day. Thus the Romans succeeded where the Greeks had failed; but where they felt their national genius inferior to the Greek, as in literature, art, architecture, and philosophy, they showed their admiration by a humble imitation and by passing on the legacy of Greece to later generations. Thus the modern world owes Rome a double debt: both for her own achievements, and for preserving and transmitting the achievements of Greece.

But if Carthage had won the battle of Zama and had been enabled to crush Rome, the world we live in might have been a very different place. For Carthage herself could offer little: no great literature or art, no profound ideals of law or government; a city of middlemen, her citizens preferred to handle the money-making products of commerce and industry rather than to pass on the heritage of thought and beauty which Greece had given to mankind. Thus Zama was in a real sense one of the decisive battles of the world. In the conflict itself, for one dramatic moment all hung in the balance: would the Roman cavalry break off their pursuit of the enemy's horsemen in time to hurl themselves upon the rear of the Carthaginian infantry before it succeeded in breaking the Roman line? How it came about that the fate of the civilized world was so precariously balanced on the field of Zama we must now consider by tracing briefly the earlier history of Rome and Carthage.

Carthage had been founded as a trading settlement by Phoenicians from Tyre about 814 B.C. on the coast of what is known to-day as the Bay of Tunis. A better position could scarcely have been chosen: situated on a low hill on a peninsula which afforded both room for expansion and protection from the natives, the city lay sheltered in the heart of the bay. The hinterland was fertile, and her prominent position in the mid-Mediterranean allowed Carthage to trade with east and west and to control trans-Mediterranean shipping. Thus the city prospered and its merchants sailed far afield, Himilco to explore the Atlantic tin-routes which led to Britain, Hanno to bring back gold and ivory from the west coast of Africa. Carthage soon outstripped the other Phoenician trading stations in the Western Mediterranean, and gradually built up a far-flung empire which embraced much of the coastal district of North Africa, the western end of Sicily, Sardinia and a large part of Spain. Thus the western half of the Mediterranean became a Carthaginian preserve, which was closed to foreign shipping. But although the strength of the arm of Carthage was felt far afield and the condition of her subjects may on the whole have been tolerable, there is little ground to believe that she was able to infuse a spirit of loyalty and devotion into this empire, which was held together rather by force and common commercial interests.

The felicity of this empire depended largely on the unusual stability of the Carthaginian constitution, which attracted the interest of Greek political thinkers such as Aristotle. At the head of the State we find two annually-elected magistrates: the Romans called them Suffetes, but the Carthaginian form of the word is Shophetim, which is the same word that the Hebrews, the kinsmen of the Semitic Carthaginians, used to describe the Judges of early Israel. The conduct of State affairs rested with a Council of Thirty (called the 'seniores' by Livy), which included the Suffetes, and with a Senate of Three Hundred. There was an Assembly of all the citizens, which elected the Suffetes, the members of both Councils and the generals, but beyond this it had little power; and even in the elections systematic bribery, which was one of the most vicious features of Carthaginian life, may have left the real decision in the hands of the nobles. The real power, however, lay with a group of magistrates whom the Carthaginians called Pentarchies or Boards of Five; they elected a Council of One Hundred and Four Judges who had supreme judicial power. These two groups, Pentarchs and Judges, worked hand-in-glove, and controlled affairs to such an extent that the State gradually succumbed to their domination and Carthage was at the mercy of a corrupt oligarchy of nobles.

To support her Empire, Carthage needed money, men, and ships. The first she derived from tribute and custom dues. Her army by the third century B.C. was formed largely of her subjects and hired mercenaries; the Carthaginians themselves avoided military service, and preferred to force, or to pay, others to protect their interests. Thus the Carthaginian army often comprised a motley crowd with little or no national feeling, which might turn against its paymaster if things went ill; but when disciplined and organized by a general of genius, it developed into a first-class fighting machine. The skill of the seamen and

B

navigators of Carthage was well known, but it is unlikely that she normally found it necessary to keep a large navy afloat to safeguard her commerce or to threaten her subjects. In time of peace many vessels would be laid up in the dockyards, and the crews would only be called up in time of need. But when danger threatened, she could send a formidable fleet to sea.

Carthaginian civilization is not attractive. Her commerce and carrying trade made her rich in this world's goods, but there is little evidence to show that she sought the things of the spirit. Even her industry aimed at mass-production and cheapness rather than beauty. Her art was unoriginal and unattractive, save when it followed Greek or Egyptian models. The Punic language, which is akin to Hebrew, showed some virility; but there is no suggestion that any great literature was produced. Carthaginian cult and religion were cruel, gloomy, and licentious. The Canaanitish deities, Baal, Tanit, and Astarte, inspired in their worshippers a fanatical devotion which did not shrink from self-immolation or human sacrifice, so that in hours of national crisis infants from noble families continued to be " passed through the fire " to Moloch. To the end the Carthaginians remained Oriental and unpopular in the Western world. But though the Greeks and Romans regarded them as cringing and salaaming hucksters whose god was Mammon, men indifferent to the goodwill of their subjects which they could not win, yet it is well to remember with Cicero that they would scarcely have held an Empire for 600 years if they had lacked all political wisdom and statecraft, and that some of the world's greatest soldiers came from the Punic house of Barca.

The Romans had created a very different way of life and tradition. Before meeting the Carthaginians in war they had extended their power throughout Italy, but this success had been achieved not by following a selfish policy of exploitation ; rather it was the result of wise and generous statecraft. Rome had built up a political framework which embraced the various peoples of Italy in one common Confederacy, and so had welded together a nation, proud of its unity and loyal to its leader. The two guiding principles of Roman policy were Incorporation and Alliance. Some or all of the rights and privileges of Roman citizenship had been extended to a large part of Central Italy, while the other peoples of the peninsula remained in theory independent states bound to Rome by treaties of alliance. These allies surrendered their foreign policy to Rome's direction, but retained their local self-government and paid no tribute to Rome, except in the form of military service. Only Roman citizens were called upon to pay taxes, but citizens and allies alike were expected to fight in defence of their common freedom.

Gradually the reign of law superseded lawlessness throughout the peninsula. As early as the middle of the fifth century B.C., by a remarkable achievement, the Romans, who were only a small community of peasant-proprietors, had established a body of law which found its sanction not in the authority of a divine or human law-giver, but in a sense of justice and equity which was inherent in the peculiar genius of the Latin race. But Rome's greatest gift to Italy was the *pax Romana*: peace was substituted for war as the normal condition, and from the fourth century onwards foreign invaders, save only Pyrrhus and Hannibal, were held at arm's length. Rome was thus not primarily a dominating military Power, but the head of a confederacy which gave Italy some kind of political, economic, and social unity; and the moral justification of her conquest of Italy is that when foreign invaders, such as Pyrrhus and Hannibal, attacked Italy in the expectation that the various peoples would flock to their standards in revolt against the supposed tyrannical rule of Rome, they found instead that the peoples of Italy preferred to remain members of a confederacy to which they were bound by ties of loyalty as well as of self-interest.

This skilfully constructed Confederacy was one cause of

the Roman advance to world power. To this we may add
the advantages derived from their geographical position,
their superior man-power and war-craft. Polybius, a
Greek historian who lived in the second century B.C.,
emphasized two further causes: their excellent constitution and their moral qualities, points which deserve a
little more attention. Superficially the machinery of their
central government might resemble that of Carthage:
they had two magistrates at the head of the executive, a
senate, and a popular assembly. But the men who
administered the two constitutions worked in a different
spirit. Carthage was dominated by a corrupt oligarchy,
while the Roman constitution, as Polybius points out, was
the well-balanced product of three fundamental principles·
the consuls representing regal power, the Senate aristocratic, and the People democratic. In fact, it was the
Senate that drove the chariot of state; but seldom did the
magistrates or people try to kick over the traces. For the
Roman Senate was far more representative and democratic
than that of Carthage. It was recruited from magistrates
and ex-magistrates, drawn mainly from the nobles, but
not to the complete exclusion of the common people.
Further, it formed a reservoir of political wisdom and
experience, so that it came to exercise by custom and
through its prestige a control over the State which far
exceeded its strict legal powers. The assembly of the
People was far from being obliterated by the Senate. It
elected the magistrates, who in turn formed the Senate;
it was frequently consulted, and legally the resolutions of
the Senate gained the force of law only when approved by
the People. The magistrates, though seldom men of
genius, were generally good soldiers and upright adminis-
trators, loyal to the wishes of the Central Government.
It was the Greek historian, Polybius, who wrote 'if a
single talent is entrusted to a Greek statesman, ten auditors,
as many seals, and twice as many witnesses are required
for the security of the bond, yet even so faith is not observed;
while a Roman official or diplomat who handles vast sums

of money, keeps faith through the mere moral obligation of the oath he has sworn. Amongst the Romans the corrupt official is as rare as a financier with clean hands among other peoples.' Polybius here doubtless had in mind the Carthaginians as well as his own fellow-countrymen.

Thus the spirit behind the Roman constitution was even more important than the actual form, excellent though that was in its flexibility and balance. And the spirit ultimately was determined by the common citizen. Rome had her roots deep in the soil: her people were farmers, and agriculture, not commerce, formed the basis of her early prosperity. She had no professional army, but in time of need called her sons from their farms to form a citizen-militia. Thus early there grew up a sense of unity and discipline, and amid the austerities of a simple agricultural life of which the family formed the unit there grew up a code of conduct, the *mos maiorum*, which aimed at promoting such qualities as *grauitas, continentia, industria, diligentia*, and *constantia*. If the early Roman took himself rather too seriously and lacked some of the graces of life, at any rate his ideal of a ' uir fortis et strenuus ' contrasts favourably with the portrait of the average Carthaginian, and goes far to explain the success of Rome over her rival. If all his fellow-countrymen had had a greater share in the noble qualities of Hannibal, the story of the Punic Wars might well have been very different.

Thus the struggle between Rome and Carthage was largely a conflict of national ideals. The two peoples had little in common. Different in race, culture, and religion, with divergent moral and material interests, they would tend to gravitate towards conflict when once the minor states between them had been eliminated or assimilated. Later, in the second century, Rome came into contact with the Hellenistic East, where a common culture held in a precarious Balance of Powers the three great monarchies of Macedonia, Syria and Egypt. As Rome had by then absorbed something of that culture, she adapted her policy in order to try to maintain that balance, although the experiment ultimately failed. But in the West rivalry would lead to war: compromise was difficult, if not impossible. No war is inevitable, but neither Rome nor Carthage made any real effort to bridge the gap that lay between them or to build up some political system which would allow their divergent interests to work harmoniously side by side. Both peoples therefore drifted towards a series of wars, which could end only in the final extinction of the weaker.

2. THE PUNIC WARS

THE early relations of Rome and Carthage had been friendly. Treaties had been negotiated in 509 and 348 B.C. in which the Romans recognized Carthaginian trading rights in the Western Mediterranean in exchange for a promise that Carthage would not interfere in Latium. Only the fact that Rome's interests were entirely bound up in agriculture and Italian affairs explains why she so readily allowed Carthage to turn the Western Mediterranean into a ' mare clausum '. Later, when Pyrrhus, King of Epirus, invaded Italy, Carthage, so far from helping him, made a friendly agreement with Rome. Pyrrhus' adventure was unsuccessful: he was driven from Italy by the Romans, and he failed to sweep the Carthaginians out of Western Sicily. When he left the shores of Sicily he is reported to have remarked, ' What a cockpit we are now leaving for Carthaginian and Roman to fight in '; and he was right, for it was there that the First Punic War broke out.

After the defeat of Pyrrhus, the Greek cities of South Italy had joined the Italian Confederacy, and thus the Roman sphere of interest was extended to the narrow straits which separate Sicily from the toe of Italy. Carthage held the greater part of Sicily, and in 264 had thrown a garrison into Messana (now Messina) to help a company of bandits called the Mamertines or Sons of Mars, who had seized the town some years before. The Mamertines soon tired of their new guests, and appealed to Rome for help to get rid of them. Could the Romans disregard the appeal, and still more the existence of a Carthaginian garrison at Messana, a key position which barred access to Sicily and constituted a base whence the Carthaginians might sail against Rome's new allies on the southern coast of Italy? The Romans decided to help the

Mamertines and secure an outpost which was necessary
to the safety of Italy, although this action might involve
war with Carthage.

The details of the war which dragged on for twenty-
three years need not be recalled here. Suffice it to say
that it forced Rome to become a sea Power. She built a
fleet, and without previous naval experience defeated the
Carthaginians, with their centuries of sea-faring experience
behind them, in a series of six encounters, suffering only
one naval defeat herself; but, owing to lack of skilled
seamanship, she suffered terrific losses from tempests.
After a slow advance in Sicily, the Romans tried to end the
war by sending an expeditionary force under M. Atilius
Regulus to Africa to attack Carthage itself (258); but in
vain, as Regulus was defeated and his force was smashed
in the following spring. This failure in her first overseas
expedition would not encourage Rome to try the experiment again. At last in 241, when both sides were completely exhausted, the Roman fleet, under C. Lutatius
Catulus, won a decisive victory at the Aegates Islands off
the western end of Sicily. Carthage capitulated: she
paid a heavy indemnity and evacuated Sicily, which
became the first overseas possession of Rome, her first
province. The victory was won by the moral qualities of
the Roman people, by the patriotism of a citizen army, by
the loyalty of the Italian allies, and by the steadiness of
the Senatorial government.

After the war Carthage had to face a very serious revolt
of her mercenaries, during which Sardinia rebelled. Rome
then stepped in and bluntly annexed the island (238).
For this piece of wanton aggression there was no shadow
of excuse, but there was a very real reason: Sardinia was
so closely connected geographically with Italy and would
form so admirable a base for an attack on Italy that the
Romans feared to allow the Carthaginians to continue
to control it. Thus the Romans seized the opportunity and acted with decision and without scruple: the
result was permanently to embitter relations with her

old rival just when they were becoming more friendly. Carthage replied to the loss of Sardinia by strengthening her hold on Spain, which had weakened. The southern part was quickly reduced by Hamilcar Barca. On his death in 228 he was succeeded by his son-in-law Hasdrubal, who achieved more by diplomacy than force. As a military and naval base he founded the city of Carthago Nova (to-day Cartagena) on a peninsula which commands one of the best harbours in the Mediterranean. By 226 he had advanced the Carthaginian frontier as far north as the Ebro, and arranged a treaty with Rome by which that river was recognized as dividing the spheres of influence of the two Powers. When he was killed in 221, he was succeeded by Hannibal, the son of Hamilcar, now aged twenty-five. As a boy, Hannibal had accompanied his father to Spain, and it was said that before they left Carthage the father had made his nine-years-old son swear at the altar of Baal eternal hatred of Rome. We cannot be certain how far the object of this new empire-building in Spain was offensive or how far defensive—that is, whether it was deliberately planned in order to make feasible a war of revenge on Rome, or whether it merely aimed at compensating Carthage for the loss of Sardinia. If it was deliberately hostile, the leadership in Spain could not have fallen into better hands than those of Hannibal. A born leader who won the devotion of his troops, endowed with great powers of endurance, swift in mind and action, he was one of the great soldiers of all time.

The new general reverted to his father's warlike policy. In a lightning campaign he stormed the central plateau of Spain, and then turned against the native Iberian city of Saguntum (now Sagunto, about 20 miles north of Valencia), the only town south of the Ebro which still withstood him. But Saguntum was an ally of Rome. Relying on help from Rome, the Saguntines refused to surrender, and for eight months withstood Hannibal's blockade. But the help never came, and the town at length fell by assault. The Romans had their hands full elsewhere, both in the north and east. They were busy founding colonies at Placentia and Cremona in North Italy to secure their northern frontier against the Gauls, who had invaded Italy in 226 and were only gradually being driven back beyond the River Po. Further, they had been forced to fight two wars against the Illyrians (230–228 and 221–219) to free the Adriatic from piracy, and had not finished the second when news of events in Spain reached them. Hannibal had made skilful use of their preoccupation to storm Saguntum; but whatever the precise juridical position may have been, he must have known that this action would force the Romans into war. In March 218 the Carthaginian Government received a Roman ultimatum, and when they refused to disavow Hannibal's action, Rome declared war.

The Romans acted promptly. One consul, Sempronius, was sent to Sicily with orders to invade Africa; the other, Publius Cornelius Scipio, was sent by sea to Massilia (Marseilles) to invade Spain. But Hannibal had been quicker. He had taken the momentous decision to abandon his base in Spain and, by a rapid march over the Alps, to pounce on Italy. Thus, on reaching the Rhone, Scipio found that Hannibal had already slipped past and was on his way across the Alps. He wisely, however, sent his brother Gnaeus to Spain with most of his forces to prevent reinforcements from following Hannibal; he himself hastened back to Italy to await Hannibal's arrival. There he hoped to use the tributaries of the Po to fight a series of delaying actions until he was joined by his colleague Sempronius, who was hastily recalled from Sicily. Hannibal soon swept down from the Alps and defeated Scipio in a cavalry engagement on the Ticinus. When Sempronius joined Scipio in North Italy he insisted on fighting at once on the Trebia, a small tributary of the Po. Two-thirds of the Roman force was wiped out. In the following spring (217) Hannibal crossed the Apennines, and by enticing the Roman army into an ambush, won another overwhelming victory on the banks of Lake

Trasimene. The way to Rome lay open. But Hannibal had not brought siege-engines which would enable him to storm a large fortified city. Rather, he expected to disrupt the Italian Confederacy and so undermine Rome's power. Here he met his first rebuff, when he found that none of the cities of Umbria, Etruria, or Campania would open their gates to him. Hence he could only ravage the fertile district of Campania and try to provoke the Romans to a further battle. After wintering in Apulia, he met the Roman legions on the plain of Cannae, and administered the severest defeat yet known to Roman arms. Some 25,000 Romans fell, while 10,000 were captured A large part of South Italy went over to Hannibal, and this example was followed by Capua, the second city in Italy, and other Campanian towns. Hannibal must have thought that the war was over. But if so, he under-estimated the dogged perseverance of his foes. Though the flower of their man-hood was slain and part of Italy was in revolt, the Romans never faltered nor thought of peace. Latium, Umbria, and Etruria remained loyal, and Rome herself was safe within her walls. If she could avoid another pitched battle, she might still wear down Hannibal's strength: he was cut off from reinforcements, while the reservoirs of man-power in Italy were immense.

Hannibal devised a new strategy to break the will of his foes. This aimed at extending the theatre of war and raising up a circle of enemies around Rome. In the west the war was to be prosecuted vigorously in Spain and a landing effected in Sardinia; in the north were the hostile Gauls; in the east an alliance was made with Philip, King of Macedon, who would try to drive the Romans from Illyria; in the south the Greek cities of Sicily would be encouraged to revolt to Carthage, more readily when she was allied with Philip. Thus from all sides Carthage sought to encompass Rome. But the attempt failed. In Spain the Romans had already won a decisive naval victory off the mouth of the Ebro, after which the Car-thaginians were forced to abandon any large-scale naval operations (217). The Romans strengthened their resisting power in Spain by sending out reinforcements under Publius Scipio to join his brother Gnaeus. In 215 the brothers had to face a critical situation: Hannibal's brother Hasdrubal advanced to the Ebro to put everything to the hazard, only to suffer a crushing defeat. The Scipios then cautiously took the offensive, and after the capture of Saguntum (212) advanced farther south in two divisions. But this gallant attempt over-strained their resources: they were defeated and killed. Although the gains of the previous four years were thus lost, the Romans still managed to hold the line of the Ebro and prevented reinforcements reaching Hannibal in Italy.

Elsewhere they were even more successful in parrying the Carthaginian thrusts. The Punic landing in Sardinia failed. Although the war in Greece forced the Romans to send out an expeditionary force, they gained the support of the Aetolians and a large part of Southern Greece, so that they were gradually able to transfer the burden of the war to the shoulders of their allies, until peace was made with King Philip in 205. In Sicily the Carthaginians brought about the revolt of Rome's ally Syracuse, but despite the engineering skill of Archimedes, the city surrendered in 211 to the Roman commander Marcellus after a siege of more than two and a half years; thus fell Syracuse, chief among the Greek cities of the west for the last three centuries. Finally, in Italy Hannibal achieved little success. True, Tarentum went over to him in 213, but thanks to the guiding hand of Q. Fabius Maximus, surnamed the Delayer (Cunctator), the Romans, by following a strategy of attrition, avoided further pitched battles and a second Cannae. They recovered Capua in 211 and Tarentum in 209, while Hannibal was being steadily forced farther down into South Italy.

It was in Spain that the first hopes of final victory dawned for Rome. Though her armies had been wiped out and the two Scipios slain, fresh forces were sent out in 210 under the command of Publius Cornelius Scipio, son of one of

the dead generals. Aged twenty-five, courageous, re-
sourceful, self-confident, and wise, the young Scipio had
an extraordinary power of inspiring confidence in others.
His character was a curious blend of the man of action and
the religious mystic; his unusual enthusiasm was moderated
by Greek culture and Roman common sense. Although
technically unqualified for a high command, being a mere
' priuatus ', he was invested by the Roman people with
proconsular imperium to conduct the war in Spain. In
209 he disregarded the three Carthaginian armies in
Central Spain and swooped down on their base at New
Carthage, which he took by a sudden assault. It was one of
the most daring exploits of the war, and deprived the
Carthaginians not only of their base in Spain, but also
of the sinews of war, because the district was rich in silver
mines. Scipio spent the rest of the year building up a
New Model Army which he hoped would one day be able
to face Hannibal himself in the field: his tactical reforms,
the details of which will be considered later, were one of
the chief factors which enabled Rome ultimately to deliver
the knock-out blow. In 208 Hasdrubal Barca determined
to make one final attempt to break out of Spain and join
his brother Hannibal in Italy: he suffered a severe defeat
at Scipio's hands at Baecula, but managed to slip away
with part of his army, which he increased en route by
recruiting Gauls and Ligurians. By 207 he was in North
Italy, marching against the consul Marcus Livius Salinator.
But the other consul, Marcus Claudius Nero, who was
holding Hannibal in check in the south, had the good
fortune to intercept Hasdrubal's dispatches to his brother,
Hannibal. Realizing the danger, he determined to join
Livius, in the hope of defeating Hasdrubal with their joint
forces and of returning to his southern command before
Hannibal had realized his absence. And so it fell out.
The two consuls met Hasdrubal on the River Metaurus,
not very far from Ariminum in North-east Italy, and won
a decisive victory. Hasdrubal was killed, Nero hastened
back to the south, and the first news that Hannibal received

of this overwhelming disaster was when his brother's head was flung into his camp. Meantime Scipio had wisely refrained from going on a wild-goose chase after Hasdrubal: he left the Roman forces in Italy to deal successfully with that danger. There were still two unconquered Carthaginian armies in Spain, and these Scipio met in battle near Ilipa (Alcala del Rio, near Seville) in 206. By skilful tactics he outflanked the enemy and won the decisive battle of the war in Spain. The Carthaginians were swept out of the Peninsula and their Empire in Spain had fallen, while Scipio returned to Rome conquering and yet to conquer.

3. THE AFRICAN CAMPAIGN

ON his return from Spain, Scipio was rewarded, not by a triumph which as a *priuatus cum imperio* he could not claim, but by being elected consul for 205, amid great popular enthusiasm. It was now well known that he wished to carry the war into Africa, a plan which provoked much bitter opposition on political and strategic grounds. Some Romans, like Fabius, did not look beyond Italy for Rome's future: they wanted to finish the war with all speed, to heal the wounds it had inflicted on the Italian countryside, to pursue an isolationist policy, and to withstand the tide of Greek ideas which was flooding Rome at the time. Others, like Scipio, realized that a purely continental Italian policy was obsolete, and that Rome must become a Mediterranean Power. The military views of the two parties varied correspondingly. The Fabians wished by a defensive strategy to force Hannibal from Italy. Scipio wished to defeat Hannibal and secure Rome's future safety by humbling Carthage. Hence he determined to disregard the enemy's main forces, strike at their base by leading an expeditionary force to Africa, and so force Hannibal to return there to fight the decisive battle, which Scipio might hope to win, thanks to the tactical reforms which he had been introducing into the Roman army.

Scipio at last forced the Senate to acquiesce in this policy, but the Fabian Opposition hampered him by securing that he was only granted the command of two legions stationed in Sicily. However, he increased his forces by appealing for volunteers, and spent some time in Sicily training his new army for its future adventure. By the spring of 204 all was ready, and the expeditionary force, numbering perhaps 30,000 men, set sail for Africa amid great enthusiasm.

Meanwhile Hannibal was being pressed ever farther

southwards into Bruttium, the toe of Italy, where he still controlled the strongholds of Locri and Croton. But in 205 Scipio slipped across from Sicily and succeeded in snatching Locri from his grasp. At the same time the Carthaginian Government made one last attempt to help Hannibal and to keep Scipio in Italy; Mago sailed from the Balearic Islands and captured Genoa, where he received reinforcements from Carthage. The Romans met this danger of a fresh invasion from the north by stationing two armies at Arretium and Ariminum. But Mago was not yet ready to take the offensive; the Gallic tribes, who had been abandoned by Hannibal and had Hasdrubal's fate at Metaurus before their eyes, were lukewarm in their support, while it took Mago a long time to organize the hill tribes of Liguria. At length, in 203, he advanced into the valley of the Po with some 30,000 men, but was defeated in a serious engagement, which Livy describes in Chapters xviii–xix of this book; he received orders to return to Carthage, but died on the voyage as a result of wounds received in battle. Hannibal had been holding on desperately in Bruttium like a lion at bay. All hope of success in Italy was dead, and he could only try to prevent reinforcements being sent to Scipio in Africa, where success after success was reported, until finally in the autumn of 203 he received orders to return home in order to defend Carthage.

Hannibal's recall was occasioned by Scipio's victories. The latter had landed in the spring of 204 near Utica, a town some twenty miles west of Carthage, where he pitched his camp on some high ground to the south of the town. He had further tried to pave the way for his African adventure by seeking the alliance of two native African princes, Syphax, who ruled over Numidia, with his capital at Cirta (now Constantine in Algeria), and Masinissa, a claimant for the throne of the Massyli, who lived between Numidia and Carthage. Though at the moment in exile, Masinissa proved a valuable ally, and soon joined Scipio with a band of cavalry, an arm in which the Romans were

weak. Scipio was, however, not so successful with Syphax,
who, although pledged to support the Romans, was won
over to the Carthaginian cause by Sophoniba, Hasdrubal
Gisgo's beautiful daughter, whom he now married. But
despite the support of Syphax, the Carthaginians were
alarmed at the approach of the Romans, the more so
when a cavalry squadron under Hasdrubal's son Hanno
was ambushed and defeated in some hills just south-west
of Utica. After this victory Scipio pressed forward the
siege of Utica by land and sea, but winter came on and the
town still resisted. Threatened by the approach of
Hasdrubal and Syphax, Scipio withdrew for the winter
to a sharp headland projecting into the sea about two miles
east of Utica, which was later known as the Castra Cornelia.

The rest of the campaign is described in this book of
Livy, but the events may be briefly outlined. In the
winter (204/3) Syphax attempted to negotiate a peace on
behalf of Carthage. Although unwilling to accept the
terms offered, Scipio treacherously prolonged negotiations
in order that his envoys by frequent visits might obtain
detailed topographical information about the enemies'
quarters. For Syphax and Hasdrubal were encamped
during the winter on two adjacent hills, which formed the
southern termination of the ridge which in the north ended
at Castra Cornelia, some six miles away. In the spring
of 203 Scipio broke off negotiations and renewed the
blockade of Utica. When the enemies' suspicions were
lulled, he launched a sudden night attack on their camps,
which ended in a terrific disaster for the Carthaginians
(chapters iii–vi). A month later, when Hasdrubal and
Syphax were mustering a fresh army in the quiet of the
desert at the Great Plains some seventy-five miles south-
west of Utica, Scipio again struck unexpectedly. While
part of his army continued to besiege Utica, the rest
swooped down on Campi Magni, and won a great tactical
victory (chapter viii). Scipio followed up this success by
capturing Tunis, only fifteen miles from Carthage, where
he could command the enemy's land communications.

c

The Carthaginians made a desperate counter-attack on his fleet at Utica, but he marched back just in time to thwart it (chapters ix–x). Meantime after the Battle of Campi Magni, Scipio's friend Laelius and Masinissa had pursued Syphax to his own country and defeated him near Cirta (Constantine), which they took, while Syphax was captured and sent to Rome (chapters xi–xv). The situation at Carthage was now desperate, and Hannibal was at length recalled to defend his country. But the peace party of merchants and landowners prevailed, and it was decided to sue for peace. Severe but not crushing terms were offered by Scipio, and were accepted: an armistice was arranged while they were referred for confirmation to the Roman Senate, which at first hesitated, as rival nobles, jealous of Scipio's success, were working against him (chapters xvi, xvii, xx–xxiii).

While the peace was being ratified in Rome, Hannibal landed in Africa, and was soon joined by the other army from Italy which Mago had commanded. When a storm drove a Roman convoy ashore near Carthage, the populace of the overcrowded and ill-supplied city seized the supplies. The envoys whom Scipio sent to complain of this violation of the armistice were dismissed and treacherously ambushed on their return voyage. Thus the war party at Carthage, trusting in Hannibal, had again prevailed (chapters xxiv, xxv, xxviii). Scipio in anger stormed up the Bagradas valley, cutting Carthage off from her economic base. He hastily summoned Masinissa, who was fighting in Western Numidia, and advanced farther and farther inland to meet him, as he dared not face the enemy without the Numidian cavalry. Thereupon Hannibal advanced from Hadrumetum to Zama, hoping to cut Scipio's communications and to force him to fight without the cavalry. But at Naraggara Scipio was joined by Masinissa, and then advanced eastwards. After an ineffective interview between the two generals, the two armies faced one another. In the battle which followed Hannibal's army was destroyed, and the fate of Rome and Carthage was decided (chapters xxix–xxxv).

After making a demonstration before Carthage, Scipio received a peace deputation at Tunis. For Hannibal, who had escaped to Carthage, was counselling peace, especially as news came that Syphax's son Vermina had just been defeated. Further resistance was useless, and might involve the destruction of the city. Scipio was also ready for peace, because the siege of Carthage would involve fresh efforts when Italy most needed rest, and because he wished to disarm, but not to destroy. Accordingly terms were arranged which left Carthage in possession of her own territory in Africa but ended her career as a Mediterranean Power (chapters xxxvi–xxxviii, 5). After a certain amount of political intrigue at Rome, which Livy describes in the closing chapters of the book, the peace terms were ratified in Rome and executed in Africa. And so the long war ended, and Scipio returned victorious to Rome, where he was surnamed after the land he had conquered—Africanus.

4. THE ROMAN ARMY AND SCIPIO'S TACTICS[1]

THE Roman army at this period was a citizen-militia, not a professional force of paid soldiers. It was recruited normally by conscription from the Roman citizens and the allied states of Italy, although its numbers might be increased at time of need by volunteers, such as the 7,000 men who hastened to join Scipio's African expedition. The citizens were organized in legions of infantry and *turmae* of cavalry, a legion normally consisting of 4,200 men. Of these, 1,200 were light-armed skirmishers (*uelites*). The remaining 3,000 heavy-armed troops were divided into three lines: (1) the *hastati*, a first line of young soldiers; (2) the *principes*, men in the prime of life; and (3) the *triarii*, a rear line of veterans. Each of these three lines was divided into ten smaller units called maniples, and each of these was again subdivided into two centuries. This term no longer implied that these centuries consisted of 100 men. In fact in the two front lines (the *hastati* and *principes*) each of the twenty centuries contained sixty men, whilst those of the *triarii* comprised only thirty men each. The organization of the legion was therefore as follows:—

Hastati (10 maniples of 120 men divided into 20 centuries of 60 men) 1200
Principes (10 maniples of 120 men divided into 20 centuries of 60 men 1200
Triarii (10 maniples of 60 men divided into 20 centuries of 30 men) 600
Velites 1200

4200

To each legion were attached ten *turmae*, each of thirty horsemen (*equites*). The *hastati* and *principes* carried a long, convex shield (*scutum*), a short sword (*gladius*) and

[1] Further details will be explained where necessary in the notes.

two throwing-javelins (*pila*). The *triarii* had a thrusting
spear (*hasta*) in place of the *pilum*.

The normal procedure was to volley with the pila, and
then to rush in and meet the enemy hand-to-hand. But
the three lines were kept separate. First the *hastati* went
into action, and were only supported by the *principes* when
necessary, and the latter in turn by the *triarii*. The purpose
of the division into maniples was to give each line a certain
flexibility; gaps were left between the maniples of each
line, and these were covered by the maniples of the line
behind, an arrangement called the Quincunx, which is
represented in the diagram which follows

Hastati	□ □ □ □ □ □ □ □ □ □
Principes	□ □ □ □ □ □ □ □ □
Triarii	□ □ □ □ □ □ □ □ □ □

But the Roman army suffered from three great weaknesses at the beginning of the Hannibalic war: inelasticity,
lack of cavalry, and insufficient training to make the
individual effective when he broke away from the compact
mass. Although the introduction of manipular tactics
had superseded a more rigid phalanx system of earlier
days, the battle-line was not sufficiently flexible: it relied
on mere push and weight, and could not wheel or turn
with any ease. When faced by a more mobile enemy, the
Roman legions collapsed. At the battle of Cannae the
Roman wings were inadequately covered by small bodies
of horsemen, and were soon exposed by Hannibal's superior
cavalry; the infantry were thus outflanked, and gradually
drawn into the flexible net of Hannibal's line. Unable to
bend to face the fresh attacks on their flanks and rear, the
legionaries were gradually crushed together and massacred.

It was these weaknesses that Scipio reformed. In Spain
he built up a New Model Army. To make the individual
more effective, he was given an adequate training in arms
drill, while his weapons were improved: the Spanish

sword with a well-tempered point was adopted, and the *pilum* was probably improved from Spanish models. Lack of cavalry was counteracted by alliance with the native princes of Spain, and later of Numidia, who supplied horsemen. But Scipio's greatest tactical contribution was that he abandoned the close maintenance of the triple line and created lines which operated independently. This more flexible weapon was used with increasing skill at Baecula (where, under a screen of light troops, Scipio divided his main army, and detachments swept up on to the two flanks of the enemy), at Ilipa (where he pinned the enemy's main forces in useless inactivity while his wings carried out an outflanking movement), and at Campi Magni (the tactics of which are described in this book), until finally it crushed Hannibal at Zama. Scipio has indeed many claims to be ranked among the world's greatest soldiers, but not the least part of his military genius was displayed in the sheer brilliance of his tactical reforms. And it is in this book of Livy that we can see the new weapon finally perfected at Campi Magni, and then turned with fatal effect against one whom the world has always ranked among its greatest captains. The historical interest of the book depends partly on the world issues staked on the field of Zama, but partly also on the fact that we can watch two of the greatest soldiers known playing the game of diamond-cut-diamond.

5. LIVY'S PREDECESSORS

LIVY (59 B.C.–A.D. 17) passed the second part of his life in the reign of Augustus, who brought peace to a war-weary world. The emperor not only re-established a stable government after the period of revolution in which the Roman Republic had collapsed, but also attempted to restore the ancient Roman virtues. In this task he was helped by poets like Virgil and Horace and by writers like Livy, who determined to compose a history of the Roman people from earliest times until his own day, a history which should above all be a pageant of the worthies of the Roman state, and should show clearly the ancient virtues, the *mos maiorum*, which had made Rome great. But if a man in the reign of Augustus set himself such a task, where could he find his material? In other words, on what sources could Livy draw for his account of the end of the Hannibalic war, for it is with that period that we are alone concerned?

First and foremost there was the Greek historian Polybius, who, although writing some sixty years after the Battle of Zama, had met and talked with men who had fought in it, including Masinissa and Scipio's right-hand man Laelius. Further, he had lived in Italy in close touch with official circles, where he won the friendship of Scipio Aemilianus, the adopted grandson of the elder Africanus, and thus had access to private family papers as well as to official documents. His object was to write a history of the whole inhabited world and to show how it fell under the domination of Rome in the fifty years that followed Zama. His style is somewhat dull, but he was so anxious to give an accurate account of what happened that he eschewed the attractive rhetoric with which many of his contemporaries adorned their highly coloured and exaggerated works, which resembled historical novels more than the truthful accounts which they claimed to be. To his more sober task Polybius brought the critical faculties of a trained historian and the wisdom of an experienced and widely travelled statesman. So here Livy had a first-class authority to follow, and something like two-thirds of Book XXX is derived from Polybius, often in the form of an almost literal translation from the Greek, for the attitude of ancient writers to what we call plagiarism was very different from ours. And, furthermore, it must be admitted that Livy's acknowledgement of this great debt is very ' shabby ', for in the only passage referring to Polybius, Livy describes him as ' haudquaquam spernendus auctor ' (XXX, xlv, 5), hardly a generous tribute.

Secondly, an Augustan author could turn to Roman writers for information; here he would find no lack of material, but work of very varied quality. The earlier Roman historians, or annalists as they were called, fall into two groups: one group in the first half of the second century wrote mostly in Greek, and their work was essentially trustworthy. They were followed by a later group, who lived from the time of the Gracchi (133) to the end of the Republic; many of these wrote in Latin highly rhetorical and unreliable accounts which glorified the exploits of Roman leaders with little regard to the truth. Their purpose was rather to interest their readers and to give a highly biassed account of Rome's past. One of the most unreliable of all these was Valerius Antias. Another, named Coelius Antipater, wrote a monograph on the Second Punic War, which was somewhat more reliable (since it was based in part on Polybius), but it was also marred by rhetorical exaggeration. Livy used both these authors in this book. He also drew on some official sources for the lists of legions and magistrates which he records at the beginning of each year.

Thus it will be seen that Livy's value as a historical writer depends very largely upon the sources which he himself used in any given part of his narrative. In about two-thirds of the present book he followed Polybius, and so is reliable (although here and there he adds details from other less good sources), while for the other third he used the later annalists, and here he must be treated with more caution by the historian who wishes to establish the truth. Such, then, was the quarry from which he hewed his material. With what aims and by what methods he worked it up into a glorious work of art are discussed more fully in the next section.

6. TITUS LIVIUS

Born at Patavium (*Padua*) 59 B.C.   Died A.D. 17

LIVY, whose long life began ten years before the outbreak of the Civil War and ended in the reign of Tiberius, though far from being the greatest of historians, was one of the greatest stylists that ever turned their hands to the writing of history.

Neither his aims nor his methods were those of the modern historian. The aim of the modern is to discover as far as possible what actually happened, to trace the causes of events and set all down without fear or favour. History may have valuable lessons for mankind, but the ideal of the historian is not that of the moralist. The moral, if any, is but a by-product of the work as a whole. The historian of to-day has, moreover, vast stores of material on which to draw. Besides the work of earlier historians, he has the accumulated wealth of the archives of Europe as a field for his researches; while if he studies the records of antiquity he may find some consolation for the loss of the vast bulk of ancient historical writings in the stores of knowledge provided by archaeological discovery, the vast collections of ancient inscriptions, and the relics of remote ages which have been brought to light by the spade of the excavator. Indeed, he has often better means for forming a judgement on certain points than the ancient historians themselves, whose material was not thus collected for them and who had comparatively restricted opportunities of travel. History has become scientific, with the result that the artistic side of the work is sometimes unduly neglected. For the ancient historian, on the other hand, the artistic element is of immense, if not of primary, importance, and he rarely loses sight of a practical or even a definitely moral purpose. Livy, for example, has told us his purpose in the preface to his first book.

' What chiefly makes the study of history wholesome and profitable is this, that you behold the lessons of every kind of experience set forth as on a conspicuous monument; from these you may choose for yourself and your own state what to imitate, from these mark for avoidance what is shameful in the conception and shameful in the result. For the rest, either love of the task I have set myself deceives me, or no state was ever greater, none more righteous or richer in good examples; none ever was where avarice and luxury came into the social order so late, or where humble means and thrift were so highly esteemed and so long held in honour. Of late, riches have brought in avarice and excessive pleasures have created the longing to carry wantonness and licence to the point of ruin for oneself and destruction for the community.' [1] In other words his aim is primarily moral and secondly patriotic. It is a lofty ideal, but it does not fulfil the whole duty of a historian. What of the search for truth? Livy is far from neglecting it. But he had a very difficult task. The early history of Rome was vague and legendary. Even when the mythical period comes to an end and records begin, he has to rely on dry and not too informative public records or on mere tradition as recorded by writers of the last two centuries before Christ. For it must be remembered that Rome had no prose literature till after the Second Punic War. For many of his inconsistencies and improbabilities, therefore, Livy must not be blamed. He realized the difficulties before him and duly warned his readers. By the time, however, that he reaches the Second Punic War he has one reliable guide. Where Livy follows Polybius, he did the best that could be done and, at the cost perhaps of some precision and accuracy, lends life and colour to the somewhat ungainly narrative of the Greek. The faults of Livy are in any case not, as a rule, due to lack of industry. He has studied the state records and the available historians with care, but he lacks the careful accuracy and the critical spirit of the greatest

[1] Foster's translation (Loeb Series) slightly altered.

historians. Further, his patriotic fervour is apt to lead him astray, and at times he does scant justice to the enemies of Rome. For example, while he feels the greatness of Hannibal as a leader of men and as a master in the art of war, there is little to justify him when in his famous character-sketch of the Carthaginian hero (XXI. 4) he says that ' great as his virtues were they were equalled by the enormity of his vices. His cruelty was inhuman, his treachery worse than Carthaginian. Righteousness and truth were not in him; he feared no god in heaven, counted perjury as nothing and was devoid of any sort of scruple.' And, apart from this special bias, his passion for artistic expression and, above all, for rhetoric led him, perhaps not necessarily astray, but certainly away from the narrow path along which the science of history would have us walk. The great speeches which form such a prominent and attractive feature in his work are rhetorical fictions, employed in part, it is true, to express in dramatic form the situation of the moment, but even more, perhaps, to lend brilliance and colour to his narrative. Rhetoric formed the basis of Roman education, and Livy had astonishing gifts for this form of art. We could not wish such speeches away; Quintilian speaks of their ' incredible eloquence ', and the modern reader can scarcely fail to receive a similar impression. His battles are less successful than his speeches. They are brilliant in style and thrilling to read. But they are not clear in outline; the detail, notably the topographical detail, is confused and inadequate, and it is often hard to reconstruct the plan of the battle as we should desire, or to discover where precisely it was fought. The battle of Zama provides a good example. Amid many uncertainties the one thing we can say with certainty is that it was not fought at Zama. Again, although Livy's account of the actual fight has a specious appearance of clearness, yet if it be compared with the account given in Polybius on which it is based, it will be found that it gives a false impression.

But these defects, such as they are, are largely the result

of the conditions under which he wrote and the ideals of his time. His task was one of amazing difficulty; he had not the scientific mind of Polybius or his wide experience of life. But he has supreme gifts of style and makes history live. He is at his greatest in his treatment of the Second Punic War, that great drama to which the First War is but a confused and formless prelude and the Third a pitiable epilogue. The book contained in this little volume shows us the final act of the central tragedy. It cannot give us quite the thrill of the two books in which Livy describes the colossal victories of Hannibal during the opening years of the great conflict (Books XXI, XXII). Rome is manifestly on the verge of victory, and there is nothing of the element of suspense which we feel in the Twenty-seventh Book when Livy is leading up to the victory of the Metaurus which placed Rome's ultimate triumph almost beyond a doubt though the war had five long years yet to run. But the denouement of a great drama has seldom been described with greater dignity or eloquence. Livy is above all a patriot, but here at least the patriotic note is never overemphasized. Amid all his rhetoric and richness of colour he keeps his emotion under a just control, and the result is marvellously effective. Above all, the figures of the two chief actors rivet the attention. The young commander Scipio, with honours thick upon him, quietly efficient, a master of tact and diplomacy as well as of war, self-controlled and supremely self-confident, is a convincing and a living figure. Livy has, it is true, depicted an almost flawless character, but (largely by allowing his acts to speak for themselves) has escaped the danger of presenting to his readers a portrait of almost inhuman perfection. No less striking is the picture of Hannibal, a soldier from his boyhood, the victor of Cannae and Trasimene, forced after fifteen years' campaigning in his enemy's country to return to his home which he has not seen since the days of his childhood. He is not long before our eyes, but he fills the stage; the bitterness of his departure from the scene of his triumphs, the extraordinary skill and eloquence of his

great speech to Scipio, the masterly disposition of his troops
in the final battle, and the last tragic scene in the Carthaginian Senate when he, the hero of the war-party,
rebukes, with laughter on his lips, but despair in his heart,
the last advocate of resistance—all these are depicted by a
master hand and illumined by the pity, admiration, and
sympathy demanded by the fall of Rome's greatest enemy, a
foeman worthy of her steel.   Nor is it only in dealing with
the two protagonists and the main issues of the war that
Livy shows his greatness.   In Masinissa, the Numidian
prince who, driven from his kingdom and hunted ' like a
partridge upon the mountains ', is forced into the arms of
Rome, to be, after Scipio, the chief factor in her success,
and in the very hour of his most brilliant success darkens
his triumph by the mad folly of his passion for Sophoniba,
Livy found a character who provided him with a matchless
opportunity for the exercise of his gifts as a romantic
historian.   Here and in Book XXIX Rome itself is kept in the
background.   We are told all that it is necessary to know; we
have a few vivid pictures of the jealousy excited among
older rivals by Scipio's success and of the suspicion aroused
by his sympathy with Hellenic culture; we see attempts
made to supplant him and to reap the fruits of his victory,
attempts which culminate in the tragi-comic ' Odyssey '
of Tiberius Claudius.   But with the exception of the
ghastly tragedy of Locri, sacked by its Roman governor,
the scandal of which came near to besmirching the fair
fame of Scipio,[1] and a very few other incidents of minor
importance, the interest of the reader is deliberately riveted
on Africa.   The two books therefore have a unity such as
was not always within Livy's power to obtain; and he
rises nobly to the occasion.   For he has every gift as a
narrator.   Other historians both ancient and modern have
had a wider outlook, a more philosophic temperament,
and a more scrupulously scientific intelligence.   For richness and warmth of colour, for sheer eloquence and vivid-
ness of presentation, he has never been surpassed.

[1] See XXIX, 6-9, 26-22.

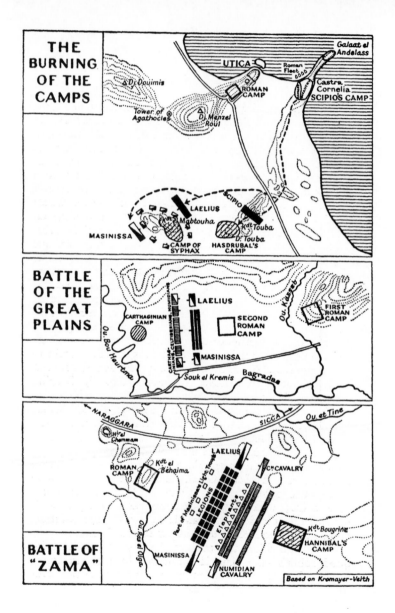

THE BURNING OF THE CAMPS

Galaat el Andelass
UTICA
Roman Fleet
Dj. Douimis
ROMAN CAMP
Castra Cornelia
SCIPIOS CAMP
Tower of Agathocles
Dj. Menzel Roul
LAELIUS
SCIPIO
K.dt el Mabtouha
MASINISSA
K.dt Touba
Dr. Touba
CAMP OF SYPHAX
HASDRUBAL'S CAMP

BATTLE OF THE GREAT PLAINS

CARTHAGINIAN CAMP
LAELIUS
SECOND ROMAN CAMP
Ou. Kasseb
FIRST ROMAN CAMP
Ou. Bou Heurtma
CARTHAG. & NUMID. CELTIBERIAN. INFANTRY
MASINISSA
Souk el Kremis
Bagradas

BATTLE OF "ZAMA"

NARAGGARA
Sidi el Chemmam
SICCA
Ou. et Tine
ROMAN CAMP
K.dt el Behaima
LAELIUS
C.n CAVALRY
Part of Masinissas Light Troops
LEGIONS
Elephants
K.dt Bougrine
HANNIBAL'S CAMP
Ou. Ras el Oliga
MASINISSA
NUMIDIAN CAVALRY
Based on Kromayer-Veith

TITI LIVII

LIBER XXX

I. Cn. Seruilius et C. Seruilius consules—sextus deci-
mus is annus belli Punici erat—cum de republica belloque
2 et prouinciis ad senatum rettulissent, censuerunt patres, ut
consules inter se compararent sortirenturue, uter Bruttios
aduersus Hannibalem, uter Etruriam ac Ligures prouinciam
3 haberet; cui Bruttii euenissent, exercitum a P. Sempronio
acciperet: P. Sempronius—ei quoque enim proconsuli
imperium in annum prorogabatur—P. Licinio succederet;
4 is Romam reuerteretur, bello quoque bonus habitus ad
cetera, quibus nemo ea tempestate instructior ciuis habebatur. congestis omnibus humanis ab natura fortunaque
5 bonis, nobilis idem ac diues erat; forma uiribusque
corporis excellebat, facundissimus habebatur seu causa
oranda, seu in senatu et apud populum suadendi ac dis-
6 suadendi locus esset; iuris pontificii peritissimus; super
haec bellicae quoque laudis consulatus compotem fecerat.
quod in Bruttiis prouincia, idem in Etruria ac Liguribus
7 decretum: M. Cornelius nouo consuli tradere exercitum
iussus, ipse prorogato imperio Galliam prouinciam obtinere
cum legionibus iis quas L. Scribonius priore anno habuisset.
8 sortiti deinde prouincias: Caepioni Bruttii, Seruilio
9 Gemino Etruria euenit. tum praetorum prouinciae in
sortem coniectae: iuris dictionem urbanam Paetus Aelius,
Sardiniam P. Lentulus, Siciliam P. Villius, Ariminum cum
duabus legionibus—sub Lucretio Spurio eae fuerant—
10 Quinctilius Varus est sortitus. et Lucretio prorogatum
imperium, ut Genuam oppidum a Magone Poeno dirutum
exaedificaret. P. Scipioni non temporis sed rei gerendae
fine, donec debellatum in Africa foret, prorogatum im-
11 perium est; decretumque, ut supplicatio fieret, quod is
in Africam prouinciam traiecisset, ut ea res salutaris
populo Romano ipsique duci atque exercitui esset.

II. In Siciliam tria milia militum sunt scripta, quia,
quod roboris ea prouincia habuerat, in Africam trans-
uectum fuerat; et quia, antequam classis ex Africa trai-

D   33

ceret, quadraginta nauibus custodiri placuerat Siciliae
2 maritimam oram, tredecim nouas naues Villius secum
3 in Siciliam duxit, ceterae in Sicilia ueteres refectae. huic
classi M. Pomponius, prioris anni praetor, prorogato
imperio praepositus nouos milites ex Italia aduectos in
4 naues imposuit. parem nauium numerum Cn. Octauio,
praetori item prioris anni, cum pari iure imperii ad tuendam Sardiniae oram patres decreuerunt: Lentulus praetor
5 duo milia militum dare in naues iussus. et Italiae ora,
quia incertum erat quo missuri classem Carthaginienses
forent (uidebantur autem quidquid nudatum praesidiis
esset petituri), M. Marcio, praetori prioris anni, cum totidem
6 nauibus tuenda data est. tria milia militum in eam
classem ex decreto patrum consules scripserunt et duas
7 legiones urbanas ad incerta belli. Hispaniae cum exercitibus imperioque ueteribus imperatoribus, L. Lentulo et
L. Manlio Acidino, decretae. uiginti omnino legionibus
et centum sexaginta nauibus longis res Romana eo anno
gesta.
8   Praetores in prouincias ire iussi; consulibus imperatum
ut priusquam ab urbe proficiscerentur, ludos magnos
facerent, quos T. Manlius Torquatus dictator in quintum
9 annum uouisset, si eodem statu res publica staret. et
nouas religiones excitabant in animis hominum prodigia
ex pluribus locis nuntiata. aurum in Capitolio corui non
10 lacerasse tantum rostris crediti sed etiam edisse: mures
Antii coronam auream adrosere: circa Capuam omnem
agrum locustarum uis ingens, ita ut unde aduenissent pa-
11 rum constaret, compleuit: eculeus Reate cum quinque
pedibus natus: Anagniae sparsi primum ignes in caelo,
12 dein fax ingens arsit: Frusinone arcus solem tenui linea
amplexus est; circulum deinde ipsum maior solis orbis
extrinsecus inclusit: Arpini terra campestri agro in in-
13 gentem sinum consedit: consulum alteri primam hostiam
immolanti caput iecineris defuit. ea prodigia maioribus
hostiis procurata; editi a collegio pontificum dei quibus
sacrificaretur.
      III. His transactis, consules praetoresque in prouincias

profecti; omnibus tamen, uelut eam sortitis, Africae cura
erat, seu quia ibi summam rerum bellique uerti cernebant,
seu ut Scipioni gratificarentur, in quem tum omnis uersa
2 ciuitas erat. itaque non ex Sardinia tantum, sicut ante
dictum est, sed ex Sicilia quoque et Hispania uestimenta
frumentumque, et arma etiam ex Sicilia et omne genus
3 commeatus eo portabantur. nec Scipio ullo tempore
hiemis belli opera remiserat, quae multa simul undique
eum circumstabant: Vticam obsidebat; castra in conspectu Hasdrubalis erant; Carthaginienses deduxerant
naues; classem paratam instructamque ad commeatus
4 intercipiendos habebant. inter haec ne Syphacis quidem
reconciliandi curam ex animo miserat, si forte iam satias
5 amoris in uxore ex multa copia cepisset. ab Syphace
magis pacis cum Carthaginiensibus condiciones, ut Romani
Africa, Poeni Italia excederent quam, si bellaretur, spes
6 ulla desciturum adferebatur. haec per nuntios acta
magis equidem crediderim—et ita pars maior auctores
sunt—quam ipsum Syphacem, ut Antias Valerius prodit,
7 in castra Romana ad colloquium uenisse. primo eas
condiciones imperator Romanus uix auribus admisit;
postea, ut causa probabilis suis commeandi foret in castra
hostium, mollius eadem illa abnuere ac spem facere saepius
ultro citroque agitantibus rem conuenturam.

8   Hibernacula Carthaginiensium, congesta temere ex
9 agris materia exaedificata, lignea ferme tota erant. Numidae praecipue harundine textis storeaque pars maxima
tectis passim nullo ordine, quidam, ut sine imperio occu-
patis locis, extra fossam etiam uallumque habitabant.
10 haec relata Scipioni spem fecerant castra hostium per
occasionem incendendi.

IV. Cum legatis, quos mitteret ad Syphacem, calonum
loco primos ordines spectatae uirtutis atque prudentiae
2 seruili habitu mittebat, qui, dum in colloquio legati essent,
uagi per castra, alius alia aditus exitusque omnes, situm
formamque et uniuersorum castrorum et partium, qua
Poeni qua Numidae haberent, quantum interualli inter
3 Hasdrubalis ac regia castra esset, specularentur moremque

simul noscerent stationum uigiliarumque, nocte an interdiu
opportuniores insidianti essent et inter crebra colloquia
alii atque alii de industria, quo pluribus omnia nota essent,
4 mittebantur. cum saepius agitata res certiorem spem
pacis in dies et Syphaci et Carthaginiensibus per eum
faceret, legati Romani uetitos se reuerti ad imperatorem
5 aiunt, nisi certum responsum detur: proinde, seu ipsi
staret iam sententia, promeret sententiam, seu consulendus
Hasdrubal et Carthaginienses essent, consuleret: tempus
6 esse aut pacem componi aut bellum nauiter geri. dum
consulitur Hasdrubal et Carthaginienses, et speculatores
omnia uisendi et Scipio ad comparanda ea quae in rem
7 erant tempus habuit; et mentione ac spe pacis neglegentia,
ut fit, apud Poenos Numidamque orta cauendi, ne quid
8 hostile interim paterentur. tandem relatum responsum
quibusdam, quia nimis cupere Romanus pacem uidebatur,
iniquis per occasionem adiectis; quae peropportune
9 cupienti tollere indutias Scipioni causam praebuere; ac
nuntio regis, cum relaturum se ad consilium dixisset,
postero die respondit se uno frustra tendente nulli alii
pacem placuisse: renuntiaret igitur nullam aliam spem
pacis quam relictis Carthaginiensibus Syphaci cum
10 Romanis esse. ita tollit indutias, ut libera fide incepta
exsequeretur; deductisque nauibus—et iam ueris principium erat—machinas tormentaque, uelut a mari adgres-
11 surus Vticam, imponit; et duo milia militum ad capiendum
quem antea tenuerat tumulum super Vticam mittit, simul
ut ab eo quod parabat in alterius rei curam conuerteret
12 hostium animos, simul ne qua, cum ipse ad Syphacem
Hasdrubalemque profectus esset, eruptio ex urbe et impetus
in castra sua relicta cum leui praesidio fieret.

V. His praeparatis aduocatoque consilio et dicere
exploratoribus iussis, quae comperta adferrent, Masinissaque, cui omnia hostium nota erant, postremo ipse quid
2 pararet in proximam noctem proponit; tribunis edicit
ut, ubi praetorio dimisso signa concinuissent, extemplo
3 educerent castris legiones. ita ut imperauerat signa sub
occasum solis efferri sunt coepta. ad primam ferme uigi-

liam agmen explicauerunt; media nocte—septem enim
milia itineris erant—modico gradu ad castra hostium
4 peruentum est. ibi Scipio partem copiarum Laelio Masinissamque ac Numidas attribuit et castra Syphacis inua-
5 dere ignesque conicere iubet. singulos deinde separatim
Laelium ac Masinissam deductos obtestatur ut, quantum
nox prouidentiae adimat, tantum diligentia expleant cura-
6 que; se Hasdrubalem Punicaque castra adgressurum:
ceterum non ante coepturum quam ignem in regiis castris
7 conspexisset. neque ea res morata diu est: nam ut
proximis casis iniectus ignis haesit, extemplo proxima
quaeque et deinceps continua amplexus totis se passim
8 dissipauit castris. et trepidatio quidem, quanta necesse
erat, in nocturno effuso tam late incendio orta est: ceterum fortuitum non hostilem ac bellicum ignem rati esse,
sine armis ad restinguendum incendium effusi in armatos
9 incidere hostes, maxime Numidas ab Masinissa notitia
regiorum castrorum ad exitus itinerum idoneis locis dis-
10 positos. multos in ipsis cubilibus semisomnos hausit
flamma; multi in praecipiti fuga ruentes super alios alii in
angustiis portarum obtriti sunt.

VI. Relucentem flammam primo uigiles Carthaginiensium, deinde excitati alii nocturno tumulto cum conspexis-
sent, ab eodem errore credere et ipsi sua sponte incendium
2 ortum; et clamor, inter caedem et uulnera sublatus an
ex trepidatione nocturna esset, confusus sensum ueri
3 adimebat. igitur pro se quisque inermes, ut quibus nihil
hostile suspectum esset, omnibus portis, qua cuique proximum erat, ea modo quae restinguendo igni forent portantes,
4 in agmen Romanum ruebant. quibus caesis omnibus
praeterquam hostili odio etiam ne quis nuntius effugeret,
extemplo Scipio neglectas ut in tali tumultu portas inuadit;
5 ignibusque in proxima tecta coniectis effusa flamma primo
uelut sparsa pluribus locis reluxit, dein per continua ser-
6 pens uno repente omnia incendio hausit. ambusti homines
iumentaque foeda primum fuga, dein strage obruebant
itinera portarum: quos non oppresserat ignis, ferro ab-
7 sumpti, binaque castra clade una deleta. duces tamen

ambo et ex tot milibus armatorum duo milia peditum et
quingenti equites semermes, magna pars saucii adflatique
8 incendio effugerunt. caesa aut hausta flammis quadraginta milia hominum sunt, capta supra quinque milia,
9 multi Carthaginiensium nobiles, undecim senatores; signa
militaria centum septuaginta quattuor, equi Numidici
supra duo milia septingenti; elephanti sex capti, octo
ferro flammaque absumpti; magna uis armorum capta:
ea omnia imperator Volcano sacrata incendit.

VII. Hasdrubal ex fuga cum paucis Afrorum urbem
proximam petierat, eoque omnes qui supererant, uestigia
ducis sequentes, se contulerant: metu deinde, ne dede-
2 retur Scipioni, urbe excessit. mox eodem patentibus portis
Romani accepti, nec quicquam hostile, quia uoluntate
concesserant in dicionem, factum. duae subinde urbes
captae direptaeque: ea praeda et quae castris incensis ex
igne rapta erat militi concessa est. Syphax octo milium
3 ferme inde spatio loco communito consedit; Hasdrubal
Carthaginem contendit, ne quid per metum ex recenti
4 clade mollius consuleretur. quo tantus primo terror est
adlatus, ut omissa Vtica Carthaginem crederent extemplo
5 Scipionem obsessurum. senatum itaque sufetes, quod
6 uelut consulare imperium apud eos erat, uocauerunt. ibi
tribus sententiis certatum: una de pace legatos ad Scipionem decernebat, altera Hannibalem ad tuendam ab exitia-
bili bello patriam reuocabat, tertia Romanae in aduersis
7 rebus constantiae erat: reparandum exercitum Syphacem-
que hortandum, ne bello absisteret, censebat. haec
sententia, quia Hasdrubal praesens Barcinaeque omnes
8 factionis bellum malebant, uicit. inde dilectus in urbe
agrisque haberi coeptus, et ad Syphacem legati missi,
summa ope et ipsum reparantem bellum, cum uxor non
iam ut ante blanditiis, satis potentibus ad animum amantis,
9 sed precibus et misericordia ualuisset, plena lacrimarum ob-
testans, ne patrem suum patriamque proderet isdemque
flammis Carthaginem, quibus castra conflagrassent, ab-
10 sumi sineret. spem quoque opportune oblatam adferebant legati: quattuor milia Celtiberorum circa urbem

nomine Obbam, ab conquisitoribus suis conducta in Hispania, egregiae iuuentutis sibi occurrisse, et Hasdrubalem
propediem adfore cum manu haudquaquam contemnenda.
11 igitur non benigne modo legatis respondit, sed ostendit
etiam multitudinem agrestium Numidarum, quibus per
eosdem dies arma equosque dedisset, et omnem iuuen-
12 tutem adfirmat ex regno exciturum: scire incendio, non
proelio cladem acceptam: eum bello inferiorem esse, qui
13 armis uincatur. haec legatis responsa, et post dies paucos
rursus Hasdrubal et Syphax copias iunxerunt. is omnis
exercitus fuit triginta ferme milium armatorum.

VIII. Scipionem, uelut iam debellato, quod ad Syphacem Carthaginiensesque attineret, Vticae oppugnandae
intentum iamque machinas admouentem muris auer-
2 tit fama redintegrati belli; modicisque praesidiis ad speciem modo obsidionis terra marique relictis ipse cum
3 robore exercitus ire ad hostes pergit. primo in tumulo
quattuor milia ferme distante ab castris regiis consedit;
postero die cum equitatu in Magnos—ita uocant—campos
subiectos ei tumulo degressus, succedendo ad stationes
hostium lacessendoque leuibus proeliis diem absumpsit.
4 et per insequens biduum tumultuosis hinc atque illinc
excursionibus in uicem nihil dictu satis dignum fecerunt:
5 quarto die in aciem utrimque descensum est. Romanus
principes post hastatorum prima signa, in subsidiis triarios
constituit; equitatum Italicum ab dextro cornu, ab
6 laeuo Numidas Masinissamque opposuit. Syphax Has-
drubalque Numidis aduersus Italicum equitatum, Carthaginiensibus contra Masinissam locatis, Celtiberos in
mediam aciem aduersus signa legionum accepere. ita
7 instructi concurrunt. primo impetu simul utraque cornua
et Numidae et Carthaginienses pulsi: nam neque Numidae, maxima pars agrestes, Romanum equitatum, neque
Carthaginienses, et ipse nouus miles, Masinissam recenti
8 super cetera uictoria terribilem sustinuere. nudata utrimque cornibus Celtiberum acies stabat, quod nec in fuga
salus ulla ostendebatur locis ignotis, neque spes ueniae
ab Scipione erat, quem bene meritum de se et gente sua

mercennariis armis in Africam oppugnatum uenissent.
9 igitur circumfusis undique hostibus alii super alios ca-
dentes obstinate moriebantur; omnibusque in eos uersis,
aliquantum ad fugam temporis Syphax et Hasdrubal prae-
ceperunt. fatigatos caede diutius quam pugna uictores
nox oppressit.

IX. Postero die Scipio Laelium Masinissamque cum
omni Romano et Numidico equitatu expeditisque militum
ad persequendos Syphacem atque Hasdrubalem mittit.
2 ipse cum robore exercitus urbes circa, quae omnes Carthaginiensium dicionis erant, partim spe partim metu
3 partim ui subigit. Carthagini erat quidem ingens terror,
et circumferentem arma Scipionem omnibus finitimis raptim perdomitis ipsam Carthaginem repente adgressurum
4 credebant. itaque et muri reficiebantur propugnaculisque
armabantur, et pro se quisque, quae diutinae obsidionis
5 tolerandae sunt, ex agris conuehit. rara mentio est pacis,
frequentior legatorum ad Hannibalem arcessendum mit-
6 tendorum; pars maxima classem, quae ad commeatus ex-
cipiendos parata erat, mittere iubent ad opprimendam
stationem nauium ad Vticam incaute agentem: forsitan
etiam naualia castra, relicta cum leui praesidio, oppres-
7 suros. in hoc consilium maxime inclinant; legatos tamen
ad Hannibalem mittendos censent: quippe classi ut feli-
cissime gerantur res, parte aliqua leuari Vticae obsidio-
8 nem: Carthaginem ipsam qui tueatur, neque imperatorem
alium quam Hannibalem neque exercitum alium quam
9 Hannibalis superesse. deductae ergo postero die naues,
simul et legati in Italiam profecti. raptimque omnia stimu-
lante fortuna agebantur, et in quo quisque cessasset,
prodi ab se salutem omnium rebatur.

10   Scipio grauem iam spoliis multarum urbium exercitum trahens, captiuis aliaque praeda in uetera castra ad
Vticam missis, iam in Carthaginem intentus occupat re-
11 lictum fuga custodum Tyneta. abest a Carthagine quindecim milia ferme passuum locus cum operibus tum
12 suapte natura tutus, et qui et ab Carthagine conspici et
praebere ipse conspectum in circumfusum mare urbi

possit. X. Inde, cum maxime uallum Romani iacerent,
conspecta classis hostium est Vticam a Carthagine petens.
2 igitur omisso opere pronuntiatum iter, signaque raptim
ferri sunt coepta, ne naues in terram et obsidionem uersae
3 ac minime nauali proelio aptae opprimerentur. qui enim
restitissent agili et nautico instrumento aptae et armatae
classi naues tormenta machinasque portantes et aut in
onerariarum usum uersae aut ita appulsae muris, ut pro
aggere ac pontibus praebere ascensum possent?
4   Itaque Scipio, postquam eo uentum est, contra quam
in nauali certamine solet, rostratis, quae praesidio aliis esse
5 poterant, in postremam aciem receptis prope terram,
onerariarum quadriplicem ordinem pro muro aduersus
hostem opposuit, easque ipsas, ne in tumultu pugnae turbari
ordines possent, malis antennisque de naue in nauem
traiectis ac ualidis funibus uelut uno inter se uinculo
6 illigatis comprendit, tabulasque superinstrauit, ut peruium
in totum nauium ordinem esset, et sub ipsis pontibus
interualla fecit, qua procurrere speculatoriae naues in
7 hostem ac tuto recipi possent. his raptim pro tempore
instructis, mille ferme delecti propugnatores onerariis
imponuntur; telorum missilium, ut quamuis longo
8 certamine sufficerent, uis ingens congeritur. ita parati
atque intenti hostium aduentum opperiebantur.

Carthaginienses, qui, si maturassent, omnia permixta
9 turba trepidantium primo impetu oppressissent, perculsi
terrestribus cladibus atque inde ne mari quidem, ubi ipsi
plus poterant, satis fidentes, die segni nauigatione absumpto
sub occasum solis in portum—Rusucmona Afri uocant—
10 classe appulere. postero die sub ortum solis instruxere ab
alto naues uelut ad iustum proelium nauale et tamquam
11 exituris contra Romanis. cum diu stetissent, postquam
nihil moueri ab hostibus uiderunt, tum demum onerarias
12 adgrediuntur. res erat minime certamini nauali similis,
proxime speciem muros oppugnantium nauium. altitu-
13 dine aliquantum onerariae superabant; ex rostratis Poeni
uana pleraque, utpote supino iactu, tela in locum superio-
rem mittebant; grauior ac pondere ipso libratior superne

14 ex onerariis ictus erat. speculatoriae naues ac leuia alia
nauigia, quae sub constratis pontium per interualla excur-
rebant, primo ipsae tanto impetu et magnitudine rostra-
15 tarum obruebantur; deinde et propugnatoribus quoque
incommodae erant, quod permixtae cum hostium nauibus
inhibere saepe tela cogebant metu, ne ambiguo ictu suis
16 inciderent. postremo asseres ferreo unco praefixi—harpagones uocantur—ex Punicis nauibus inici in Romanas
17 coepti. quos cum neque ipsos neque catenas quibus sus-
pensi iniciebantur incidere possent, ut quaeque retro in-
18 hibita rostrata onerariam haerentem unco traheret, scindi
uideres uincula, quibus alia aliis innexa erat, seriem aliam
19 simul plurium nauium trahi. hoc maxime modo lacerati
quidem omnes pontes, et uix transiliendi in secundum
ordinem nauium spatium propugnatoribus datum est.
20 sexaginta ferme onerariae puppibus abstractae Carthaginem
sunt. maior quam pro re laetitia, sed eo gratior, quod
inter adsiduas clades ac lacrimas unum quantumcumque
ex insperato gaudium adfulserat, cum eo ut appareret
haud procul exitio fuisse Romanam classem, ni cessatum a
praefectis suarum nauium foret et Scipio in tempore
subuenisset.

XI. Per eosdem forte dies cum Laelius et Masinissa
quinto decimo ferme die in Numidiam peruenissent, Maesulii, regnum paternum Masinissae, laeti ut ad regem diu
2 desideratum concessere. Syphax pulsis inde praefectis
praesidiisque suis uetere se continebat regno, neutiquam
3 quieturus. stimulabat aegrum amore uxor socerque, et
ita uiris equisque abundabat, ut subiectae oculis regni
per multos florentis annos uires etiam minus barbaro
4 atque impotenti animo spiritus possent facere. igitur
omnibus, qui bello apti erant, in unum coactis equos arma
tela diuidit; equites in turmas, pedites in cohortes, sicut
quondam ab Romanis centurionibus didicerat, distribuit.
5 exercitu haud minore quam quem prius habuerat, ceterum
omni prope nouo atque incondito, ire ad hostes pergit.
6 et castris in propinquo positis primo pauci equites ex tuto
speculantes ab stationibus progredi, dein iaculis summoti

recurrere ad suos; inde excursiones in uicem fieri et,
7 cum pulsos indignatio accenderet, plures subire, quod
irritamentum certaminum equestrium est, cum aut
uincentibus spes aut pulsis ira adgregat suos.

8   Ita tum a paucis proelio accenso omnem utrimque
postremo equitatum certaminis studium effundit. ac
dum sincerum equestre proelium erat, multitudo Masaesuliorum, ingentia agmina Syphace emittente, sustineri uix
9 poterat: deinde ut pedes Romanus repentino per turmas
suas uiam dantes intercursu stabilem aciem fecit absterruit-
que effuse inuehentem sese hostem, primo barbari segnius
10 permittere equos, dein stare, ac propere turbati nouo genere
pugnae postremo non pediti solum cedere, sed ne equitem
11 quidem sustinere peditis praesidio audentem. iam signa
quoque legionum adpropinquabant. tum uero Masaesulii
non modo primum impetum sed ne conspectum quidem
signorum atque armorum tulerunt: tantum seu memoria
priorum cladium seu praesens terror ualuit. XII. Ibi Syphax, dum obequitat hostium turmis, si pudore, si peri-
2 culo suo fugam sistere posset, equo grauiter icto effusus
opprimitur capiturque et uiuus, laetum ante omnes Masinissae praebiturus spectaculum, ad Laelium pertrahitur.

3   Cirta caput regni Syphacis erat, eoque se ingens ho-
4 minum contulit uis. caedes in eo proelio minor quam
uictoria fuit, quia equestri tantummodo proelio certatum
5 fuerat. non plus quinque milia occisa, minus dimidium
eius hominum captum est impetu in castra facto, quo
6 perculsa rege amisso multitudo se contulerat. Masinissa
sibi quidem dicere nihil esse in praesentia pulchrius quam
uictorem recuperatum tanto post interuallo patrium
inuisere regnum; sed tam secundis quam aduersis rebus
7 non dari spatium ad cessandum: si se Laelius cum equitatu uinctoque Syphace Cirtam praecedere sinat, trepida
omnia metu se oppressurum: Laelium cum peditibus
8 subsequi modicis itineribus posse. adsentiente Laelio
praegressus Cirtam euocari ad colloquium principes Cir-
tensium iubet. sed apud ignaros regis casus nec quae
acta essent promendo nec minis nec suadendo ante ualuit,

9 quam rex uinctus in conspectum datus esset. tum ad
spectaculum tam foedum comploratio orta, et partim pa-
uore moenia sunt deserta, partim repentino consensu
gratiam apud uictorem quaerentium patefactae portae.
10 et Masinissa praesidio circa portas opportunaque moenium
dimisso, ne cui fugae pateret exitus, ad regiam occupan-
dam citato uadit equo.
11 Intranti uestibulum in ipso limine Sophoniba, uxor
Syphacis, filia Hasdrubalis Poeni, occurrit; et cum in
medio agmine armatorum Masinissam insignem cum armis
tum cetero habitu conspexisset, regem esse, id quod erat,
12 rata, genibus aduoluta eius: " omnia quidem ut posses "
inquit " in nobis, di dederunt uirtusque et felicitas tua:
sed si captiuae apud dominum uitae necisque suae uocem
supplicem mittere licet, si genua, si uictricem attingere
13 dextram, precor quaesoque per maiestatem regiam, in
qua paulo ante nos quoque fuimus, per gentis Numidarum
nomen, quod tibi cum Syphace commune fuit, per huiusce
regiae deos, qui te melioribus ominibus accipiant quam
14 Syphacem hinc miserunt, hanc ueniam supplici des, ut
ipse quodcumque fert animus de captiua statuas neque
me in cuiusquam Romani superbum et crudele arbitrium
15 uenire sinas. si nihil aliud quam Syphacis uxor fuissem,
tamen Numidae atque in eadem mecum Africa geniti
16 quam alienigenae et externi fidem experiri mallem: quid
Carthaginiensi ab Romano, quid filiae Hasdrubalis timen-
dum sit, uides. si nulla re alia potes, morte me ut
17 uindices ab Romanorum arbitrio oro obtestorque." forma
erat insignis et florentissima aetas: itaque cum modo
genua modo dextram amplectens in id, ne cui Romano
traderetur, fidem exposceret, propiusque blanditias oratio
18 esset quam preces, non in misericordiam modo prolapsus
est animus uictoris, sed, ut est genus Numidarum in
uenerem praeceps, amore captiuae uictor captus. data
dextra in id quod petebatur obligandae fidei, in regiam
19 concedit. insistit deinde reputare secum ipse, quem ad
modum promissi fidem praestaret. quod cum expedire
non posset, ab amore temerarium atque impudens mu-

20 tuatur consilium: nuptias in eum ipsum diem parari repente iubet, ne quid relinqueret integri aut Laelio aut
ipsi Scipioni consulendi uelut in captiuam, quae Masi-
21 nissae iam nupta foret. factis nuptiis superuenit Laelius,
et adeo non dissimulauit improbare se factum, ut primo
etiam cum Syphace et ceteris captiuis detractam eam lecto
22 geniali mittere ad Scipionem conatus sit. uictus deinde
precibus Masinissae orantis, ut arbitrium, utrius regum
duorum fortunae accessio Sophoniba esset, ad Scipionem
reiceret, misso Syphace et captiuis ceteras urbes Numidiae, quae praesidiis regiis tenebantur, adiuuante Masinissa
recipit.

    XIII. Syphacem in castra adduci cum esset nuntia-
tum, omnis uelut ad spectaculum triumphi multitudo effusa
2 est. praecedebat ipse uinctus, sequebatur grex nobilium
Numidarum. tum, quantum quisque plurimum poterat
magnitudini Syphacis famaeque gentis uictoriam suam au-
3 gendo addebat: illum esse regem, cuius tantum maiestati
duo potentissimi in terris tribuerint populi, Romanus Car-
thaginiensisque, ut Scipio imperator suus ad amicitiam
4 eius petendam, relicta prouincia Hispania exercituque,
5 duabus quinqueremibus in Africam nauigauerit, Hasdrubal Poenorum imperator non ipse modo ad eum in regnum
uenerit, sed etiam filiam ei nuptum dederit. habuisse eum
uno tempore in potestate duos imperatores, Poenum Ro-
6 manumque. sicut ab dis immortalibus pars utraque hostiis mactandis pacem petisset, ita ab eo utrimque pariter
7 amicitiam petitam. iam tantas habuisse opes, ut Masinissam regno pulsum eo redegerit, ut uita eius fama
mortis et latebris, ferarum modo in siluis rapto uiuentis,
tegeretur.
8   His sermonibus circumstantium celebratus rex in
praetorium ad Scipionem est perductus. mouit et Scipionem cum fortuna pristina uiri praesenti fortunae collata,
tum recordatio hospitii dextraeque datae et foederis
9 publice ac priuatim iuncti. eadem haec et Syphaci animum dederunt in adloquendo uictorem. nam cum Scipio
quid sibi uoluisset quaereret, qui non societatem solum

10 abnuisset Romanam, sed ultro bellum intulisset, tum ille
peccasse quidem sese atque insanisse fatebatur, sed non
tum demum cum arma aduersus populum Romanum ce-
11 pisset; exitum sui furoris eum fuisse, non principium: tum
se insanisse, tum hospitia priuata et publica foedera omnia
ex animo eiecisse, cum Carthaginiensem matronam do-
12 mum acceperit. illis nuptialibus facibus regiam confla-
grasse suam, illam furiam pestemque omnibus delenimentis
animum suum auertisse atque alienasse, nec conquiesse,
donec ipsa manibus suis nefaria sibi arma aduersus ho-
13 spitem atque amicum induerit. perdito tamen atque ad-
flicto sibi hoc in miseriis solatii esse, quod in omnium
hominum inimicissimi sibi domum ac penates eandem
14 pestem ac furiam transisse uideat. neque prudentiorem
neque constantiorem Masinissam quam Syphacem esse,
etiam iuuenta incautiorem: certe stultius illum atque in-
temperantius eam quam se duxisse.

XIV. Haec non hostili modo odio sed amoris etiam
stimulis amatam apud aemulum cernens cum dixisset,
2 non mediocri cura Scipionis animum pepulit. et fidem
criminibus raptae prope inter arma nuptiae neque consulto
neque exspectato Laelio faciebant, tamque praeceps
festinatio, ut quo die captam hostem uidisset, eodem
matrimonio iunctam acciperet et ad penates hostis sui
3 nuptiale sacrum conficeret. et eo foediora haec uidebantur
Scipioni, quod ipsum in Hispania iuuenem nullius forma
pepulerat captiuae. haec secum uolutanti Laelius ac
Masinissa superuenerunt; quos cum pariter ambo et
benigno uultu excepisset et egregiis laudibus frequenti
praetorio celebrasset, abductum in secretum Masinissam
4 sic adloquitur: " aliqua te existimo, Masinissa, intuentem
in me bona et principio in Hispania ad iungendam mecum
amicitiam uenisse, et postea in Africa te ipsum spesque
5 omnes tuas in fidem meam commisisse. atqui nulla earum
uirtus est propter quas tibi appetendus uisus sim, qua ego
aeque ac temperantia et continentia libidinum gloriatus
5 fuerim. hanc te quoque ad ceteras tuas eximias uirtutes,
Masinissa, adiecisse uelim. non est, non—mihi crede—

tantum ab hostibus armatis aetatis nostrae periculi,
7 quantum ab circumfusis undique uoluptatibus. qui eas
temperantia sua frenauit ac domuit, multo maius decus
maioremque uictoriam sibi peperit quam nos Syphace
8 uicto habemus. quae me absente strenue ac fortiter
fecisti, libenter et commemoraui et memini: cetera te
ipsum reputare tecum quam me dicente erubescere malo.
Syphax populi Romani auspiciis uictus captusque est.
9 itaque ipse, coniunx, regnum, ager et oppida, homines qui
incolunt, quidquid denique Syphacis fuit, praeda populi
10 Romani est; et regem coniugemque eius, etiamsi non
ciuis Carthaginiensis esset, etiamsi non patrem eius imperatorem hostium uideremus, Romam oporteret mitti, ac
senatus populique Romani de ea iudicium atque arbitrium
esse, quae regem socium nobis alienasse atque in arma
11 egisse praecipitem dicatur. uince animum: caue deformes
multa bona uno uitio, et tot meritorum gratiam maiore
culpa, quam causa culpae est, corrumpas."
XV. Masinissae haec audienti non rubor solum suffusus
sed lacrimae etiam obortae; et cum se quidem in potestate
futurum imperatoris dixisset, orassetque eum ut, quantum
2 res sineret, fidei suae temere obstrictae consuleret—
promisisse enim se in nullius potestatem eam traditurum—
ex praetorio in tabernaculum suum confusus concessit.
3 ibi arbitris remotis cum crebro suspiritu et gemitu, quod
facile ab circumstantibus tabernaculum exaudiri posset,
4 aliquantum temporis consumpsisset, ingenti ad postremum
edito gemitu fidum e seruis uocat, sub cuius custodia regio
more ad incerta fortunae uenenum erat, et mixtum in
5 poculo ferre ad Sophonibam iubet, ac simul nuntiare
Masinissam libenter primam ei fidem praestaturum fuisse,
quam uir uxori debuerit: quoniam eius arbitrium qui
possint adimant, secundam fidem praestare, ne uiua in
6 potestatem Romanorum ueniat: memor patris imperatoris patriaeque et duorum regum, quibus nupta fuisset,
sibi ipsa consuleret. hunc nuntium ac simul uenenum
7 ferens minister cum ad Sophonibam uenisset, "accipio"
inquit "nuptiale munus, neque ingratum, si nihil maius

uir uxori praestare potuit: hoc tamen nuntia, melius me
8 morituram fuisse, si non in funere meo nupsissem." non
locuta est ferocius quam acceptum poculum nullo trepida-
9 tionis signo dato impauide hausit. quod ubi nuntiatum
est Scipioni, ne quid aeger animi ferox iuuenis grauius
10 consuleret, accitum eum extemplo nunc solatur, nunc,
quod temeritatem temeritate alia luerit, tristioremque rem
11 quam necesse fuerit fecerit, leniter castigat. postero die,
ut a praesenti motu auerteret animum eius, in tribunal
escendit et contionem aduocari iussit. ibi Masinissam,
primum regem adpellatum eximiisque ornatum laudibus,
aurea corona, aurea patera, sella curuli et scipione eburno,
12 toga picta et palmata tunica donat. addit uerbis honorem:
neque magnificentius quicquam triumpho apud Romanos
neque triumphantibus ampliorem eo ornatum esse, quo
unum omnium externorum dignum Masinissam populus
13 Romanus ducat. Laelium deinde et ipsum collaudatum
aurea corona donat. et alii militares uiri, prout a quoque
14 nauata opera erat, donati. his honoribus mollitus regis
animus, erectusque in spem propinquam sublato Syphace
omnis Numidiae potiundae.

XVI. Scipio C. Laelio cum Syphace aliisque captiuis
Romam misso, cum quibus et Masinissae legati profecti
sunt, ipse ad Tyneta rursus castra refert et quae muni-
2 menta inchoauerat permunit. Carthaginienses non breui
solum sed prope uano gaudio ab satis prospera in praesens oppugnatione classis perfusi, post famam capti
Syphacis, in quo plus prope quam in Hasdrubale atque
3 exercitu suo spei reposuerunt, perculsi, iam nullo auctore
belli ultra audito oratores ad pacem petendam mittunt
triginta seniorum principes; id erat sanctius apud illos
consilium maximaque ad ipsum senatum regendum uis.
4 qui ubi in castra Romana et in praetorium peruenerunt,
more adulantium—accepto, credo, ritu ex ea regione ex
5 qua oriundi erant—procubuerunt. conueniens oratio tam
humili adulationi fuit, non culpam purgantium, sed trans-
ferentium initium culpae in Hannibalem potentiaeque eius
6 fautores. ueniam ciuitati petebant ciuium temeritate bis

iam euersae, incolumi futurae iterum hostium beneficio;
7 imperium ex uictis hostibus populum Romanum non perni-
ciem petere. paratis obedienter seruire imperaret, quae
uellet.

8   Scipio et uenisse ea spe in Africam se ait, et spem
suam prospero belli euentu auctam, uictoriam se non pacem
9 domum reportaturum esse: tamen, cum uictoriam prope
in manibus habeat, pacem non abnuere, ut omnes gentes
sciant populum Romanum et suscipere iuste bella et finire.
10 leges pacis se has dicere: captiuos et perfugas et fugitiuos restituant; exercitus ex Italia et Gallia deducant;
Hispania abstineant; insulis omnibus, quae inter Italiam
11 atque Africam sint, decedant; naues longas praeter uiginti omnes tradant, tritici quingenta, hordei trecenta
12 milia modium. pecuniae summam quantam imperauerit,
parum conuenit: alibi quinque milia talentum, alibi quinque milia pondo argenti, alibi duplex stipendium militibus
13 imperatum inuenio. " his condicionibus " inquit " pla-
ceatne pax, triduum ad consultandum dabitur. si pla-
cuerit, mecum indutias facite, Romam ad senatum mittite
14 legatos." ita dimissi Carthaginienses nullas recusandas
condiciones pacis cum censuissent, quippe qui moram
temporis quaererent, dum Hannibal in Africam traiceret,
15 legatos alios ad Scipionem, ut indutias facerent, alios
Romam ad pacem petendam mittunt, ducentes paucos in
speciem captiuos perfugasque et fugitiuos, quo impetrabilior
pax esset.

   XVII. Multis ante diebus Laelius cum Syphace pri-
moribusque Numidarum captiuis Romam uenit, quaeque
in Africa gesta essent, omnia ordine exposuit patribus,
ingenti hominum et in praesens laetitia et in futurum spe.
2 consulti inde patres regem in custodiam Albam mittendum
censuerunt, Laelium retinendum, donec legati Carthagi-
3 nienses uenirent. supplicatio in quadriduum decreta est.
P. Aelius praetor senatu misso et contione inde aduocata
4 cum C. Laelio in rostra escendit. Ibi uero audientes fusos
Carthaginiensium exercitus, deuictum et captum ingentis
nominis regem, Numidiam omnem egregia uictoria pera-

E

5 gratam, tacitum continere gaudium non poterant, quin
clamoribus quibusque aliis multitudo solet laetitiam im-
6 modicam significarent. itaque praetor extemplo edixit,
uti aeditui aedes sacras tota urbe aperirent, circumeundi
salutandique deos agendique grates per totum diem populo
potestas fieret.

7   Postero die legatos Masinissae in senatum introduxit.
gratulati primum senatui sunt, quod P. Scipio prospere
8 res in Africa gessisset; deinde gratias egerunt, quod
Masinissam non adpellasset modo regem sed fecisset
restituendo in paternum regnum, in quo post Syphacem
sublatum, si ita patribus uisum esset, sine metu et certa-
9 mine esset regnaturus, dein collaudatum pro contione
amplissimis decorasset donis; quibus ne indignus esset et
10 dedisse operam Masinissam et porro daturum esse. petere
ut regium nomen ceteraque Scipionis beneficia et munera
11 senatus decreto confirmaret: et ad haec, nisi molestum
esset, illud quoque petere Masinissam, ut Numidas captiuos,
qui Romae in custodia essent, remitterent: id sibi amplum
12 apud populares futurum esse. ad ea responsum legatis:
rerum gestarum prospere in Africa communem sibi cum
rege gratulationem esse; Scipionem recte atque ordine
uideri fecisse quod eum regem appellauerit, et quidquid
aliud fecerit, quod cordi foret Masinissae, id patres compro-
13 bare ac laudare. munera quoque quae legati ferrent regi,
decreuerunt sagula purpurea duo cum fibulis singulis et
lato clauo tunicis, equos duo phaleratos, bina equestria
arma cum loricis, et tabernacula militaremque supellecti-
14 lem, qualem praeberi consuli mos esset. haec regi praetor
mittere iussus, legatis in singulos dona ne minus quinum
milium, comitibus eorum singulorum milium aeris, et
uestimenta bina legatis, singula comitibus Numidisque
qui ex custodia emissi redderentur regi: ad hoc aedes
liberae, loca, lautia legatis decreta.

    XVIII. Eadem aestate, qua haec decreta Romae et
in Africa gesta sunt, P. Quinctilius Varus praetor et
M. Cornelius proconsul in agro Insubrum Gallorum cum
2 Magone Poeno signis collatis pugnarunt. praetoris legio-

nes in prima acie fuerunt: Cornelius suas in subsidiis tenuit,
ipse ad prima signa equo aduectus; proque duobus
cornibus praetor ac proconsul milites ad inferenda in
3 hostes signa summa ui hortabantur. postquam nihil commouebant, tum Quinctilius Cornelio: "lentior, ut uides,
fit pugna, et induratur praeter spem resistendo hostium
4 timor, ac ne uertat in audaciam periculum est. equestrem
procellam excitemus oportet, si turbare ac statu mouere
uolumus. itaque uel tu ad prima signa proelium sustine,
ego inducam in pugnam equites; uel ego hic in prima
acie rem geram, tu quattuor legionum equites in hostem
5 emitte." utram uellet praetor muneris partem proconsule
accipiente, Quinctilius praetor cum filio, cui Marco praenomen erat, impigro iuuene ad equites pergit, iussosque
6 escendere in equos repente in hostem emittit. tumultum
equestrem auxit clamor ab legionibus additus, nec stetis-
set hostium acies, ni Mago ad primum equitum motum
7 paratos elephantos extemplo in proelium induxisset; ad
quorum stridorem odoremque et aspectum territi equi
uanum equestre auxilium fecerunt. et ut, turbae permixtus ubi cuspide uti et comminus gladio posset, roboris
maioris Romanus eques erat, ita in ablatum pauentibus
procul equis melius ex interuallo Numidae iaculabantur.
8 simul et peditum legio duodecima, magna ex parte caesa,
9 pudore magis quam uiribus tenebat locum; nec diutius
tenuisset, ni ex subsidiis tertia decima legio in primam
aciem inducta proelium dubium excepisset. Mago quoque
10 ex subsidiis Gallos integrae legioni opposuit. quibus haud
magno certamine fusis hastati legionis undecimae conglo-
bant sese atque elephantos iam etiam peditum aciem
11 turbantes inuadunt. in quos cum pila confertos coniecis-
sent, nullo ferme frustra emisso omnes retro in aciem
suorum auerterunt; quattuor grauati uulneribus corrue-
12 runt. tum primum commota hostium acies, simul omnibus equitibus, ut auersos uidere elephantos, ad augendum
pauorem ac tumultum effusis. sed donec stetit ante signa
Mago, gradum sensim referentes ordines et tenorem pugnae
13 seruabant; postquam femine transfixo cadentem auferrique

ex proelio prope exsanguem uidere, extemplo in fugam
omnes uersi. ad quinque milia hostium eo die caesa, et
14 signa militaria duo et uiginti capta. nec Romanis incruenta
uictoria fuit: duo milia et trecenti de exercitu praetoris,
pars multo maxima ex legione duodecima, amissi. inde
15 et tribuni militum duo, M. Cosconius et M. Maeuius. ter-
tiae decimae quoque legionis, quae postremo proelio ad-
fuerat, C. Heluius tribunus militum in restituenda pugna
cecidit, et duo et uiginti ferme equites illustres obtriti
ab elephantis cum centurionibus aliquot perierunt. et
longius certamen fuisset, ni uulnere ducis concessa uictoria
esset.

XIX. Mago proximae silentio noctis profectus, quantum pati uiae per uulnus poterat itineribus extentis, ad
2 mare in Ligures Ingaunos peruenit. ibi eum legati ab
Carthagine paucis ante diebus in sinum Gallicum appulsis
nauibus adierunt, iubentes primo quoque tempore in
3 Africam traicere: id et fratrem eius Hannibalem—nam ad
eum quoque isse legatos eadem iubentes—facturum;
non in eo esse Carthaginiensium res, ut Galliam atque Ita-
4 liam armis obtineant. Mago non imperio modo senatus
periculoque patriae motus sed metuens etiam, ne uictor
hostis moranti instaret, Liguresque ipsi, relinqui Italiam
a Poenis cernentes, ad eos quorum mox in potestate futuri
5 essent deficerent, simul sperans leniorem in nauigatione
quam in uia iactationem uulneris fore et curationi omnia
commodiora, impositis copiis in naues profectus, uixdum
superata Sardinia ex uulnere moritur. naues quoque aliquot Poenorum disiectae in alto a classe Romana, quae
6 circa Sardiniam erat, capiuntur. haec terra marique in
parte Italiae, qua iacet ad Alpes, gesta.

Consul C. Seruilius nulla memorabili re in prouincia
Etruria Galliaque—nam eo quoque processerat—gesta,
7 patre C. Seruilio et C. Lutatio ex seruitute post sextum
decimum annum receptis, qui ad uicum Tannetum a
8 Boiis capti fuerant, hinc patre hinc Catulo lateri circumdatis priuato magis quam publico decore insignis Romam
9 rediit. latum ad populum est, ne C. Seruilio fraudi esset

quod, patre qui sella curuli sedisset uiuo, cum id igno-
raret, tribunus plebis atque aedilis plebis fuisset, contra
quam sanctum legibus erat. hac rogatione perlata in prouinciam rediit.

10   Ad Cn. Seruilium consulem, qui in Bruttiis erat, Consentia Aufugum Bergae Besidiae Ocriculum Lymphaeum
Argentanum Clampetia multique ignobiles populi, sen-
11 escere Punicum bellum cernentes, defecere. idem consul
cum Hannibale in agro Crotoniensi acie conflixit. obscura
eius pugnae fama est. Valerius Antias quinque milia
hostium caesa ait; quae tanta res est, ut aut impudenter
12 ficta sit aut neglegenter praetermissa. nihil certe ultra rei
in Italia ab Hannibale gestum. nam ad eum quoque legati
ab Carthagine uocantes in Africam, iis forte diebus quibus
ad Magonem, uenerunt. XX. frendens gemensque ac
uix lacrimis temperans dicitur legatorum uerba audisse.
2 postquam edita sunt mandata, " iam non perplexe " inquit
" sed palam reuocant, qui uetando supplementum et
3 pecuniam mitti iam pridem retrahebant. uicit ergo
Hannibalem non populus Romanus totiens caesus fugatus-
que, sed senatus Carthaginiensis obtrectatione atque
4 inuidia. neque hac deformitate reditus mei tam P.
Scipio exsultabit atque efferet sese quam Hanno, qui
domum nostram, quando alia re non potuit, ruina Carthaginis oppressit."

5   Iam hoc ipsum praesagiens animo praeparauerat ante
naues. itaque inutili militum turba praesidii specie in
oppida Bruttii agri, quae pauca magis metu quam fide
continebantur, dimissa, quod roboris in exercitu erat in
6 Africam transuexit, multis Italici generis, quia in Africam
secuturos abnuentes concesserant in Iunonis Laciniae
delubrum inuiolatum ad eam diem, in templo ipso foede
7 interfectis. raro quemquam alium patriam exsilii causa
relinquentem tam maestum abisse ferunt quam Hannibalem
hostium terra excedentem; respexisse saepe Italiae litora
et deos hominesque accusantem in se quoque ac suum
8 ipsius caput execratum, quod non cruentum ab Cannensi
uictoria militem Romam duxisset; Scipionem ire ad

Carthaginem ausum, qui consul hostem Poenum in Italia
9 non uidisset: se, centum milibus armatorum ad Trasumennum aut Cannas caesis, circa Casilinum Cumasque et
Nolam consensuisse. haec accusans querensque ex diutina
possessione Italiae est detractus.

XXI. Romam per eosdem dies et Magonem et Hannibalem profectos adlatum est. cuius duplicis gratulatio-
nis minuit laetitiam et quod parum duces in retinendis iis,
cum id mandatum ab senatu esset, aut animi aut uirium
2 habuisse uidebantur et quod solliciti erant, omni belli
mole in unum exercitum ducemque inclinata, quo euasura
3 esset res. per eosdem dies legati Saguntini uenerunt com-
prensos cum pecunia adducentes Carthaginienses, qui ad
4 conducenda auxilia in Hispaniam traiecissent. ducenta et
quinquaginta auri, octingenta pondo argenti in uestibulo
5 curiae posuerunt. hominibus acceptis in carcerem condi-
tis, auro argentoque reddito, gratiae legatis actae, atque
insuper munera data ac naues, quibus in Hispaniam re-
6 uerterentur. mentio deinde ab senioribus facta est segnius
homines bona quam mala sentire; transitu in Italiam Hannibalis quantum terroris pauorisque esse meminisse; quas
7 deinde clades, quos luctus incidisse! uisa castra hostium
e muris urbis: quae uota singulorum uniuersorumque
fuisse! quotiens in conciliis uoces manus ad caelum por-
8 rigentium auditas, en umquam ille dies futurus esset, quo
uacuam hostibus Italiam bona pace florentem uisuri es-
9 sent! dedisse id deos tandem sexto decimo demum anno,
nec esse, qui deis grates agendas censeant: adeo ne ad-
uenientem quidem gratiam homines benigne accipere, ne-
10 dum ut praeteritae satis memores sint. conclamatum
deinde ex omni parte curiae est, uti referret P. Aelius
praetor; decretumque, ut quinque dies circa omnia puluinaria supplicaretur uictimaeque maiores immolarentur
centum uiginti.

11 Iam dimisso Laelio legatisque Masinissae cum Carthaginiensium legatos de pace ad senatum uenientes Puteolis uisos, inde terra uenturos adlatum esset, reuocari
12 C. Laelium placuit, ut coram eo de pace ageretur. Q. Ful-

uius Gillo, legatus Scipionis, Carthaginienses Romam
adduxit: quibus uetitis ingredi urbem hospitium in uilla
publica, senatus ad aedem Bellonae datus est. XXII. Orationem eandem ferme quam apud Scipionem habuerunt,
culpam omnem belli a publico consilio in Hannibalem
2 uertentes; eum iniussu senatus non Alpes modo sed Hiberum quoque transgressum, nec Romanis solum, sed
ante etiam Saguntinis priuato consilio bellum intulisse;
3 senatui ac populo Carthaginiensi, si quis uere aestimet,
4 foedus ad eam diem inuiolatum esse cum Romanis. itaque nihil aliud sibi mandatum esse uti peterent quam ut
in ea pace, quae postremo cum consule Lutatio facta es-
5 set, manere liceret. cum more tradito patribus potestatem interrogandi, si quis quid uellet, legatos praetor
fecisset, senioresque, qui foederibus interfuerant, alia alii
interrogarent, nec meminisse per aetatem—etenim omnes
6 ferme iuuenes erant—dicerent legati, conclamatum ex
omni parte curiae est Punica fraude electos qui ueterem
pacem repeterent, cuius ipsi non meminissent.

XXIII. Emotis deinde curia legatis sententiae interro-
gari coeptae. M. Liuius C. Seruilium consulem, qui
propior esset, arcessendum, ut coram eo de pace ageretur,
2 censebat; cum de re maiore, quam quanta ea esset, con-
sultatio incidere non posset, non uideri sibi absente consulum altero ambobusue eam rem agi satis ex dignitate
3 populi Romani esse. Q. Metellus, qui triennio ante consul
dictatorque fuerat: cum P. Scipio caedendo exercitus,
agros populando in eam necessitatem hostes compulisset,
4 ut supplices pacem peterent, et nemo omnium uerius
existimare posset, qua mente ea pax peteretur, quam tum
qui ante portas Carthaginis bellum gereret, nullius alterius
consilio quam Scipionis accipiendam abnuendamue pacem
5 esse. M. Valerius Laeuinus, qui bis consul fuerat, speculatores non legatos uenisse arguebat, iubendosque Italia
excedere et custodes cum iis usque ad naues mittendos,
6 Scipionique scribendum, ne bellum remitteret. Laelius
Fuluiusque adiecerunt, et Scipionem in eo positam habuisse
spem pacis, si Hannibal et Mago ex Italia non reuocaren-

7 tur; omnia simulaturos Carthaginienses duces eos exercitusque exspectantes; deinde quamuis recentium foederum
et deorum omnium oblitos bellum gesturos. eo magis in
8 Laeuini sententiam discessum. legati pace infecta ac
prope sine responsu dimissi.

XXIV. Per eos dies Cn. Seruilius consul, haud dubius quin pacatae Italiae penes se gloria esset, uelut pulsum ab se Hannibalem persequens, in Siciliam, inde et in
2 Africam transiturus, traiecit. quod ubi Romae uolgatum est, primo censuerant patres, ut praetor scriberet con-
3 suli, senatum aequum censere in Italiam reuerti eum; dein cum praetor spreturum eum litteras suas diceret, dictator ad id ipsum creatus P. Sulpicius pro iure maioris imperii
4 consulem in Italiam reuocauit. reliquum anni cum M. Seruilio magistro equitum circumeundis Italiae urbibus, quae bello alienatae fuerant, noscendisque singularum causis consumpsit.

5 Per indutiarum tempus et ex Sardinia ab Lentulo praetore centum onerariae naues cum commeatu uiginti rostratarum praesidio et ab hoste et ab tempestatibus mari
6 tuto in Africam transmiserunt. Cn. Octauio ducentis onerariis triginta longis nauibus ex Sicilia traicienti non ea-
7 dem fortuna fuit. in conspectum ferme Africae prospero cursu uectum primo destituit uentus, deinde uersus in
8 Africum turbauit ac passim naues disiecit. ipse cum rostratis per aduersos fluctus ingenti remigum labore enisus
9 Apollinis promunturium tenuit: onerariae pars maxima ad Aegimurum—insula ea sinum ab alto claudit, in quo sita Carthago est, triginta ferme milia ab urbe—, aliae aduersus urbem ipsam ad Calidas Aquas delatae sunt.
10 omnia in conspectu Carthaginis erant. itaque ex tota urbe in forum concursum est: magistratus senatum uocare, populus in curiae uestibulo fremere, ne tanta ex oculis ma-
11 nibusque amitteretur praeda. cum quidam pacis petitae, alii indutiarum—necdum enim dies exierat—fidem opponerent, permixto paene senatus populique concilio consensum est, ut classem quinquaginta nauium Hasdrubal Aegimurum traiceret, inde per litora portusque dispersas

12 Romanas naues colligeret. desertae fuga nautarum primum ab Aegimuro, deinde ab Aquis onerariae Carthaginem puppibus tractae sunt.

XXV. Nondum ab Roma reuerterant legati. neque sciebatur, quae senatus Romani de bello aut pace sen-
2 tentia esset, necdum indutiarum dies exierat: eo, indigniorem iniuriam ratus Scipio, ab iis, qui petissent pacem et indutias, et spem pacis et fidem indutiarum uiolatam esse, legatos Carthaginem L. Baebium M. Sergium L. Fa-
3 bium extemplo misit. qui cum multitudinis concursu prope uiolati essent nec reditum tutiorem futurum cernerent, petierunt a magistratibus, quorum auxilio uis prohibita erat, ut naues mitterent quae se prosequerentur.
4 datae triremes duae cum ad Bagradam flumen peruenissent, unde castra Romana conspiciebantur, Carthaginem rediere.
5 classis Punica ad Vticam stationem habebat. ex ea tres quadriremes—seu clam misso a Carthagine nuntio uti fieret, seu Hasdrubale, qui classi praeerat, sine publica
6 fraude auso facinus—quinqueremem Romanam superantem promunturium ex alto repente adgressae sunt. sed neque rostro ferire celeritate subterlabentem poterant, neque transilire armati ex humilioribus in altiorem nauem,
7 et defendebatur egregie quoad tela suppeditarunt. quis deficientibus iam nulla alia res eam quam propinquitas terrae multitudoque a castris in litus effusa tueri potuisset.
8 concitatam enim remis quanto maximo impetu poterant in terram cum immisissent, nauis tantum iactura facta, in-
9 columes ipsi euaserunt. ita alio super aliud scelere cum haud dubie indutiae ruptae essent, Laelius Fuluiusque ab
10 Roma cum legatis Carthaginiensibus superuenerunt. quibus Scipio, etsi non indutiarum fides modo a Carthaginiensibus sed ius etiam gentium in legatis uiolatum esset, tamen se nihil nec institutis populi Romani nec suis moribus indignum in iis facturum esse cum dixisset, dimissis legatis bellum parabat.
11 Hannibali iam terrae appropinquanti iussus e nauticis unus escendere in malum, ut specularetur, quam tenerent regionem, cum dixisset sepulchrum dirutum proram

12 spectare, abominatus praeteruehi iusso gubernatore ad
Leptim adpulit classem atque ibi copias exposuit.

XXVI. Haec eo anno in Africa gesta: insequentia
excedunt in eum annum, quo M. Seruilius, qui tum magister equitum erat, et Tib. Claudius Nero consules facti
2 sunt. ceterum exitu superioris anni cum legati sociarum
urbium ex Graecia questi essent uastatos agros ab regiis
praesidiis profectosque in Macedoniam legatos ad res re-
3 petendas non admissos ad Philippum regem, simul nun-
tiassent quattuor milia militum cum Sopatro duce traiecta
in Africam dici, ut essent Carthaginiensibus praesidio, et
4 pecuniae aliquantum una missum, legatos ad regem, qui
haec aduersus foedus facta uideri patribus nuntiarent,
mittendos censuit senatus. missi C. Terentius Varro C.
Mamilius M. Aurelius. iis tres quinqueremes datae.

5 Annus insignis incendio ingenti, quo cliuus Publicius
ad solum exustus, et aquarum magnitudine, sed annonae
uilitate fuit, praeterquam quod pace omnis Italia erat
6 aperta, etiam quod magnam uim frumenti ex Hispania
missam M. Valerius Falto et M. Fabius Buteo aediles cu-
rules quaternis aeris uicatim populo discripserunt.

7 Eodem anno Quintus Fabius Maximus moritur exactae aetatis, si quidem uerum est augurem duos et sexa-
8 ginta annos fuisse, quod quidam auctores sunt. uir certe
fuit dignus tanto cognomine, uel si nouum ab eo inciperet.
superauit paternos honores, auitos aequauit. uictoriis
et maioribus proeliis auus insignis Rullus: sed omnia
9 aequare unus hostis Hannibal potest. cautior tamen quam
promptior hic habitus; et sicut dubites, utrum ingenio
cunctator fuerit, an quia ita bello proprie, quod tum ge-
rebatur, aptum erat, sic nihil certius est quam unum ho-
minem nobis cunctando rem restituisse, sicut Ennius ait.
10 augur in locum eius inauguratus Quintus Fabius Maximus
filius; in eiusdem locum pontifex—nam duo sacerdotia
habuit—Ser. Sulpicius Galba.

11 Ludi Romani diem unum, plebeii ter toti instaurati
ab aedilibus M. Sextio Sabino et Cn. Tremellio Flacco. ii
ambo praetores facti et cum iis C. Liuius Salinator et

12 C. Aurelius Cotta. comitia eius anni utrum C. Seruilius
consul habuerit, an, quia eum in Etruria tenuerint quaestiones ex senatus consulto de coniurationibus principum
habentem, dictator ab eo dictus P. Sulpicius, incertum ut
sit diuersi auctores faciunt.

XXVII. Principio insequentis anni M. Seruilius et Tib.
Claudius senatu in Capitolium uocato de prouinciis rettu-
2 lerunt. Italiam atque Africam in sortem conici, Africam
ambo cupientes, uolebant; ceterum Q. Metello maxime
3 adnitente neque negata neque data est Africa. consules
iussi cum tribunis plebis agere, ut, si iis uideretur, populum rogarent, quem uellent in Africa bellum gerere.
4 omnes tribus P. Scipionem iusserunt. nihilo minus consules prouinciam Africam—ita enim senatus decreuerat—in
5 sortem coniecerunt. Tib. Claudio Africa euenit, ut quinquaginta nauium classem, omnes quinqueremes, in Africam traiceret, parique imperio cum P. Scipione imperator
6 esset; M. Seruilius Etruriam sortitus. in eadem prouincia
et C. Seruilio prorogatum imperium, si consulem manere
7 ad urbem senatu placuisset. praetores M. Sextius Galliam
est sortitus, ut duas legiones prouinciamque traderet ei
P. Quinctilius Varus; C. Liuius Bruttios cum duabus legionibus, quibus P. Sempronius proconsul prioris anni
8 praefuerat; Cn. Tremelius Siciliam, ut a P. Villio Tappulo
praetore prioris anni prouinciam et duas legiones acciperet; Villius pro praetore uiginti nauibus longis, militibus
9 mille oram Siciliae tutaretur; M. Pomponius uiginti nauibus reliquis mille et quingentos milites Romam deporta-
ret; C. Aurelio Cottae urbana euenit. ceteris ita, uti quisque obtinebant prouincias exercitusque, prorogata imperia.
10 sedecim non amplius eo anno legionibus defensum impe-
11 rium est. et ut placatis dis omnia inciperent agerentque,
ludos, quos M. Claudio Marcello T. Quinctio consulibus
T. Manlius dictator quasque hostias maiores uouerat, si
per quinquennium res publica eodem statu fuisset, ut eos
ludos consules, priusquam ad bellum proficiscerentur, fa-
12 cerent. ludi in circo per quadriduum facti, hostiaeque
quibus uotae erant dis caesae.

XXVIII. Inter haec simul spes simul cura in dies
crescebat; nec satis certum constare apud animos poterat, utrum gaudio dignum esset Hannibalem post sextum
decimum annum ex Italia decedentem uacuam possessio-
nem eius reliquisse populo Romano, an magis metuendum,
2 quod incolumi exercitu in Africam transisset; locum nimirum, non periculum mutatum; cuius tantae dimicatio-
nis uatem, qui nuper decessisset, Q. Fabium haud frustra
canere solitum grauiorem in sua terra futurum hostem
3 Hannibalem, quam in aliena fuisset. nec Scipioni aut cum
Syphace, inconditae barbariae rege, cui Statorius semilixa
ducere exercitus solitus sit, aut cum socero eius Hasdrubale, fugacissimo duce, rem futuram, aut cum tumultuariis
exercitibus ex agrestium semermi turba subito conlectis,
4 sed cum Hannibale, prope nato in praetorio patris, fortissimi ducis, alito atque educato inter arma, puero quon-
5 dam milite, uixdum iuuene imperatore, qui senex uincendo
factus Hispanias Gallias Italiam ab Alpibus ad fretum mo-
numentis ingentium rerum complesset. ducere exercitum
aequalem stipendiis suis, duratum omnium rerum patien-
tia, quas uix fides fiat homines passos, perfusum milliens
cruore Romano, exuuias non militum tantum sed etiam
6 imperatorum portantem. multos occursuros Scipioni in
acie, qui praetores, qui imperatores, qui consules Romanos sua manu occidissent, muralibus uallaribusque insignes coronis, peruagatos capta castra, captas urbes
7 Romanas. non esse hodie tot fasces magistratibus populi
Romani, quot captos ex caede imperatorum praeferre
posset Hannibal.
8   Has formidines agitando animis ipsi curas et metus
augebant, etiam quod, cum adsuessent per aliquot annos
bellum ante oculos aliis atque aliis in Italiae partibus
lenta spe in nullum propinquum debellandi finem gerere,
erexerant omnium animos Scipio et Hannibal, uelut
9 ad supremum certamen comparati duces. ei quoque, quibus erat ingens in Scipione fiducia et uictoriae spes, quo
magis in propinquam eam imminebant animis, eo curae
10 intentiores erant. haud dispar habitus animorum Cartha-

giniensibus erat, quos modo petisse pacem, intuentes
Hannibalem ac rerum gestarum eius magnitudinem, pae-
11 nitebat, modo cum respicerent bis sese acie uictos, Syphacem captum, pulsos se Hispania, pulsos Italia,
atque ea omnia unius uirtute et consilio Scipionis facta,
uelut fatalem eum ducem in exitium suum natum horre-
bant.

XXIX. Iam Hadrumetum peruenerat Hannibal,
unde, ad reficiendum ex iactatione maritima militem paucis
diebus sumptis, excitus pauidis nuntiis omnia circa Carthaginem obtineri armis adferentium, magnis itineribus
2 Zamam contendit. Zama quinque dierum iter a Carthagine abest. inde praemissi speculatores cum excepti a
custodibus Romanis deducti ad Scipionem essent, traditos
eos tribunis militum iussosque omisso metu uisere omnia
3 per castra qua uellent circumduci iussit; percontatusque,
satin per commodum omnia explorassent, datis qui pro-
4 sequerentur, retro ad Hannibalem dimisit. Hannibal
nihil quidem eorum quae nuntiabantur—nam et Masinissam cum sex milibus peditum, quattuor equitum uenisse
eo ipso forte die adferebant—laeto animo audiuit, maxime
hostis fiducia, quae non de nilo profecto concepta esset
5 percussus. itaque quamquam et ipse causa belli erat, et
aduentu suo turbauerat et pactas indutias et spem foederum,
tamen, si integer quam si uictus peteret pacem, aequiora
impetrari posse ratus, nuntium ad Scipionem misit, ut
6 colloquendi secum potestatem faceret. id utrum sua
sponte fecerit an publico consilio, neutrum cur adfirmem
7 habeo. Valerius Antias primo proelio uictum eum a
Scipione, quo duodecim milia armatorum in acie sint
caesa, mille et septingenti capti, legatum cum aliis decem
8 legatis tradit in castra ad Scipionem uenisse. ceterum
Scipio cum colloquium haud abnuisset, ambo ex composito duces castra protulerunt, ut coire ex propinquo
9 possent. Scipio haud procul Naraggara urbe cum ad
cetera loco opportuno, tum quod aquatio intra teli coniec-
10 tum erat, consedit. Hannibal tumulum a quattuor milibus inde, tutum commodumque alioqui, nisi quod longin-

quae aquationis erat, cepit. ibi in medio locus conspectus undique, ne quid insidiarum esset, delectus.

XXX. Summotis pari spatio armatis cum singulis interpretibus congressi sunt, non suae modo aetatis maximi duces, sed omnis ante se memoriae, omnium gentium cui-
2 libet regum imperatorumue pares. paulisper alter alterius conspectu, admiratione mutua prope attoniti, conticuere.
3 tum Hannibal prior: " si hoc ita fato datum erat, ut qui primus bellum intuli populo Romano, quique totiens prope in manibus uictoriam habui, is ultro ad pacem petendam uenirem, laetor te mihi sorte potissimum datum,
4 a quo peterem. tibi quoque inter multa egregia non in ultimis laudum hoc fuerit, Hannibalem, cui tot de Romanis ducibus uictoriam di dedissent, tibi cessisse, teque huic bello uestris plus quam nostris cladibus insigni, finem impo-
5 suisse. hoc quoque ludibrium casus ediderit fortuna, ut cum patre tuo consule ceperim arma, cum eodem primum Romano imperatore signa contulerim, ad filium eius iner-
6 mis ad pacem petendam ueniam. optimum quidem fuerat eam patribus nostris mentem datam ab dis esse, ut et uos
7 Italiae et nos Africae imperio contenti essemus: neque enim ne uobis quidem Sicilia ac Sardinia satis digna pretia sunt pro tot classibus, tot exercitibus, tot tam egregiis amissis ducibus. sed praeterita magis reprehendi possunt
8 quam corrigi. ita aliena appetiimus ut de nostris dimicaremus, nec in Italia solum uobis bellum, nobis in Africa esset, sed et uos in portis uestris prope ac moenibus signa armaque hostium uidistis, et nos ab Carthagine fremitum
9 castrorum Romanorum exaudimus. quod igitur nos maxime abominaremur, uos autem ante omnia optaretis, in meliore uestra fortuna de pace agitur. agimus ei, quorum maxime interest pacem esse, et qui quodcumque egerimus, ratum ciuitates nostrae habiturae sint. animo tantum nobis opus est non abhorrente a quietis consiliis.
10 Quod ad me attinet, iam aetas senem in patriam reuertentem, unde puer profectus sum, iam secundae, iam aduersae res ita erudierunt, ut rationem sequi quam fortu-
11 nam malim: tuam et adolescentiam et perpetuam felicita-

tem, ferociora utraque quam quietis opus est consiliis, metuo.
non temere incerta casuum reputat, quem fortuna num-
12 quam decepit. quod ego fui ad Trasumennum ad Cannas,
id tu hodie. uixdum militari aetate imperio accepto omnia
audacissime incipientem nusquam fefellit fortuna.
13 patris et patrui persecutus mortem ex calamitate uestrae
domus decus insigne uirtutis pietatisque eximiae cepisti;
amissas Hispanias reciperasti quattuor inde Punicis exerciti-
14 bus pulsis; consul creatus, cum ceteris ad tutandam Italiam
parum animi esset, transgressus in Africam, duobus hic
exercitibus caesis, binis eadem hora captis simul incensis-
que castris, Syphace potentissimo rege capto, tot urbibus
regni eius, tot nostri imperii ereptis, me sextum decimum
iam annum haerentem in possessione Italiae detraxisti.
15 potest uictoriam malle quam pacem animus. noui spiritus magnos magis quam utiles: et mihi talis aliquando
16 fortuna adfulsit. quodsi in secundis rebus bonam quoque
mentem darent dei, non ea solum quae euenissent, sed
etiam ea quae euenire possent, reputaremus. ut omnium
obliuiscaris aliorum, satis ego documenti in omnes casus
17 sum quem modo castris inter Anienem atque urbem uestram positis signa inferentem ac iam prope scandentem
moenia Romana uideras, hic cernas duobus fratribus,
fortissimis uiris, clarissimis imperatoribus orbatum, ante
moenia prope obsessae patriae, quibus terrui uestram
urbem, ea pro mea deprecantem.
18   Maximae cuique fortunae minime credendum est: in
bonis tuis rebus, nostris dubiis, tibi ampla ac speciosa
danti est pax, nobis petentibus magis necessaria quam
19 honesta. melior tutiorque est certa pax quam sperata
uictoria; haec in tua, illa in deorum manu est. ne tot
20 annorum felicitatem in unius horae dederis discrimen; cum
tuas uires, tum uim fortunae Martemque belli communem
propone animo. utrimque ferrum, utrimque corpora hu-
mana erunt: nusquam minus quam in bello euentus re-
21 spondent. non tantum ad id, quod data pace iam habere
potes, si proelio uiceris, gloriae adieceris, quantum ademeris, si quid aduersi eueniat. simul parta ac sperata

22 decora unius horae fortuna euertere potest. omnia in pace
iungenda tuae potestatis sunt, P. Corneli: tunc ea habenda
23 fortuna erit, quam di dederint. inter pauca felicitatis
uirtutisque exempla M. Atilius quondam in hac eadem
terra fuisset, si uictor pacem petentibus dedisset patribus
nostris: non statuendo felicitati modum nec cohibendo
efferentem se fortunam, quanto altius elatus erat, eo foe-
dius corruit.

24 Est quidem eius qui dat, non qui petit, condiciones
dicere pacis: sed forsitan non indigni simus, qui nobismet
25 ipsi multam irrogemus. non recusamus quin omnia, propter
quae ad bellum itum est, uestra sint, Sicilia Sardinia
Hispania, quidquid insularum toto inter Africam Italiam-
26 que continetur mari: Carthaginienses inclusi Africae
litoribus uos, quando ita dis placuit, externa etiam terra
27 marique uideamus regentes imperio. haud negauerim,
propter non nimis sincere petitam aut expectatam nuper
pacem suspectam esse uobis Punicam fidem. multum,
per quos petita sit, ad fidem tuendae pacis pertinet, Scipio
28 (uestri quoque, ut audio, patres, nonnihil etiam ob hoc,
quia parum dignitatis in legatione erat, negauerunt
29 pacem): Hannibal peto pacem, qui neque peterem, nisi
utilem crederem, et propter eandem utilitatem tuebor eam
30 propter quam petii. et quemadmodum, quia a me bellum
coeptum est, ne quem eius paeniteret, quoad id ipsi
inuidere dei, praestiti, ita adnitar, ne quem pacis per me
partae paeniteat."

XXXI. Aduersus haec imperator Romanus in hanc
fere sententiam respondit: "non me fallebat, Hannibal,
aduentus tui spe Carthaginienses et praesentem indu-
2 tiarum fidem et spem pacis turbasse: neque tu id sane
dissimulas, qui de condicionibus superioribus pacis omnia
subtrahas praeter ea quae iam pridem in nostra potestate
3 sunt. ceterum ut tibi curae est sentire ciues tuos, quanto
per te onere leuentur, sic mihi laborandum est, ne
quae tunc pepigerunt hodie subtracta ex condicionibus
4 pacis praemia perfidiae habeant. indigni, quibus eadem
pateat condicio, etiam ut prosit uobis fraus petitis. neque

patres nostri priores de Sicilia, neque nos de Hispania
fecimus bellum: et tunc Mamertinorum sociorum periculum, et nunc Sagunti excidium nobis pia ac iusta indue-
5 runt arma. uos lacessisse et tu ipse fateris et dei testes
sunt, qui et illius belli exitum secundum ius fasque dede-
6 runt et huius dant et dabunt. quod ad me attinet, et hu-
manae infirmitatis memini et uim fortunae reputo, et
omnia quaecumque agimus subiecta esse mille casibus
7 scio: ceterum quemadmodum superbe et uiolenter me
faterer facere, si, priusquam in Africam traiecissem, te
tua uoluntate cedentem Italia et imposito in naues exercitu ipsum uenientem ad pacem petendam aspernarer;
8 sic nunc, cum prope manu conserta restitantem ac ter-
giuersantem in Africam attraxerim, nulla sum tibi uere-
9 cundia obstrictus. proinde si quid ad ea, in quae tum pax
conuentura uidebatur—quae sit multa nauium cum commeatu per indutias expugnatarum legatorumque uiolato-
rum—adicitur, est quod referam ad consilium: sin illa
quoque grauia uidentur, bellum parate, quoniam pacem
pati non potuistis."

10 Ita infecta pace ex colloquio ad suos cum se rece-
pissent, frustra uerba praelata renuntiant: armis decer-
nendum esse habendamque eam fortunam, quam dei
dedissent. XXXII. In castra ut est uentum, pronuntiant
ambo, arma expedirent milites animosque ad supremum
certamen, non in unum diem sed in perpetuum, si feli-
2 citas adesset, uictores: Roma an Carthago iura gentibus
darent, ante crastinam noctem scituros; neque enim Africam aut Italiam, sed orbem terrarum uictoriae praemium
fore: par periculum praemio, quibus aduersa pugnae
3 fortuna fuisset. nam neque Romanis effugium ullum pate-
bat in aliena ignotaque terra, et Carthagini supremo
auxilio effuso adesse uidebatur praesens excidium.

4 Ad hoc discrimen procedunt postero die duorum
opulentissimorum populorum duo longe clarissimi duces,
duo fortissimi exercitus, multa ante parta decora aut cu-
5 mulaturi eo die aut euersuri. anceps igitur spes et metus
miscebant animos; contemplantibusque modo suam modo
F

hostium aciem, cum oculis magis quam ratione pensarent
uires, simul laeta simul tristia obuersabantur; quae ipsis
sua sponte non succurrebant, ea duces admonendo atque
6 hortando subiciebant. Poenus sedecim annorum in terra
Italia res gestas, tot duces Romanos, tot exercitus occidione
occisos, et sua cuique decora, ubi ad insignem alicuius
7 pugnae memoria militem uenerat, referebat. Scipio
Hispanias et recentia in Africa proelia et confessionem
hostium, quod neque non petere pacem propter metum
neque manere in ea prae insita animis perfidia potuissent.
8 ad hoc colloquium Hannibalis in secreto habitum ac
9 liberum fingenti qua uolt flectit; ominatur, quibus
quondam auspiciis patres eorum ad Aegates pugnauerint
insulas, ea illis exeuntibus in aciem portendisse deos.
10 adesse finem belli ac laboris, in manibus esse praedam
Carthaginis, reditum domum in patriam ad parentes
11 liberos coniuges penatesque deos. celsus haec corpore,
uultuque ita laeto, ut uicisse iam crederes, dicebat.

Instruit deinde primos hastatos, post eos principes,
triariis postremam aciem clausit. XXXIII. non con-
fertas autem cohortes ante sua quamque signa instruebat,
sed manipulos aliquantum inter se distantes, ut esset
spatium qua elephanti hostium acti nihil ordines turbarent.
2 Laelium, cuius ante legati, eo anno quaestoris extra
sortem ex senatus consulto opera utebatur, cum Italico
equitatu ab sinistro cornu, Masinissam Numidasque ab
3 dextro opposuit. uias patentes inter manipulos antesignanorum uelitibus—ea tunc leuis armatura erat—
compleuit, dato praecepto, ut ad impetum elephantorum
aut post directos refugerent ordines, aut in dextram lae-
uamque discursu applicantes se antesignanis uiam, qua
irruerent in ancipitia tela, beluis darent.
4 Hannibal ad terrorem primos elephantos—octoginta
autem erant, quot nulla umquam in acie ante habuerat—
5 instruxit, deinde auxilia Ligurum Gallorumque Baliaribus
Maurisque admixtis; in secunda acie Carthaginienses
6 Afrosque et Macedonum legionem; modico deinde
interuallo relicto subsidiariam aciem Italicorum militum—

Bruttii plerique erant, ui ac necessitate plures quam sua
7 uoluntate decedentem ex Italia secuti—instruxit. equitatum et ipse circumdedit cornibus, dextrum Carthaginienses,
8 sinistrum Numidae tenuerunt. uaria adhortatio erat in
exercitu inter tot homines, quibus non lingua, non mos, non
lex, non arma, non uestitus habitusque, non causa militandi
9 eadem esset. auxiliaribus et praesens et multiplicata ex
praeda merces ostentabatur; Galli proprio atque insito in
Romanos odio accenduntur; Liguribus campi uberes
Italiae deductis ex asperrimis montibus in spem uictoriae
10 ostentantur; Mauros Numidasque Masinissae impotenti
futuro dominatu terret; aliae aliis spes ac metus iactantur.
11 Carthaginiensibus moenia patriae, di penates, sepulchra
maiorum, liberi cum parentibus coniugesque pauidae,
aut excidium seruitiumque aut imperium orbis terrarum,
nihil aut in metum aut in spem medium, ostentatur.
12 Cum maxime haec imperator apud Carthaginienses,
duces suarum gentium inter populares, pleraque per in-
terpretes inter immixtos alienigenis agerent, tubae cor-
13 nuaque ab Romanis cecinerunt, tantusque clamor ortus,
ut elephanti in suos, sinistro maxime cornu, uerterentur,
Mauros ac Numidas. addidit facile Masinissa perculsis
terrorem, nudauitque ab ea parte aciem equestri auxilio.
14 paucae tamen bestiarum intrepidae in hostem actae inter
uelitum ordines cum multis suis uulneribus ingentem stra-
15 gem edebant. resilientes enim ad manipulos uelites, cum
uiam elephantis, ne obtererentur, fecissent, in ancipites
ad ictum utrimque coniciebant hastas, nec pila ab ante-
16 signanis cessabant, donec undique incidentibus telis exacti
ex Romana acie hi quoque in suo dextro cornu ipsos
Carthaginiensium equites in fugam uerterunt. Laelius ut
turbatos uidit hostes, addidit perculsis terrorem.

XXXIV. Utrimque nudata equite erat Punica acies,
cum pedes concurrit, nec spe nec uiribus iam par. ad
hoc dictu parva, sed magna eadem in re gerenda momenta: congruens clamor a Romanis eoque maior et ter-
ribilior, dissonae illis, ut gentium multarum discrepantibus
2 linguis, uoces; pugna Romana stabilis et suo et armorum

pondere incumbentium in hostem, concursatio et uelocitas
3 illinc maior quam uis. igitur primo impetu extemplo mouere loco hostium aciem Romani. ala deinde et umbone
pulsantes, in summotos gradu illato, aliquantum spatii
4 uelut nullo resistente incessere, urgentibus et nouissimis
primos, ut semel motam aciem sensere; quod ipsum uim
5 magnam ad pellendum hostem addebat. apud hostes
auxiliares cedentes secunda acies, Afri et Carthaginienses,
adeo non sustinebant, ut contra etiam, ne resistentes per-
tinaciter primos caedendo ad se perueniret hostis, pedem
6 referrent. igitur auxiliares terga dant repente, et in suos
uersi partim refugere in secundam aciem, partim non recipientes caedere, ut et paulo ante non adiuti et tunc
7 exclusi. et prope duo iam permixta proelia erant, cum Carthaginienses simul cum hostibus simul cum suis cogerentur
8 manus conserere. non tamen ita perculsos iratosque in
aciem accipere, sed densatis ordinibus in cornua uacuumque
circa campum extra proelium eiecere, ne pauido fuga
uulneribusque milite sinceram et integram aciem miscerent.
9   Ceterum tanta strages hominum armorumque locum,
in quo steterant paulo ante auxiliares, compleuerat,
ut prope difficilior transitus esset, quam per con-
10 fertos hostes fuerat. itaque, qui primi erant, hastati per
cumulos corporum armorumque et tabem sanguinis qua
quisque poterat sequentes hostem et signa et ordines
confuderunt. principum quoque signa fluctuari coeperant
11 uagam ante se cernendo aciem. quod Scipio ubi uidit, receptui propere canere hastatis iussit; et sauciis in postremam aciem subductis principes triariosque in cornua in-
ducit, quo tutior firmiorque media hastatorum acies esset.
12 ita nouum de integro proelium ortum est: quippe ad
ueros hostes peruentum erat, et armorum genere et usu
militiae et fama rerum gestarum et magnitudine uel spei
13 uel periculi pares. sed et numero superior Romanus erat,
et animo, quod iam equites iam elephantos fuderat, iam
prima acie pulsa in secundam pugnabat. XXXV. in
tempore Laelius ac Masinissa, pulsos per aliquantum spatii
secuti equites, reuertentes in auersam hostium aciem in-

2 currere. is demum equitum impetus fudit hostem. multi circumuenti in acie caesi; multi per patentem circa campum fuga sparsi tenente omnia equitatu passim interierunt.
3 Carthaginiensium sociorumque caesa eo die supra milia uiginti, par ferme numerus captus cum signis militaribus centum triginta duobus, elephantis undecim. uictores ad mille et quingenti cecidere.

4   Hannibal cum paucis equitibus inter tumultum elap-
sus Hadrumetum perfugit, omnia et in proelio et ante
5 aciem, priusquam excederet pugna expertus, et confes-
sione etiam Scipionis omniumque peritorum militiae
illam laudem adeptus, singulari arte aciem eo die in-
6 struxisse: elephantos in prima fronte, quorum fortuitus
impetus atque intolerabilis uis signa sequi et seruare ordines, in quo plurimum spei ponerent, Romanos prohi-
7 berent; deinde auxiliares ante Carthaginiensium aciem,
ne homines mixti ex colluuione omnium gentium, quos
non fides teneret sed merces, liberum receptum fugae
8 haberent, simul primum ardorem atque impetum hostium
excipientes fatigarent ac, si nihil aliud, uulneribus suis
9 ferrum hostium hebetarent; tum, ubi omnis spes esset,
milites Carthaginienses Afrosque, ut omnibus rebus aliis
pares, eo quod integri cum fessis ac sauciis pugnarent,
superiores essent; Italicos, incertos, socii an hostes essent, in
10 postremam aciem summotos. hoc edito uelut ultimo uirtutis opere Hannibal cum Hadrumetum refugisset accitus-
que inde Carthaginem sexto ac tricesimo post anno, quam
puer inde profectus erat, redisset, fassus in curia est non
proelio modo se sed bello uictum, nec spem salutis alibi
quam in pace impetranda esse.

      XXXVI. Scipio confestim a proelio expugnatis ho-
stium castris direptisque cum ingenti praeda ad mare ac
2 naues rediit, nuntio adlato P. Lentulum cum quinquaginta
rostratis, centum onerariis, cum omni genere commeatus
3 ad Vticam accessisse. admouendum igitur undique terrorem perculsae Carthagini ratus, misso Laelio Romam
cum uictoriae nuntio, Octauium terrestri itinere ducere
legiones Carthaginem iubet: ipse ad suam ueterem noua

Lentuli classe adiuncta profectus ab Vtica portum Car-
4 thaginis petit. haud procul aberat, cum uelata infulis
ramisque oleae Carthaginiensium occurrit nauis. decem
legati erant principes ciuitatis, auctore Hannibale missi
5 ad petendam pacem. qui cum ad puppim praetoriae nauis
accessissent uelamenta supplicum porrigentes, orantes
6 implorantesque fidem ac misericordiam Scipionis, nullum
iis aliud responsum datum, quam ut Tynetem uenirent:
eo se moturum castra. ipse ad contemplandum Carthaginis situm prouectus non tam noscendi in praesentia quam
deprimendi hostis causa, Vticam, eodem et Octauio reuo-
cato, rediit.

7   Inde procedentibus ad Tynetem nuntius adlatus
Verminam Syphacis filium cum equitibus pluribus quam
8 peditibus uenire Carthaginiensibus auxilio. pars exercitus cum omni equitatu [Saturnalibus primis] agmen ad-
gressa Numidarum leui certamine fudit. exitu quoque
fugae intercluso, a parte omni circumdatis equitibus, quindecim milia hominum caesa, mille et ducenti uiui capti sunt,
et equi Numidici mille et quingenti, signa militaria duo et
septuaginta. regulus ipse inter tumultum cum paucis effugit.
9 tum ad Tynetem eodem quo ante loco castra posita,
legatique triginta a Carthagine ad Scipionem uenerunt.

Et illi quidem multo miserabilius quam antea, quo
magis cogebat fortuna, egerunt, sed aliquanto minore
cum misericordia ab recenti memoria perfidiae auditi
10 sunt. in consilio quamquam iusta ira omnes ad delendam
stimulabat Carthaginem, tamen cum et quanta res esset,
quam longi temporis obsidio tam munitae et tam ualidae
11 urbis reputarent, et ipsum Scipionem exspectatio succes-
soris uenturi ad paratum uictoriae fructum, alterius labore
ac periculo finiti belli famam, sollicitaret, ad pacem omnium
animi uersi sunt. XXXVII. postero die reuocatis legatis
et cum multa castigatione perfidiae monitis, ut tot cladibus
edocti tandem deos et ius iurandum esse crederent, con-
2 diciones pacis dictae, ut liberi legibus suis uiuerent; quas
urbes quosque agros quibusque finibus ante bellum tenuis-
sent, tenerent, populandique finem eo die Romanus

3 faceret: perfugas fugitiuosque et captiuos omnes redderent
Romanis, et naues rostratas praeter decem triremes trade-
rent elephantosque quos haberent domitos, neque doma-
4 rent alios: bellum neue in Africa neue extra Africam
iniussu populi Romani gererent: Masinissae res redderent
5 foedusque cum eo facerent: frumentum stipendiumque
auxiliis, donec ab Roma legati redissent, praestarent:
decem milia talentum argenti, discripta pensionibus ae-
6 quis in annos quinquaginta, soluerent: obsides centum
arbitratu Scipionis darent, ne minores quattuordecim
annis neu triginta maiores. indutias ita se daturum, si per
priores indutias naues onerariae captae quaeque fuissent
in nauibus restituerentur: aliter nec indutias nec spem
pacis ullam esse.
7   Has condiciones legati cum domum referre iussi in
contione ederent, et Gisgo ad dissuadendam pacem pro-
cessisset audireturque a multitudine inquieta eadem et
8 imbelli, indignatus Hannibal dici ea in tali tempore audi-
rique arreptum Gisgonem manu sua ex superiore loco
detraxit. quae insueta liberae ciuitati species cum fremi-
9 tum populi mouisset, perturbatus militaris uir urbana
libertate "nouem" inquit "annorum a uobis profectus
post sextum et tricesimum annum redii. militares artes,
quas me a puero fortuna nunc priuata nunc publica docuit,
probe uideor scire: urbis ac fori iura, leges, mores uos
10 me oportet doceatis." excusata imprudentia de pace
multis verbis disseruit, quam nec iniqua et necessaria esset.
11 id omnium maxime difficile erat, quod ex nauibus per
indutias captis nihil praeter ipsas comparebat naues; nec
inquisitio erat facilis, aduersantibus paci qui arguerentur.
12 placuit naues reddi et homines utique inquiri; cetera quae
abessent aestimanda Scipioni permitti, atque ita pecunia
13 luere Carthaginienses. Sunt qui Hannibalem ex acie ad
mare peruenisse, inde praeparata naue ad regem Antiochum
extemplo profectum tradant; postulantique ante omnia
Scipioni, ut Hannibal sibi traderetur, responsum esse
Hannibalem in Africa non esse.
    XXXVIII. Postquam redierunt ad Scipionem legati,

quae publica in nauibus fuerant ex publicis descripta
rationibus quaestores, quae priuata, profiteri domini iussi:
2 pro ea summa pecuniae uiginti quinque milia pondo argenti praesentia exacta; indutiaeque Carthaginiensibus
3 datae in tres menses. additum ne per indutiarum tempus
alio usquam quam Romam mitterent legatos, et quicum-
que legati Carthaginem uenissent, ne ante dimitterent eos
quam Romanum imperatorem, qui et quae petentes
4 uenissent, certiorem facerent. cum legatis Carthaginiensibus Romam missi L. Veturius Philo et M. Marcius
5 Ralla et L. Scipio imperatoris frater. per eos dies
commeatus ex Sicilia Sardiniaque tantam uilitatem
annonae fecerunt, ut pro uectura frumentum nautis
mercator relinqueret.
6   Romae ad nuntium primum rebellionis Carthaginiensium trepidatum fuerat, iussusque erat Tib. Claudius ma-
ture classem in Siciliam ducere atque inde in Africam
traicere, et alter consul M. Seruilius ad urbem morari,
7 donec quo statu res in Africa essent sciretur. segniter
omnia in comparanda deducendaque classe ab Tib. Claudio consule facta erant, quod patres de pace Scipionis
potius arbitrium esse, quibus legibus daretur, quam
8 consulis censuerant. prodigia quoque nuntiata sub ipsam
famam rebellionis terrorem attulerant: Cumis solis orbis
minui uisus et pluit lapideo imbri, et in Veliterno agro
terra ingentibus cauernis consedit, arboresque in pro-
9 fundum haustae; Ariciae forum et circa tabernae, Frusinone murus aliquot locis et porta de caelo tacta; et in
Palatio lapidibus pluit. id prodigium more patrio nouem-
10 diali sacro, cetera hostiis maioribus expiata. inter quae
etiam aquarum insolita magnitudo in religionem uersa:
nam ita abundauit Tiberis, ut ludi Apollinares circo inun-
dato extra portam Collinam ad aedem Erycinae Veneris
11 parati sint. ceterum ludorum ipso die subita serenitate
orta pompa duci coepta ad portam Collinam reuocata
deductaque in circum est, cum recessisse inde aquam nun-
12 tiatum esset: laetitiamque populo et ludis celebritatem
addidit sedes sua sollemni spectaculo reddita.

XXXIX. Claudium consulem, profectum tandem
ab urbe, inter portus Cosanum Loretanumque atrox uis
2 tempestatis adorta in metum ingentem adduxit. Populonium inde cum peruenisset stetissetque ibi, dum reliquum tempestatis exsaeuiret, Iluam insulam et ab Ilua
Corsicam, a Corsica in Sardiniam traiecit. ibi superantem
Insanos montes multo et saeuior et infestioribus locis
3 tempestas adorta disiecit classem. multae quassatae ar-
mamentisque spoliatae naues, quaedam fractae; ita uexata
ac lacerata classis Carales tenuit. ubi dum subductae
reficiuntur naues, hiems oppressit, circumactumque anni
tempus et, nullo prorogante imperium, priuatus Tib. Clau-
4 dius classem Romam reduxit. M. Seruilius, ne comitiorum causa ad urbem reuocaretur, dictatore dicto C. Seruilio Gemino, in prouinciam est profectus; dictator ma-
5 gistrum equitum P. Aelium Paetum dixit. saepe comitia
indicta perfici tempestates prohibuerunt; itaque cum pridie idus Martias ueteres magistratus abissent, noui suffecti
non essent, res publica sine curulibus magistratibus erat.
6 T. Manlius Torquatus pontifex eo anno mortuus: in
locum eius suffectus C. Sulpicius Galba. ab L. Licinio
Lucullo et Q. Fuluio aedilibus curulibus ludi Romani ter
7 toti instaurati. pecuniam ex aerario scribae uiatoresque
aedilicii clam egessisse per indicem damnati sunt, non
8 sine infamia Luculli aedilis. P. Aelius Tubero et L. Lae-
torius aediles plebis uitio creati magistratu se abdicaue-
runt, cum ludos ludorumque causa epulum Ioui fecissent
et signa tria ex multaticio argento facta in Capitolio po-
suissent. Cerialia ludos dictator et magister equitum ex
senatus consulto fecerunt.

XL. Legati ex Africa Romani simul Carthaginiensesque cum uenissent Romam, senatus ad aedem Bello-
2 nae habitus est. ubi cum L. Veturius Philo pugnatum cum
Hannibale esse suprema Carthaginiensibus pugna finem-
que tandem lugubri bello impositum ingenti laetitia
3 patrum exposuisset, adiecit Verminam etiam Syphacis
filium, quae parua bene gestae rei accessio erat, deuictum.
in contionem prodire iussus gaudiumque id populo

4 impertire. tum patefacta gratulationi omnia in urbe templa, supplicationesque in triduum decretae. legatis Carthaginiensium et Philippi regis—nam hi quoque uenerant—petentibus ut senatus sibi daretur, responsum iussu patrum ab dictatore est consules nouos iis senatum daturos
5 esse. comitia inde habita. creati consules Cn. Cornelius Lentulus P. Aelius Paetus; praetores M. Iunius Pennus, cui sors urbana euenit, M. Valerius Falto Bruttios, M. Fabius Buteo Sardiniam, P. Aelius Tubero Siciliam est
6 sortitus. de prouinciis consulum nihil ante placebat agi quam legati Philippi regis et Carthaginiensium auditi essent: belli finem alterius, alterius principium prospiciebant animis.
7   Cn. Lentulus consul cupiditate flagrabat prouinciae Africae, seu bellum foret, facilem uictoriam fore, seu iam
8 finiretur, finiti tanti belli se consule gloriam petens. negare itaque prius quicquam agi passurum quam sibi prouincia Africa decreta esset, concedente collega, moderato uiro et prudenti, qui gloriae eius certamen cum Scipione, praeterquam quod iniquum esset, etiam impar futurum cernebat.
9 Q. Minucius Thermus et M'. Acilius Glabrio tribuni plebis rem nequiquam temptatam ab Tib. Claudio consule Cn.
10 Cornelium temptare aiebant: ex auctoritate patrum latum ad populum esse, cuius uellent imperium in Africa esse: omnes quinque et triginta tribus P. Scipioni id
11 imperium decreuisse. multis contentionibus et in senatu et ad populum acta res postremo eo deducta est, ut senatui
12 permitterent. patres igitur iurati—ita enim conuenerat— censuerunt, uti consules prouincias inter se compararent sortirenturue, uter Italiam, uter classem nauium quin-
13 quaginta haberet; cui classis obuenisset, in Siciliam nauigaret; si pax cum Carthaginiensibus componi nequisset, in Africam traiceret; consul mari, Scipio eodem quo
14 adhuc iure imperii terra rem gereret; si condiciones conuenirent pacis, tribuni plebis populum rogarent, utrum consulem an P. Scipionem iuberent pacem dare, et quem, si deportandus exercitus uictor ex Africa esset, deportare.
15 si pacem per P. Scipionem dari atque ab eodem exercitum

deportari iussissent, ne consul ex Sicilia in Africam traiceret.
16 alter consul, cui Italia euenisset, duas legiones a M. Sextio
praetore acciperet. XLI. P. Scipioni cum exercitibus quos
haberet in prouincia Africa prorogatum imperium. praetori M. Valerio Faltoni duae legiones in Bruttiis, quibus
2 C. Liuius priore anno praefuerat, decretae. P. Aelius
duas legiones in Sicilia ab Cn. Tremelio acciperet. legio
una M. Fabio in Sardiniam, quam P. Lentulus pro praetore
3 habuisset, decernitur. M. Seruilio prioris anni consuli
cum suis duabus item legionibus in Etruria prorogatum
4 imperium est. quod ad Hispanias attineret, aliquot annos
iam ibi L. Cornelium Lentulum et L. Manlium Acidinum
esse; uti consules cum tribunis agerent, ut, si iis uideretur,
plebem rogarent, cui iuberent in Hispania imperium esse;
5 is ex duobus exercitibus in unam legionem conscriberet
Romanos milites et in quindecim cohortes socios Latini
nominis, quibus prouinciam obtineret; ueteres milites
6 L. Cornelius et L. Manlius in Italiam deportarent. Consuli
quinquaginta nauium classis ex duabus classibus, Cn.
Octauii, quae in Africa esset, et P. Villii, quae Siciliae
oram tuebatur, decreta, ut quas uellet naues deligeret.
7 P. Scipio quadraginta naues longas, quas habuisset,
haberet; quibus si Cn. Octauium, sicut praefuisset, prae-
esse uellet, Octauio pro praetore in eum annum imperium
8 esset: si Laelium praeficeret, Octauius Romam decederet,
reduceretque naues quibus consuli usus non esset. et M.
9 Fabio in Sardiniam decem longae naues decretae. et
consules duas urbanas legiones scribere iussi, ut quattuordecim legionibus eo anno, centum nauibus longis res
publica administraretur.

XLII. Tum de legatis Philippi et Carthaginiensium
2 actum. priores Macedonas introduci placuit; quorum
uaria oratio fuit, partim purgantium quae questi erant
missi ad regem ab Roma legati de populatione sociorum,
partim ultro accusantium quidem et socios populi Ro-
3 mani, sed multo infestius M. Aurelium, quem ex tribus
ad se missis legatis dilectu habito substitisse et se bello
lacessisse contra foedus et saepe cum praefectis suis signis

4 collatis pugnasse, et postulantium, ut Macedones duxque
eorum Sopater, qui apud Hannibalem mercede militassent,
5 tum capti in uinclis essent, sibi restituerentur. aduersus
ea M. Furius, missus ad id ipsum ab Aurelio ex Macedonia,
disseruit Aurelium relictum, ne socii populi Romani
fessi populationibus ui atque iniuria ad regem deficerent,
6 finibus sociorum non excessisse; dedisse operam, ne
impune in agros eorum populatores transcenderent.
Sopatrum ex purpuratis et propinquis regis esse: eum
cum quattuor milibus Macedonum et pecunia missum
nuper in Africam esse Hannibali et Carthaginiensibus
7 auxilio. de his rebus interrogati Macedones cum perplexe
responderent, neque ipsi mite responsum tulerunt: bellum
quaerere regem, et si pergat, propediem inuenturum.
8 dupliciter ab eo foedus uiolatum, et quod sociis populi
Romani iniurias fecerit ac bello armisque lacessiuerit, et
9 quod hostes auxiliis et pecunia iuuerit. et P. Scipionem
recte atque ordine fecisse uideri et facere, quod eos, qui
arma contra populum Romanum ferentes capti sint, ho-
10 stium numero in uinclis habeat, et M. Aurelium ex re
publica facere, gratumque id senatui esse, quod socios populi Romani, quando iure foederis non possit, armis
tueatur.
11 Cum hoc tam tristi responso dimissis Macedonibus
legati Carthaginienses uocati; quorum aetatibus dignitati-
busque conspectis—nam longe primi ciuitatis erant—
12 tum pro se quisque dicere uere de pace agi. insignis tamen
inter ceteros Hasdrubal erat—Haedum populares cognomine appellabant—pacis semper auctor aduersusque Bar-
13 cinae factioni. eo tum plus illi auctoritatis fuit belli
culpam in paucorum cupiditatem ab re publica transferenti.
14 qui cum uaria oratione usus esset, nunc purgando crimina,
nunc quaedam fatendo, ne impudenter certa negantibus
difficilior uenia esset, nunc monendo etiam patres con-
scriptos, ut rebus secundis modeste ac moderate uterentur:
15 si se atque Hannonem audissent Carthaginienses et tempore
uti uoluissent, daturos fuisse pacis condiciones, quas tunc
peterent. raro simul hominibus bonam fortunam bonam-

16 que mentem dari: populum Romanum eo inuictum esse,
quod in secundis rebus sapere et consulere meminerit; et
17 hercule mirandum fuisse, si aliter faceret; ex insolentia, quibus noua bona fortuna sit, impotentes laetitiae insanire:
populo Romano usitata ac prope iam obsoleta ex uictoria
gaudia esse, ac plus paene parcendo uictis quam uincendo
18 imperium auxisse. ceterorum miserabilior oratio fuit com-
memorantium, ex quantis opibus quo reccidissent Carthaginiensium res; nihil iis, qui modo orbem prope terrarum
obtinuerint armis, superesse praeter Carthaginis moenia;
19 his inclusos non terra, non mari quicquam sui iuris cer-
nere; urbem quoque ipsam ac penates ita habituros, si
non in ea quoque, quo nihil ulterius sit, saeuire populus
20 Romanus uelit. cum flecti misericordia patres appareret,
senatorem unum infestum perfidiae Carthaginiensium suc-
21 clamasse ferunt, per quos deos foedus icturi essent, cum
eos, per quos ante ictum esset, fefellissent: " per eosdem "
inquit Hasdrubal, "quoniam tam infesti sunt foedera
uiolantibus."

XLIII. Inclinatis omnium ad pacem animis Cn. Lentulus consul, cui classis prouincia erat, senatus consulto
2 intercessit. tum M'. Acilius et Q. Minucius tribuni plebis
ad populum tulerunt, uellent iuberentne senatum decer-
nere, ut cum Carthaginiensibus pax fieret, et quem eam pacem dare, quemque ex Africa exercitum deportare iube-
3 rent. de pace uti rogatae erant omnes tribus iusserunt;
pacem dare P. Scipionem, eundem exercitus deportare.
4 ex hac rogatione senatus decreuit, ut P. Scipio ex decem
legatorum sententia pacem cum populo Carthaginiensi
5 quibus legibus ei uideretur faceret. gratias deinde patribus egere Carthaginienses, et petierunt, ut sibi in urbem
introire et colloqui cum ciuibus suis liceret, qui capti in
6 publica custodia essent: esse in iis partim propinquos
amicosque suos, nobiles homines, partim ad quos man-
7 data a propinquis haberent. quibus conuentis cum rursus
peterent, sibi quos uellent ex iis redimendi potestas fieret,
8 iussi nomina edere: et cum ducentos ferme ederent, senatus consultum factum est, ut legati Romani ducentos ex

captiuis, quos Carthaginienses uellent, ad P. Cornelium
in Africam deportarent, nuntiarentque ei, ut, si pax con-
9 uenisset, sine pretio eos Carthaginiensibus redderet. fetiales cum in Africam ad foedus feriendum ire iuberentur,
ipsis postulantibus senatus consultum in haec uerba factum
est, ut priuos lapides silices priuasque uerbenas secum
ferrent; uti praetor Romanus imperaret, ut foedus feri-
rent, illi praetorem sagmina poscerent. herbae id genus
ex arce sumptum fetialibus dari solet.

10   Ita dimissi ab Roma Carthaginienses cum in Africam
uenissent ad Scipionem, quibus ante dictum est legibus
11 pacem fecerunt. naues longas, elephantos, perfugas, fugitiuos, captiuorum quattuor milia tradiderunt, inter quos
12 Q. Terentius Culleo senator fuit. naues prouectas in altum
incendi iussit; quingentas fuisse omnis generis, quae remis agerentur, quidam tradunt; quarum conspectum repente incendium tam lugubre fuisse Poenis, quam si ipsa
13 Carthago arderet. de perfugis grauius quam de fugitiuis
consultum: nominis Latini qui erant, securi percussi,
Romani in crucem sublati.

    XLIV. Annis ante quadraginta pax cum Carthaginien-
sibus postremo facta erat Q. Lutatio A. Manlio consulibus.
2 bellum initum annis post tribus et uiginti P. Cornelio Tib.
Sempronio consulibus, finitum est septimo decimo anno
3 Cn. Cornelio P. Aelio Paeto consulibus. saepe postea Scipionem ferunt dixisse, Tib. Claudii primum cupiditatem,
deinde Cn. Cornelii fuisse in mora, quo minus id bellum
exitio Carthaginis finiret.

4   Carthagini cum prima collatio pecuniae diutino bello
exhaustis difficilis uideretur, maestitiaque et fletus in curia
5 esset, ridentem Hannibalem ferunt conspectum. cuius cum
Hasdrubal Haedus risum increparet in publico fletu, cum
6 ipse lacrimarum causa esset, "si quemadmodum oris
habitus cernitur oculis" inquit, "sic et animus intus cerni
posset, facile uobis appareret, non laeti sed prope amentis malis cordis hunc, quem increpitas, risum esse; qui
tamen nequaquam adeo est intempestiuus quam uestrae
7 istae absurdae atque abhorrentes lacrimae sunt. tunc

flesse decuit, cum adempta sunt nobis arma, incensae naues,
interdictum externis bellis: illo enim uulnere concidimus.
necesse est in uos odio uestro consultum ab Romanis cre-
8 datis. nulla magna ciuitas quiescere potest. si foris hostem non habet, domi inuenit, ut praeualida corpora ab
externis causis tuta uidentur, sed suis ipsa uiribus one-
9 rantur. tantum nimirum ex publicis malis sentimus, quantum ad priuatas res pertinet; nec in iis quicquam acrius
10 quam pecuniae damnum stimulat. itaque cum spolia
uictoriae Carthagini detrahebantur, cum inermem iam
ac nudam destitui inter tot armatas gentes Africae cernere-
11 tis, nemo ingemuit: nunc quia tributum ex priuato con-
ferendum est, tamquam in publico funere comploratis.
quam uereor, ne propediem sentiatis leuissimo in malo uos
hodie lacrimasse." haec Hannibal apud Carthaginienses.
12 Scipio contione aduocata Masinissam ad regnum paternum Cirta oppido et ceteris urbibus agrisque, quae ex
regno Syphacis in populi Romani potestatem uenissent,
13 adiectis donauit. Cn. Octauium classem in Siciliam
ductam Cn. Cornelio consuli tradere iussit, legatos Carthaginiensium Romam proficisci, ut, quae a se ex decem
legatorum sententia acta essent, ea patrum auctoritate
populique iussu confirmarentur. XLV. Pace terra marique parta, exercitu in naues imposito, in Siciliam Lily-
2 baeum traiecit. inde magna parte militum nauibus missa
ipse per laetam pace non minus quam uictoria Italiam,
effusis non urbibus modo ad habendos honores, sed
agrestium etiam turba obsidente uias, Romam peruenit
triumphoque omnium clarissimo urbem est inuectus.
3 argenti tulit in aerarium pondo centum uiginti tria milia.
4 militibus ex praeda quadringenos aeris diuisit. morte
subtractus spectaculo magis hominum quam triumphantis
gloriae Syphax est, Tiburi haud ita multo ante mortuus,
quo ab Alba traductus fuerat. conspecta mors tamen eius
5 fuit, quia publico funere est elatus. hunc regem in
triumpho ductum Polybius, haudquaquam spernendus
auctor, tradit. secutus Scipionem triumphantem est pilleo
capiti imposito Q. Terentius Culleo; omnique deinde

6 uita, ut dignum erat, libertatis auctorem coluit. Africani cognomen militaris prius fauor an popularis aura cele- brauerit an, sicuti Felicis Syllae Magnique Pompeii patrum memoria, coeptum ab adsentatione familiari sit, parum

7 compertum habeo. primus certe hic imperator nomine uictae a se gentis est nobilitatus. exemplo deinde huius nequaquam uictoria pares insignes imaginum titulos claraque nomina familiarum fecerunt.

NOTES

I. The book opens with a series of notices derived from a good and reliable annalistic source (cp. Introduction, p. 26). Livy gives a similar description of the situation at the beginning of each year—see below, chapters xxvii and xli.

1. **Cn. Seruilius et C. Seruilius.** On Gnaeus Seruilius Caepio see below, xix, 10–11; xxiv, 1–3. On Gaius Seruilius Geminus see xix, 6–9; xxiii, 1; xxvi, 12; xxxix, 4. Every Roman had a name (*nomen*) denoting his *gens*, a personal name (*praenomen*) and a surname (*cognomen*) which marked the family or group of families within the *gens*: e.g., Gnaeus (*praenomen*), Seruilius (*nomen*), Caepio (*cognomen*).

consules . . . ad senatum rettulissent. The consuls, together with certain other magistrates, had the right of bringing business before the Senate (*ius referendi*), which exercised a general control over the conduct of wars. It was the Senate that each year determined what were to be the provinces (*nominare prouincias*) that is, where the magistrates were to exercise their authority. A *prouincia* originally meant the sphere within which a magistrate exercised his executive authority (*imperium*), whether in Italy or abroad, but gradually came to denote more especially the foreign spheres outside Rome—i.e., the overseas provinces (as Sicily or Sardinia). Besides fixing the provinces, the Senate also decided which should be assigned to the consuls, which to the praetors; it could thus reward or punish consuls by assigning more or less important districts. Further, as it had the right to allocate money for a campaign, to provide reinforcements, and to grant a triumph in case of success, it was thus able to control the magistrates and the general conduct of the war. In 217 and 216 B.C. the People had interfered with the Senate's policy, with disastrous results, and only once again in the course of the Hannibalic War did they seek to intervene, when they elected Scipio to the Spanish command in 210.

2. **censuerunt patres. . . .** When once the senators (*patres*) had fixed the provinces, the consuls settled their allocation either by agreement or by lot, the lot (*sortitio*) becoming in time the usual practice.

comparparent. 'Should come to an agreement among themselves ': a use of *comparo* almost entirely confined to arrangements made between colleagues. This and the remaining subjunctives down to *reuerterentur* are part of the Senate's resolution (*censuerunt*).

Bruttios. The inhabitants of Bruttium (modern Calabria), the toe of Italy. Hannibal was ever being forced farther south. The military situation and the distribution of commands described in these first two chapters will be rendered more clear if a sketch-map be drawn and the position of the various commanders and forces marked. See also on ii, 7.

A full table of the legions and commanders in the Second Punic War is to be found in *Camb. Anc. Hist.*, Vol. VIII, p. 104. The situation in Bruttium was that in 204 P. Licinius Crassus served there as proconsul and P. Sempronius Tuditanus as consul; in 203 Sempronius continued as proconsul, while the place of Licinius, who returned to Rome, was taken by Seruilius Caepio the consul.

3. **P. Sempronio.** Publius Sempronius Tuditanus had had a distinguished career. After serving in Cisalpine Gaul (213–211) and holding the censorship (208), he had been sent to Greece, where he concluded the Peace with King Philip (Introduction, p. 14). As consul in 204 he had fought a successful skirmish with Hannibal near Croton, for which he dedicated a temple to Fortuna Primigenia ten years later.

imperium in annum prorogabatur. Magistrates were invested with authority (*imperium*) for one year only. But in practice it was often found desirable to keep a man in office for a longer period, especially in war-time, when it might be disastrous to supersede an efficient general at the end of one year. So as early as 326 B.C. the device was adopted of prolonging commands (*prorogare imperium*) for a year, or even longer. In fact, it was the *imperium*, and not the magistracy, that was prolonged: a man was invested with the powers of a consul without holding the office, and so was called a proconsul. This practice met a further need: in a large-scale war fought on many fronts Rome might not have enough magistrates to command the various armies, so the custom was adopted of prolonging the *imperium* of a magistrate beyond the annual limit of his magistracy, or even of conferring *imperium* on a private citizen (*priuatus cum imperio*), as e.g. on Scipio in 210 for the Spanish campaign.

P. Licinio. P. Licinius Crassus Dives is an example of the good 'all-round' type of Roman. He owed his successful career to his natural gifts, his wealth, and the support of the Scipios. In 212 he was elected Pontifex Maximus, and held the office for thirty years—a longer period than anyone else. After holding the censorship (210) and praetorship (208), he was elected consul in 205 with Scipio. As Pontifex Maximus he was not allowed to leave Italy, and so he served against Hannibal in Bruttium until 203. On his personality see Livy's digression (§§ 4–6) and Cicero, *de orat.*, III, 134.

4. **habebatur.** Indicative because it is an explanatory comment of the historian, like the parenthesis *ei . . . quoque prorogabatur* (3).

5. **nobilis.** The government of Rome was to a large extent in the hands of an aristocratic clique, the *nobiles*, which consisted of all the men who had held the consulship or were descendants of consuls; closely connected with them were the descendants of those who had held other curule magistracies. It was difficult for men outside this charmed circle to win their way to office: those who succeeded were called *noui homines*.

esset. Subjunctive of indefinite frequency, or, alternatively, expressing the thought of those by whom he was esteemed eloquent.

6. bellicae laudis. Dependent on *compotem*.

7. M. Cornelius. M. Cornelius Cethegus, who had served as consul in 204 in Etruria, was to hold a proconsular command in Cisalpine Gaul (*Gallia prouincia*) in 203, where he defeated Mago (ch. xviii). **obtinere.** Here, as always in classical Latin, to ' hold ', not ' obtain '. **L. Scribonius Libo** was *praetor peregrinus* in 204.

8. habuisset. Subjunctive in a relative clause in indirect speech, implied by *iussus*.

9. praetorum prouinciae. At this time there were four praetors: the *praetor urbanus*, who administered justice in cases between Roman citizens (*qui inter ciues ius dicit*); the *praetor peregrinus*, who dealt with lawsuits between citizens and foreigners or between foreigners, and two others who normally administered the two overseas *prouinciae* of Sicily and Sardinia. In war-time the arrangement might be upset, as the praetors might be needed in Italy. Thus in the present example the *praetor urbanus* took over at the same time the duties of the *praetor peregrinus*, who was thus freed for military service in North Italy. Like the consuls, the praetors were assigned their special functions by lot. The four praetors here mentioned are P. Aelius Paetus, who reached the consulship in 201 (xl, 5); P. Cornelius Lentulus, who later served in Africa (xxiv, 5; xxxvi, 2; xli, 2); P. Villius Tappulus, who continued to guard the coast of Sicily as propraetor in 202 (xxvii, 8; xli, 6); and P. Quinctilius Varus, who defeated Mago (ch. xviii). **Ariminum** (modern Rimini), a Latin colony which occupied an important strategic position on the Great North Road of Italy (Via Flaminia) on the Adriatic; it was the general centre of Cisalpine Gaul, and the name is often used, as here, as a synonym of the province itself. **Genuam.** For the capture of Genoa by Mago see Livy XXVIII, xlvi, 8. On Mago, see below, ch. xviii, 1.

10. P. Scipioni . . . prorogatum imperium est. Scipio had now held a continuous *imperium* for eight years. He was first invested with *imperium* as a *priuatus* in 210, and after his capture of Carthago Nova in Spain it was prolonged indefinitely: *non in annum, sed donec reuocatus ab senatu foret* (Livy, XXVII, vii, 17). On his return to Rome he was consul in 205, and was then granted proconsular *imperium* at first for one year (Livy, XXIX, xiii, 3), and finally for the duration of the war in Africa (XXX, i, 10). The truth of this last statement is uncertain, since Livy himself describes (xxvii, 7; xli, 1) how Scipio's command was prolonged amid opposition in 202 and 201, which would hardly have been necessary if he had really been appointed *donec debellatum in Africa foret*. Even if it is true, the Senate still retained the whip-hand, as a colleague invested with similar or greater authority could be sent to join Scipio in Africa.

fine. Ablative of manner: ' not fixing any limit of time other than that imposed by his carrying out the duties of his office '. **foret.** The subjunctive expresses the purpose in the mind of those who prolonged his command.

supplicatio. This religious ceremony was decreed by the Senate either as an act of humiliation in time of distress or of thanksgiving for a victory. In essence it consisted of a solemn prayer to some particular god or gods or to the gods in general, in which the whole people took part. It was thus unlike much of the formal state cult of Rome, which was celebrated by the priests alone. Cp. ch. xvii, 3; xl, 4.

11. **ea res** is the antecedent of the whole relative clause *quod . . . traiecisset* : ' that the fact of his having crossed might prove salutary, &c.'.

II. 1. **roboris** depends on *quod* : i.e., *id roboris quod habuerat*.

3. **M. Pomponius Matho**, as praetor in 204 had helped Scipio to prepare the African expeditionary force.

4. **Cn. Octavio. . . .** Livy makes a slip here. Octavius was praetor in 205, and propraetor in 204 and 203. In 205 he had captured eighty Carthaginian transports off Sardinia (XXVIII, xlvi, 14), but he was not so successful in 203 (see below, xxiv, 6–12). **duo milia militum dare in naues.** Soldiers served on shipboard as marines (*classici milites*), both to fight when ships grappled and to serve as landing-parties. The Romans tried to make up for their lack of naval skill by turning naval battles into something like land battles by the use of boarding tactics. Besides marines the fleet would need oarsmen (*remiges*) and sailors (*nautae*), who as a rule were drawn largely from the Greek allies in South Italy (*socii nauales*).

5. **esset.** Subjunctive as expressing the thought implied by *uidebantur petituri* (= ' they thought they were likely to attack ').

6. **legiones urbanas.** Two legions, composed of young recruits or elderly men, formed a guard for Rome; they were used elsewhere only in exceptional circumstances.

incerta. ' Uncertainties.'

7. **L. Lentulo. . . .** L. Cornelius Lentulus and L. Manlius Acidinus, who succeeded Scipio in the command in Spain, served there from 205 to 201 B.C. **uiginti omnino legionibus. . . .** The military dispositions were as follows. In Rome 2 urban legions; 4 legions under Cn. Servilius Caepio (consul) and P. Sempronius Tuditanus (proconsul) faced Hannibal in Bruttium; 7 legions dealt with Mago in North Italy, of which 1 occupied Genoa under Sp. Lucretius (propraetor), 2 under C. Servilius Geminus (consul) protected Etruria, and 4 under M. Cornelius Cethegus (proconsul) and P. Quinctilius Varus (praetor) fought in Cisalpine Gaul; outside Italy there were 7 more legions, 2 of which were in Sicily, under P. Villius Tappulus (praetor), with 40 ships under M. Pomponius Matho (propraetor); 2 in Spain under the propraetors L. Cornelius Lentulus and L. Manlius Acidinus; 1 in Sardinia under P. Cornelius Lentulus (praetor), with 40 ships under Cn. Octavius (propraetor); and 2 in Africa under P. Cornelius Scipio. **centum sexaginta nauibus longis.** In 208 B.C. the Romans had 280 ships at sea, but thanks to Valerius' naval victories and the peace with Philip, part of the fleet could be laid up, and in 203 B.C. the fleet at sea had sunk to 160 warships.

8. **proficiscerentur.** Subjunctive as being part of the command; cp. *foret* (i, 10). **ludos magnos.** Public shows or ' games ' (ludi) at Rome originated from religious observances. The Ludi Romani started in the sixth century B.C. and were celebrated annually after 366 B.C. They were held in honour of Jupiter, and consisted of circus-games and scenic exhibitions. They are sometimes called Ludi Magni, but this term here applies to special games (*ludi uotiui*) vowed by the praetor M. Aemilius in 217 B.C.; they were celebrated in 208 by T. Manlius Torquatus, who vowed them anew for the following lustrum—i.e., in 203. See further on xxvii, 11. **in quintum annum.** ' For the fifth year after his command.' T. Manlius Torquatus had been dictator in 208. **eodem statu**—i.e., safe and sound.

9. **religiones.** ' Religious fears.' **prodigia.** By prodigies the Romans meant events of exceptional character which seemed to suggest that good relations between the state and the gods (the *pax deorum*) was disturbed. They did not necessarily portend disaster, but they required careful attention and appeasement if the good understanding with the gods was to be restored. They were carefully recorded from early times by the college of priests (*pontifices*), and although some of the events may seem trivial or ludicrous to us, they were of real significance to the Romans, so that Roman historians thought them worthy of description. Even a practical-minded man like the Emperor Augustus paid great attention to any such signs: he even regarded it as ill-omened if in the morning he accidentally put on the wrong shoe first (see Suetonius, Aug. *c*. 90–2). On prodigies, see F. Altheim, *A History of Roman Religion*, pp. 197 ff. **Capitolio.** The temple of Jupiter Optimus Maximus on the Capitol, one of the chief hills of Rome; the roof of the temple was gilded.

10. **Antii.** Antium, the modern Anzio on the coast of Latium, south of Rome. **Capuam.** North of Naples in Campania.

11. **Reate.** A Sabine town north of Rome, Rieti. Here, as in the case of *Frusinone* below, the ablative is used for the locative in -*i*. **Anagniae.** Anagnia, a town in Latium belonging to the Hernici, now Anagni, south-east of Rome. **sparsi . . . ignes.** Falling stars. **fax,** the regular technical term for a large meteor.

12. **Frusinone.** Another city of the Hernici, now Frosinone. **arcus.** By an ' arch ' or ' bow ' Livy means an incomplete solar halo. **maior orbis.** A larger solar halo which completely enclosed the sun from without. **Arpini.** Arpinum, now Arpino, a hill town in Volscian territory above the valley of the Liris. **sinum.** ' Hollow,' ' hole '.

13. **iecineris.** The practice of divining from the livers of victims was derived from the Etruscans; the liver was plotted out into sections, marked off by lines, and omens were drawn from the condition of these sections. A bronze model of the liver, designed for the instruction of the *haruspex* or soothsayer, has been found in Italy, at Piacenza, and similar clay models have been found in Mesopotamia. **maioribus.** ' Full-grown.' **collegio pontificum.** The college of pontiffs were

charged with the supervision of religious law, and the decision of the
rites necessary in emergency would lie with them. See also note on
c. xxvi, 10. **editi.** 'Were published.'

III-VI. *Operations in Africa.   The Attack on the Camps of Syphax and Hasdrubal*

III. The general situation has been explained in the Introduction
(§ 3). Scipio had abandoned his camp south of Utica and retired
for the winter (204–3) to the Castra Cornelia on the promontory just
east of Utica. His first year's campaigning in Africa had been cautious
and not too successful. He had been forced back on to the defensive,
although he was in no actual danger as long as his communications
by sea with his base in Sicily were secured. During the winter he
planned to renew the offensive in the spring: although he had no real
intention of making peace, he negotiated with Syphax and Hasdrubal
in order to lull their suspicions, and then, when the time came, under
cover of a pretence of renewing the siege of Utica he launched an unexpected night attack on the enemies' camps. The topographical
situation will be made clear by a glance at the sketch opp. p. 33. Livy's
account is based on that by Polybius (xiv, 1–5), but he has added a
few patriotic details from Roman writers (cf. Introduction, p. 26).

1. **uelut eam sortitis.** They felt as concerned with Africa as if
they had been allotted that province themselves; and they did all
they could to help Scipio. **summam rerum.** ' The supreme issue
of Rome's fate.'

2. **ante.** See XXIX, xxxvi, 1–3.

3. **Vticam obsidebat.** *Obsideo* means ' sit down against ', and is a
little vaguer than ' besiege '. With his army shut up in the Castra
Cornelia, Scipio obviously could not have continued a formal siege
throughout the winter. **castra. . . .** The Roman and Carthaginian
camps were in fact on the opposite ends of the same ridge of hills, some
six miles apart. Livy does not make it clear here, though he does later
(e.g., iv, 2, or *bina castra*, vi, 6), that there were two Punic camps,
that of Syphax a little distance to the west of Hasdrubal's. As Polybius
has supplied details of the distances of the various camps from one
another, it is possible to be fairly sure of their exact positions to-day.

4. **si forte.** ' In case perchance.' **satias.** A word rarely found
in classical, though found in old and post-classical Latin (=*satietas*).
in uxore. Lit. ' in connexion with his wife '; Tr. ' love for his wife '.
copia. ' Access,' ' familiarity '. It was for the sake of winning Hasdrubal's daughter for his wife that Syphax had deserted the Roman and
joined the Carthaginian cause.

5. **condiciones.** Supply *adferebantur*, for which *adferebatur* (with
spes) does duty a few lines below, being singular, to agree with the nearest
subject; cp. *habuit* (iv, 6).

desciturum. Supply *illum*; the pronoun is not infrequently omitted by Livy when there is a participle to help out the sense. *esse* also has to be supplied. Such terms might have satisfied men like Fabius, but Scipio realized that Rome's future security demanded not merely the withdrawal of Hannibal from Italy, but also the humbling of Carthage. Cf. Introduction, p. 17.

6. crediderim. ' I should prefer to believe ': a potential subjunctive, often used as a means of making a polite assertion.

pars maior auctores sunt = *plures adfirmant*. This reference to the unreliable Roman annalist, Valerius Antias (on whom see Introduction, p. 26), shows how Livy turns to such Roman sources for additional or alternative information with which to supplement Polybius' account.

7. abnuere . . . facere. Historic infinitives.

ultro citroque agitantibus. Either ablative absolute or dative dependent on *rem conuenturam* (*esse*). Tr. ' the matter would be settled by frequent mutual negotiation '.

8. materia. ' Timber ': instrumental ablative dependent on *exaedificata*.

9. harundine. Probably the large ' pole-reed '. **textis.** Supply *hibernaculis*.

ut . . . locis. ' As in places occupied without orders '—i.e., the camp was not laid out on any plan.

IV. 1. quos mitteret. Subjunctive of indefinite frequency; not uncommon in Livy, but rarely found before him, though very common in later writers: ' whomsoever he sent from time to time '.

primos ordines. ' Senior centurions.' **spectatae uirtutis.** Descriptive genitive: ' of proved valour '.

2. qui . . . specularentur . . . noscerent. A clause expressing purpose.

alius alia goes with *uagi*. ' Roving about in different directions '. *alia.* Adverb. Lit. ' in other directions '; for the form cp. *qua*.

qua . . . haberent. ' Where they had their quarters.' Supply *castra* as object. **quantum . . . esset.** ' And what interval there was.' Polybius, XIV, 1, 14, gives the distance as 10 stades—i.e., just over one mile.

3. nocte an = *utrum nocte an*. **opportuniores**—i.e., ' more likely to fall victims to an ambush '. **alii atque alii.** ' More and more.'

4. detur. The present is regular after *aiunt*. But *aiunt* being a historic present, it is perfectly open to Livy to go on in past sequence as he proceeds to do. This variation of sequence is common in his works.

5. staret. ' Was already fixed.'

promeret sententiam. These words are not in the MSS. But some verb is absolutely necessary here, and the omission is easily explained by assuming the scribe's eye to have wandered to *sententiam*, when he should have written *sententia*.

nauiter. Adverb of *nauus*: an example of the adverbial termination *-iter*, which is somewhat uncommon for adjectives of the second declension.

6. **uisendi.** Genitive dependent on *tempus*. Livy might have written *ad uisenda*, but uses the perfectly normal genitive for the sake of variety. **habuit.** Singular in agreement with nearest subject, though, in view of *speculatores*, we might have expected *habuerunt*; a not uncommon usage.

7. **cauendi.** Depends on *neglegentia*.

8. **quibusdam**—i.e., certain conditions.

occasionem—i.e., that offered by the fact that the Romans seemed so eager for peace.

iniquis . . . adiectis. This version of the final reply of Syphax, which is designed to explain away Scipio's breach of good faith, is not given by Polybius, whose account implicitly seems to deny it. It is a Roman invention designed to 'whitewash' Scipio's conduct. There is no need, however, to suppose that it was a deliberate invention by Livy. He probably found it in one of his Roman sources, very likely Valerius Antias, and in his patriotic fervour accepted it, since Polybius did not explicitly say the opposite. The falsification probably arises therefore from too credulous and eager acceptance of what he read.

tollere depends on *cupienti*.

9. **relaturum.** Supply *rem* as object.

tendente. 'Striving (for peace).' **consilium** = 'council'. *concilium* = assembly. **relictis** = *si relicti essent*.

10. **libera fide.** 'Without breach of faith.' **ueris**—i.e., of 203 B.C.

deductis. The ships had been beached for the winter at the foot of Castra Cornelia and now had to be 'dragged down' to the sea. The preparations described in this and the following section were, in fact, undertaken somewhat earlier (Pol. XIV, ii, 2–4), before the breaking off of negotiations: only a few hours elapsed between the breach and Scipio's attack on the enemies' camps.

11. **tumulum.** The hill to the south of Utica on which the Roman army had encamped the previous year; the camp probably lay near a spot where later an amphitheatre was built, the site of which can still be traced.

12. **ne qua.** 'Lest at any point': the indefinite adverb, not the relative *qua* = 'where'.

V. 1. **iussis**—i.e., *exploratoribus Masinissaque*.

Masinissa. See Introduction, p. 18. This Numidian prince, who had served with the Carthaginian army in Spain from 212 to 206, was won over to the Roman side after Scipio's victory at Ilipa (206). He then returned to Africa to claim his father's kingdom, from which, however, he was driven out by Syphax; after many adventures and escapes from his pursuers he waited in hiding until Scipio landed in Africa, and then joined him with a useful force of cavalry.

2. **tribunis.** These were *tribuni militum*, who are not to be confused with the *tribuni plebis*, civil magistrates at Rome. These military tribunes were legionary officers, six in each legion.

praetorio. 'Council of war' at headquarters. See note on XIII, 8.

signa concinuissent. In the parallel passage Polybius (XIV, iii, 6) explains for his Greek readers a point which Livy could omit, as it would be familiar to most of his Roman readers: ' It is the custom among the Romans for the trumpeters and buglers to sound a call near the general's tent at supper time, that the night-watches may then take up their proper stations '.

3. **primam . . . uigiliam.** The night was divided into 4 *uigiliae*— i.e., when days and nights were of like length at the equinox, the first watch would be 6–9 p.m. But the *uigiliae* varied in length according to the season of the year, as did the hours.

explicauerunt. ' They formed their column of march.' *explico* is also used for deploying from column into line.

milia. Supply *passuum.* The length of the Roman mile was 95 yards shorter than the English mile. The *passus* = 5 feet, the Roman foot being ⅜ inch shorter than the English foot.

The army marched along the east side of the hills, where it would be protected from the enemy. Where the modern road crosses the range in a narrow cutting, Scipio halted and divided his troops, sending Laelius and Masinissa through the cutting to attack Syphax's camp, while he himself held back and prepared to attack Hasdrubal's camp when the other detachment had fired Syphax's camp.

4. **Laelio.** C. Laelius was the friend and right-hand man of Scipio, under whom he had served throughout the Spanish campaign.

5. **quantum . . . expleant.** Lit. ' By their diligence to make good just that amount of foresight of which the night deprived them '—i.e., ' by their diligence to secure themselves against the confusion inevitable in the darkness '. *prouidentiae,* genitive dependent on *quantum.*

7. **morata . . . est.** Either intransitive, ' was not long in accomplishment ', or transitive (supplying *eum*), ' did not keep him waiting long '. **deinceps continua.** ' The whole expanse of roofs one after the other.' Polybius, XIV, iv, 5, describes how Laelius and Masinissa divided their forces into two and attacked the enemy simultaneously. Livy does not trouble very much about such military details.

8. **quanta necesse erat.** Supply *oriri.* **incidere.** Third person plural of the perfect (*incidēre*).

9. **notitia.** A bold ablative of cause. ' Thanks to their knowledge of the camp.'

VI. 1. **alii.** sc. *Carthaginiensium.*

2. **confusus** = *incertus.* The noise of which they could not say whether it might not have arisen from a night alarm. The MSS. vary between *confusus* and *confusis.* If *confusis* be read, the sense will be ' the noise took away from them all realization of the truth, since they did not know, &c.'.

3. **ut quibus.** ' Like men who suspected nothing in the way of a hostile attack.' *quibus* is dative. **qua cuique proximum erat.** ' By the nearest way for each.' **quae restinguendo igni forent.** ' Such as might be suitable for extinguishing fire.' A slight extension of the

dative of purpose or action contemplated. Cp. phrases such as *soluendo esse, decemuiri sacris faciundis*, &c.

4. **praeterquam**, &c. Lit. ' besides by hatred, also to, &c.'. It is equivalent to *non modo odio, sed etiam ne quis*, &c. (a more common expression).

6. **quos** = *ii quos*.

8. Enemy casualty lists in ancient, as well as in modern times are often exaggerated by the victorious side. The total Carthaginian forces before this disaster are estimated by Polybius at 93,000, but most modern historians calculate that this figure should be reduced by more than half. He gives no exact figure for the Carthaginian losses, but says that the disaster exceeded in horror all previous events. Livy's figures, which probably derive from Valerius Antias, are not reliable, especially in view of the size of the army which Carthage could put into the field a month later.

9. **Volcano.** They were formally dedicated to the God of fire, and consumed by him.

VII. *Panic at Carthage followed by a decision to fight on*

1. **urbem proximam**, possibly named Anda. The site of this and of the place named Obba or Abba to which Syphax fled cannot be identified with any certainty.

3. **octo milium.** See on vi. 2. *milium* depends on *spatio*. ' At a distance of.' The place was named Abba or Obba (cf. § 10).

ne quid . . . consuleretur. ' Lest any weak policy should be adopted.'

5. **sufetes.** See Introduction, p. 3.

6. **decernebat.** This and the imperfects which follow indicate the tentative nature of the proposals.

sententiis certatum. These words are supplied by Madvig, on the assumption that a line was omitted by the copyist. ' Three different opinions were debated.' Early editions read *dictis sententiis* (abl. abs.).

Romanae . . . constantiae. Descriptive genitive dependent on *erat*. ' Showed courage worthy of Rome.'

7. **Barcinae . . . factionis**—i.e., the war-party who supported the policy of the house of Barca, of which the most illustrious member was Hannibal.

8. **et.** ' and also '—i.e., as well as the Carthaginians.

satis potentibus ad animum. ' Which had power to sway a lover's heart.'

10. **Celtiberorum.** Mercenaries formed a large part of the Carthaginian armies. These Celtiberians from Central Spain were marching eastward, having no doubt crossed over to Africa by the Straits of Gibraltar. Polybius (XIV, vii, 5) says it was Syphax himself (not the Carthaginian envoys, as Livy) who met them. He also names the place Abba, not Obba.

conducta. 'Hired.'

egregiae iuuentutis. In apposition with *Celtiberorum. iuuentus* means ' the prime of life ' rather than ' youth '.

11. **dedisset.** The subjunctive represents what he said; virtual Or. Obl. following on *ostendit.*

exciturum. Supply *se.*

13. **dies paucos.** Thirty days according to Polybius.

triginta milium. Possibly exaggerated. Perhaps there were some 15,000 troops. If Livy's figure is correct, it is difficult to explain why the presence of 4,000 Celtiberians should have so enheartened the Carthaginians. Also the Celtiberians played the leading role in the battle which followed : they could scarcely have done this if they were so greatly outnumbered by the other Punic forces, as Livy implies.

VIII. *Scipio defeats Hasdrubal and Syphax in a pitched battle at the Great Plains*

1. **attineret.** The subjunctive is due to the fact that *uelut debellato* expresses Scipio's thought—' considering that the war was already at an end '; impersonal abl. abs.

2. **cum robore exercitus.** Scipio took some 12,000–15,000 men, in light marching order.

3. **Magnos Campos.** Scipio arrived on the fifth day at the Great Plains, which lay by the Bagrades river, near the modern Souk el Kremis, about 75 miles from Utica. Here the Carthaginians had mustered some 20,000 men. They determined to fight a pitched battle, although it might have been wiser to try to cut off Scipio from his base at Utica and to wear him down by guerilla tactics. See the sketch opp. p. 33.

4. **in uicem.** An adverbial expression attached to a noun (*excursionibus*), virtually = *alternis*. This practice is not uncommon in Livy (cp. xxxix, 9 *circa tabernae*). In the present case it is made easier by the verbal force of *excursio.*

5. **hastatorum prima signa.** The maniples drawn up in the first line, which consisted of the *hastati*. This arrangement of the three lines was in accordance with the usual Roman practice, cf. Introduction p. 22.

6. **accepere.** ' Admitted.'

7. **terribilem.** ' Rendered formidable.'

8. **oppugnatum.** Supine; ' to attack him '.

9. **circumfusis undique hostibus.** Livy, who was not deeply interested in the details of military tactics, overlooks the essential point of Scipio's attack. After the flanks of the Celtiberian centre had been exposed by the defeat of the Punic cavalry, Scipio outflanked it by a skilful manoeuvre. Under cover of the first line of *hastati*, who engaged the Celtiberians, the *principes* and *triarii* turned into column, half to the right and half to the left, and then marched out to encircle the

Celtiberians. See Polybius XIV, viii, 11, who also points out that it was owing to the gallant stand made by the Celtiberians that Hasdrubal and Syphax were able to escape.

aliquantum goes with *temporis*.

IX. *Decision at Carthage to recall Hannibal and to attack the Roman fleet*

2. **urbes.** Probably villages rather than cities.

dicionis. Possessive gen. with *erant*; ' were under the sway of '.

3. **Carthagini.** Locative.

4. **obsidionis tolerandae sunt.** An extension of the possessive gen.; 'belong to the enduring of a lengthy siege ' = ' are necessary for, &c.'.

6. **mittere iubent.** *mitti* is perhaps the commoner idiom; but cp. Livy XXIX, vii, 6 *receptui canere cum iussisset.*

stationem . . . agentem. 'The naval force at Utica which was off its guard.'

forsitan . . . oppressuros. Or. Obliqua down to *superesse.*

7. **classi.** Ablative instr. **ut.** 'Even supposing.' **parte aliqua.** ' Only in part.'

9. **prodi.** Supply *in eo* as antecedent to *in quo.*

10. **ad Vticam.** Livy frequently uses the preposition with names of towns: in such cases *ad* generally means ' towards ': the camp was *near*, not *at* Utica.

Tyneta. Tunis lay at the western end of the Lake of Tunis, which forms a small offshoot of the main Gulf of Tunis. The northern shore of the lake runs round to Carthage.

X. *The Carthaginian attack on the Roman fleet*

1. The sudden determination of the Carthaginians to attack the Roman fleet seems to have caught Scipio unawares. It was only the sight of the Punic fleet actually under way that revealed the danger. The Roman fleet, loaded with artillery and siege weapons, had been taking an active part in the siege of Utica, and was not ready for a naval action. How Scipio met the danger is told in the following paragraphs.

1 **cum maxime.** 'Just at the moment when.'

pronuntiatum iter. ' Orders to march were given.'

3. **qui.** ' How,' originally a form of the ablative.

aptae. 'Equipped with '; participle of the obsolete verb *apere.*

pro aggere ac pontibus. In besieging a town, the Romans usually heaped up a mound (*agger*) against the wall. On or beside the mound were erected wooden towers, from the upper part of which boarding-bridges could be lodged on the top of the wall. At Utica Scipio had brought his ships close to the seaward walls, and had perhaps built towers on them up to the level of the ramparts.

6. The surviving manuscript of Polybius breaks off at this point, but there is little doubt that the rest of Livy's account of this incident follows closely the lost portion of Polybius, as may be seen from the use of the Greek accusative *Ruscumona* (§ 9) and *harpagones* (§ 16).

7. pro tempore. Lit. 'in proportion to the time '—i.e., 'as well as circumstances permitted '.

8. permixta agrees with *omnia*; 'in a state of confusion '. **turba trepidantium.** 'Owing to the disorder prevailing among the hurried workers.'

9. mari. If this is ablative ('by sea '), **fidentes** = 'having confidence in themselves '. If dative, it must be taken with *fidentes*, 'trusting in the sea,' a more poetic, but perfectly possible expression.

Rusucmona: the accusative is a Greek form. Rusucmon is to be identified with Porto Farina, north of Utica, near the end of the western horn of the Gulf of Tunis. The Phoenician word ' rosch ' means head or promontory.

10. ab alto. 'From out at sea '; we should omit ' from '.

iustum. 'Regular ', as in the phrase *iustum bellum*.

tanquam exituris. Livy uses the ablative absolute with *tanquam*, where Cicero or Caesar would have written either *ut exituris* or *tanquam exituri essent*: 'on the assumption that the Romans would come out to fight them '.

12. proxime governs the accusative because it is the superlative of the preposition *prope*. 'Being very like the appearance.'

13. utpote supino iactu. In English a verb must be supplied: 'seeing that they did so with an upward cast '. **pondere libratior.** 'Deriving greater impact from their very weight.'

15. ambiguo ictu. 'Owing to the uncertainty of their aim.' **inciderent** from *incĭdo*, ' fall on '.

16. harpagones. ' Grappling-irons '; a Greek word meaning ' snatchers ' from ἁρπάζειν.

17. incidere, from *incīdo*, ' cut '.

retro inhibita. ' Backing water.' **haerentem unco.** ' Held fast by the hook.' **traheret.** Subjunctive of repeated action after *ut* = ' whenever '; a common construction in Livy in place of which earlier writers would have used the indicative.

20. sexaginta. The figure varies in the MSS. of Livy. Some give *sex*. The higher figure is perhaps the more probable, since it would better explain the consequent joy at Carthage. Further, Scipio had brought 400 transports to Africa (Livy XXIX, xxvi, 3) and although some of these had been sent more than once to Sicily, the majority were now probably in Africa, as Scipio had not yet sent home the spoil from Campi Magni (XXX, ix, 10). As the transports were drawn up in four lines, the front line would therefore contain some 100 vessels. Livy implies that this front line was badly broken by the enemy, which would suggest the capture of sixty rather than six ships.

maior. Supply *fuit*. **pro.** ' In proportion to.' ' Their joy was out of all proportion to the facts.' **quantumcumque.** 'Such as it was.' We should rather have expected *quantulumcumque*, but Livy uses *quantuscumque* in this contemptuous sense elsewhere.

ex insperato. 'Unexpectedly.' This use of the neuter of a participle or adjective in place of an adverb is not uncommon in Livy.

cum eo ut. 'Together with the fact that.' **fuisse** is used as stating the actual fact. We must understand, to explain the pluperfect subjunctive *cessatum foret* ('if slackness had not been shown') some phrase meaning 'and would actually have been destroyed'; a common ellipse. Although Livy attributes the Roman escape to the Carthaginian commander's slackness and Scipio's timely arrival, nevertheless Scipio seems to have been guilty of some negligence in not making sure of the movements of the Carthaginian fleet before converting his own navy into a weapon of siege warfare only.

XI. *Syphax defeated by Laelius and Masinissa*

This account, at any rate as far as xii, 10, probably is based upon Polybius.

1. The Maesulii, a Numidian tribe, lived between the borders of the Carthaginian possessions to their east and the Kingdom of the Masaesulii under Syphax to their west. These tribesmen were the predecessors of the modern Berbers and racially distinct from the negroes further South. The Maesulii had been ruled over by Gaia. His son, Masinissa, had served with the Carthaginians in Spain, but had then been won over to the Roman side by Scipio's diplomacy. On Gaia's death Masinissa had returned to his kingdom, but had been driven out by Syphax. On the arrival of the Roman expeditionary force in Africa, Masinissa had hurriedly joined the Romans, and now, after the victory at Campi Magni, was given the task of pursuing his old enemy Syphax. His people, the Maesulii, welcomed back their rightful king.

quinto decimo ferme die. As the territory of the Maesulii stretched as far as Campi Magni, it would not have taken Laelius and Masinissa fifteen days to reach it. Probably Livy conveys a false impression, and in fact Masinissa, after leaving Campi Magni, passed through his own country, and reached the territory of Syphax in this time; for Cirta, the capital of Syphax, is about 200 miles from the Plains, which would involve a journey of about a fortnight.

3. **uxor socerque.** Sophoniba and Hasdrubal.

subiectae . . . uires. 'The military strength which had been placed before his eyes.' Tr. 'The contemplation of the military strength of his kingdom '. **spiritus facere.** 'Inspire.'

4. Although Syphax had seen something of Roman military methods (see Livy XXIV, ch. xlviii), he had scarcely had time to train his own troops in them, as Livy suggests.

6. **castris . . . positis.** The site of the battle is uncertain: probably it was a little to the east of Cirta, or near the River Ampsaga.

progredi and subsequent infinitives are historic.

7. **quod irritamentum est.** ' A thing provocative of cavalry combats.' **adgregat suos.** ' Brings up others of their own troops '— i.e., hope swells the ranks of the victors and anger those of the defeated.

8. **effundit.** ' Launched into the fight.' **sincerum.** Lit. ' unmixed ' —i.e., a purely cavalry combat.

Masaesuliorum. See note on § 1.

11. **audentem.** ' Emboldened by the support of the infantry.'

XII–XV. *Masinissa and Sophoniba*

The narrative down to xii, 10 derives from Polybius. Modern historians are divided on the question whether the tragic story of Sophoniba (xii, 11–xv) is also Polybian, or from the annalists; perhaps in essence it is Polybian, although not in detail.

XII. 1. **si . . . posset.** ' In case he might be able.' The capture of Syphax is also recorded in a fragment of the Roman annalist Coelius Antipater: ' Ipse regis eminus equo ferit pectus adversum; congenuculat percussus, deiecit dominum '. According to a late writer named Lydus, Syphax was riding on an elephant, not a horse.

3. **Cirta.** Now Constantine in Algeria, situated on a lofty cliff above the Ampsaga (Rumel) in an almost impregnable position.

4. **minor quam uictoria.** ' Less than the victory '—i.e., insignificant considering the magnitude of the victory.

5. **plus quinque.** *quam* is often omitted before a numeral. **eius.** ' Of that number.'

6. **dicere.** Historic infinitive, introducing Or. Obl. down to *posse.*

7. **trepida omnia,** a vague phrase, virtually equal to *omnes, dum trepidant.*

8. There are certain improbabilities in this account. Did none of the survivors of the battle, who had fled to Cirta, know and report the capture of Syphax? If Masinissa had shown his prisoner at once, he would have saved himself trouble.

datus esset. The subjunctive after *antequam* came to be used even if there was nothing more than a mere temporal connexion.

10. **opportuna moenium.** ' Suitable places along the walls.' Livy is fond of using a neuter adjective with a partitive genitive as here; a practice rare in earlier prose but common in poetry.

11. **uestibulum.** ' The forecourt.' The word is used of any open space in front of the entrance, varying from a simple recess in the front wall to a large courtyard.

Sophoniba, to whom reference has already been made, is first named here. She is better known as Sophonisba, a form which is not, however, found before a few late MSS. (fifteenth century) and early printed editions. The name is not uncommon in Punic inscriptions, where it appears as the equivalent of Safanbaal (= ' she whom Baal has protected '). The name has given Greek writers difficulty, as three different forms are used by them. Plays have been written on her story by John Marston (1606), Nathaniel Lee (1676), Corneille (1663) and James Thomson (1730). A wall painting preserved at Pompeii may depict her death. According to the Greek historians Dio Cassius and Appian, Hasdrubal had promised his daughter Sophoniba in marriage to Masinissa, but had later married her to Syphax; this therefore was the reason why Masinissa joined the Romans and took up arms against the Carthaginians and Syphax. This version, of which Livy is ignorant, is most improbable, and, in fact, Masinissa now met Sophoniba for the first time. After praising her beauty and musical and literary gifts, Dio adds that ' she was so charming that the mere sight of her or even the sound of her voice sufficed to vanquish every one, even the most indifferent '.

12. **in nobis** must be taken with *posses*: ' that you might have absolute power over us '. Lit. "in our case ".

13. **quaeso.** An old form of *quaero*, used in classical times only in the first person singular and plural (*quaesumus*). **fuit.** ' Was and is no more.' **accipiant.** ' May they welcome you.'

14. **quodcunque . . . animus.** ' Whatever your inclination leads you to decide.'

16. **morte.** ' By death.' Like Cleopatra, Sophoniba preferred death to being taken to Rome where she might be forced to walk in Scipio's triumphal procession. The Egyptian princess Arsinoe was forced to walk in chains in Julius Caesar's triumph in 46 B.C. Doubtless the fall of Cleopatra, which had occurred during Livy's lifetime, was vivid in his memory as he composed this account of Sophoniba.

17. **in id . . . fidem.** Lit. ' His promise to this that she should not be handed over to any Roman '.

18. **obligandae fidei.** Dative expressing purpose. ' To pledge his faith for the performance of that which she asked.' Cp. note on *restinguendo igni* (vi. 3).

19. **fidem praestaret.** ' Might make good the pledge of his promise ("his plighted word").' **expedire.** ' See his way to do this '; the primary meaning of *expedire* is ' disentangle '.

20. **ne quid integri** = *ne quid integrum*; the genitive being dependent on *quid*. *integer* (lit. ' untouched ') can be used to express freedom of action. **consulendi** is dependent on *integri*. ' That he might not leave Laelius or Scipio himself any freedom of decision concerning her as though she were a prisoner, now that she was already married to Masinissa.'

21. **lecto geniali.** ' From the marriage bed '; dative dependent on the compound verb *detractam*. *genius* (of which *genialis* is the adjective) is derived from *gigno* (' beget '), and in its primary meaning represents the reproductive principle. The point of Laelius's rebuke is that Sophoniba on Syphax's defeat had now become a captive of the Roman people, who alone had the right to decide her fate: see below xiv, 9-10.

22. **utrius . . . accessio.** Lit. ' to the fortune of which of the two

kings Sophoniba should be an addition '—i.e., whether she should be a captive with Syphax or a queen with Masinissa.

XIII. 2. Tum quantum . . . addebat. ' Then magnifying their own victory every Roman added as much as he could to the greatness of Syphax and the renown of his people '—i.e., exaggerated the greatness, &c. **augendo** is the modal ablative of the gerund, and is virtually equivalent to *augens*. Livy frequently uses this as ablative of the gerund as if it were an indeclinable present participle, a usage which survives in the gerunds of the modern Romance languages (with termination *-ant* in French, *-ndo* Italian and Spanish). The next four sections (4–7) give in Oratio Obliqua the substance of what they said.

3. tantum . . . tribuerint. ' Paid such tribute.' **maiestati** must be taken with *cuius*. ' To whose greatness.'

4, 5. Scipio . . . Hasdrubal. At the end of his Spanish campaign, Scipio, foreseeing the need to carry the war over into Africa, had paved the way by a visit to Syphax, whose help he sought (206 B.C. See Livy XXVIII, xvii–xviii). Hasdrubal had come at the same moment on a similar mission, and so the two generals who had fought against each other at Ilipa dined together under Syphax's roof. Scipio's magnetic personality attracted Syphax, whose goodwill was thus won to the Roman cause, and Scipio returned to Spain unable to foresee that the charms of Hasdrubal's daughter would counteract the impression he had made, and that Syphax would be won to Carthage by more subtle means.

nuptum. Supine. ' Gave in marriage.'

5. mactandis. ' By sacrificing.' The word *macto* is generally considered to be derived from the same root as *magnus*, and to mean ' magnify '. The consecration of the victim made it something greater than it had been. The verb came later to be used = ' kill ', and survives in the Spanish ' matar ', ' matador '.

7. Iam. ' Moreover.'

Masinissa. The exciting adventures of Masinissa are related by Livy XXIX xxxi–xxxii. After he had been driven from his kingdom, Masinissa was hunted down by an officer named Bucar, who drove him into a valley, from which he escaped with only fifty troopers. These were later killed in a running fight, only Masinissa, himself wounded, and four others escaping. In the pursuit two were drowned in a raging river into which Bucar dared not venture. But Masinissa found refuge in a cave, where he recovered from his wound with the help of his two surviving companions. Meantime, to save his face, Bucar had spread abroad a false rumour of Masinissa's death. **fama.** Ablative of instrument. ' By the rumour of his death.'

8. praetorium, the headquarters of a Roman camp, in which lay the general's tent (*tabernaculum*); in front was the altar on which he offered sacrifices, on the left a place where auspices were taken (*augurale*), and on the right the *tribunal*, an earthen bank on which he stood when addressing the troops or administering justice.

foederis. Livy (XXVIII, xviii, 12) says Scipio on his visit to Syphax

H

had concluded a formal treaty with him, but this is unlikely, as Scipio was there in a private capacity, not as an ambassador of Rome. Similarly below in § 9 Livy may be using *societatem* in a technical sense, but in fact Syphax was not a *socius* of the Roman people.

9. **abnuisset . . . intulisset.** Subjunctive as forming part of Scipio's question.

10. **exitum.** ' That was the outcome of his madness.'

11. **acceperit.** The tenses in dependent clauses of this passage of Oratio Obliqua are in present sequence. Cp. *uideat* (13).

12. **nuptialibus facibus.** Livy speaks of Syphax as if he was a Roman. At a Roman marriage the bride was escorted at nightfall from her father's to the bridegroom's house by a procession which included flute-players and torch-bearers.

14. **se** is the subject of *duxisse*, contrasted with *illum*.

XIV. 2. **Et fidem . . . faciebant.** The *et* is answered by *et eo* in the next section. The subjects are *raptae nuptiae* and *tam praeceps praecipitatio*. ' The charges against Masinissa were rendered credible by the suddenness of the marriage which he had carried through almost on the field of battle without consulting or awaiting Laelius and by the fact that his haste was such that,' &c.

3. Polybius (X, xix) relates that after the capture of New Carthage some Romans brought a beautiful girl captive to Scipio, who promptly returned her in safety to her father. This story of Scipio's chastity has been worked up with further romantic details by Livy, XXVI, l. **praetorio,** see note on xiii, 8.

4. **aliqua . . . commisisse.** ' I think that when first of all you came to make friends with me in Spain, and also at a later date entrusted yourself and all your hopes to my protection, you saw some good qualities in me.' There is a strong Stoic element in this speech of Scipio.

5. **uisus sim.** This has probably been attracted into the subjunctive by *gloriatus fuerim.* **gloriatus fuerim** = *gloriatus sim.* ' In which I have taken such pride.'

6. **periculi** depends on *tantum.* **aetati nostrae.** ' Men of our age.'

8. **auspiciis.** Before leading out his army from Rome, the general would take the omens (*auspicia*); when he had secured such good omens as justified his marching, he was said to lead the army *suis auspiciis.* Hence our use of the phrase ' under the auspices of ', virtually = ' under the command of '.

10. **senatus . . . esse.** ' That the power of deciding her fate should belong to the senate and Roman people.' **nobis.** Dative dependent on *alienasse.* **dicatur.** Causal subjunctive. ' Seeing that she is said '.

11. **deformes.** Subjunctive of *deformo* dependent on *caue.*

maiore culpa. I.e., the seriousness of his error is out of all proportion to the object which made him commit it.

XV. 1. **in potestate futurum.** 'Would submit himself to the commands of.' **fidei . . . consuleret.** 'Would have some regard for his rash pledge.'

3. **tabernaculum** depends on *circumstantibus*.

fidum e seruis. 'A trusted slave.'

4. **regio more.** Kings often kept poison in order to escape falling alive into the enemy's hands. Mithridates, when cornered by Pompey, took poison, but it failed to take effect, as he had fortified his constitution by antidotes, so that he was forced to induce one of his retainers to kill him.

ad incerta fortunae. 'To meet the uncertainties of fortune.'

5. **fidem primam.** The first promise—i.e. 'to love her and protect her as his wife'. **ei** is governed by *praestaturum fuisse*. **eius.** Neuter, dependent on *arbitrium*: 'the power to perform it'.

7. **si non . . . nupsissem.** 'Had not my marriage bed stood so near my grave' (Philemon Holland).

8. **ferocius.** 'More boldly.'

9. **animi.** Locative. 'Sick at heart.' **ferox.** 'Headstrong', 'impulsive'. **grauius consuleret.** 'Should take some yet more desperate decision.'

10. **luerit.** 'Had atoned for one blind folly by another.'

11. **tribunal.** Cf. on xiii, 8. **aurea corona.** A natural gift to a king, for Masinissa was now to reign under the protection of Rome; but Roman commanders, as Laelius below, were often decorated with such crowns as a reward for their services. **sella curuli.** The ivory curule chair was the official seat of the Dictator, Master of the Horse, Consul, Censor, Praetor, and curule aedile at Rome. **scipione . . . tunica.** The point of these gifts was that they were worn by Roman generals when celebrating a triumph: hence Scipio was giving Masinissa the highest honour he could devise for his defeat of Syphax. In Rome the triumphing general wore the garb of Capitoline Jupiter, which was supplied from the treasury of the temple on the Capitol—viz., a purple tunic embroidered with gold palm-leaves, a toga decorated with golden stars and circles, gilded shoes, and an ivory sceptre with an eagle on the top. The fact that Scipio's name meant a sceptre added further point to the gift.

12. **uerbis.** Ablative. **triumpho.** Ablative. 'There was nothing more magnificent than a triumph.' This festal procession through Rome at the head of his army was both the highest honour that a victorious general could receive and a solemn religious act. It was led by the magistrates and senators; then followed trumpeters, the captured spoils, painted representations of the conquered country; then garlanded sacrificial white bulls, followed by distinguished captives, the purple-tuniced lictors, musicians, priests, and finally the triumphal chariot in which stood the general in the robes of Jupiter; the troops brought up the rear.

eo. Supply *ornatu*.

13. **alii . . . donati.** Decorations such as medallions (*phalerae*), bracelets (*armillae*), necklets (*torques*), and crowns (*coronae*).

XVI. *Scipio States his Terms to the Carthaginians*

1. **ad Tyneta.** See note on *ad Vticam*, ix, 10.

3. **oratores.** 'Spokesmen', 'ambassadors'. **triginta . . . principes.** See Introduction, p. 3.

sanctius . . . consilium. 'A council regarded with special respect.'

uis. 'Influence': Tr. 'and were of great influence in directing the decisions of the senate '.

4. **ea regione.** Phoenicia.

oriundi = *orti*. A survival of the early use of the gerundive in the sense of a present participle. Cp. *uoluenda dies* = 'rolling time ' (Virgil, Aeneid, ix, 7).

5. **conueniens.** 'Suited to their grovelling flattery.' **humili.** The adjective is derived from *humus*, and here suitably describes their act of prostration on the ground.

6. **bis iam euersae.** 'Twice overthrown '—i.e., in the First Punic war as well as this, the Second.

7. Compare the famous lines of Virgil (Aeneid, vi, 851): ' tu regere imperio populos, Romane, memento|(hae tibi erunt artes), pacisque imponere morem,|parcere subiectis et debellare superbos '.

imperaret. Subjunctive of command.

8. Scipio did not aim at the destruction of Carthage itself, as the conditions which he offered now and after Zama show, although traditionally he is said to have acknowledged this aim (cf. xliv, 3). **ea spe** must be taken with *uictoriam se reportaturum esse*.

10. The terms offered would reduce Carthage to a purely African power, limited by the territory of Rome's ally Masinissa, deprived of the great resources of Spain and of her carrying trade, crippled in her recovery by a heavy indemnity and, above all, robbed of her fleet, the means of regaining or holding any distant territory. Nominally she was to remain independent, but really her future would lie in Rome's hands, and she would be little else than a client state. Such an object might well be considered an adequate war-aim. To try to reduce Carthage itself would have involved a protracted siege; as long as the Carthaginians kept their fleet, it would be difficult to starve them out, while Scipio had failed in his attempt to storm the smaller town of Utica. Further, before attempting a siege, Scipio must consider Hannibal's return. So, faced by these difficulties, he offered terms, which were accepted by the Carthaginians, by some from a real desire for peace, by others to delay matters till Hannibal's return.

perfugas. Free men who had deserted. **fugitiuos.** The regular term for ' runaway slaves '. **exercitus . . . deducant**—i.e., the army of Hannibal from Southern Italy, that of Mago from Cisalpine Gaul.

11. **modium** = *modiorum*. The *modius* = about two gallons. Africa was one of the chief sources of the corn supply. Probably this and the clause below about the *duplex stipendium* were temporary measures belonging to the armistice (indutiae, cf. 13), rather than clauses of the final peace which was to be negotiated.

12. **parum conuenit.** ' There is little agreement.'

quinque milia talentum. This is the correct figure, which is given by Polybius XV, viii, 7. By the terms of the peace after Zama, Carthage had to pay 10,000 talents of silver. The figure 5,000 pounds weight of silver, which is simply an error due to a careless or ignorant annalist, represents roughly $\frac{1}{20}$th of 5,000 talents. **pondo.** Ablative of an obsolete form *pondus, -i*; = *pondere*, ' in weight '; supply *librarum*, ' of pounds '. **duplex stipendium,** to be paid during the armistice. In Polybius' day citizen troops received 120 denarii a year, the allies some 48 modii of grain.

14. **dum . . . traiceret.** ' Until Hannibal should cross.' Purpose is implied; hence the subjunctive.

15. **in speciem.** ' For the sake of appearances.'

XVII. *Laelius and Masinissa's envoys in Rome*

1. **ingenti . . . laetitia . . . spe.** Abl. Abs.

2. **consulti.** In the absence of the consuls from Rome the praetor would preside over the Senate. **Albam.** Alba Fucens is to be distinguished from Alba Longa, which lay in the Alban Hills near Rome. It was situated in the country of the Aequi, north of the Fucine Lake, and had recently (204) been punished for refusing to supply its quota of troops to the Roman army in 209. Later Syphax was transferred to Tibur (now Tivoli), where he died (ch. xlv, 4).

3. **supplicatio.** See note on i, 10. **Aelius.** See on i, 9. **contione.** *Contio* = *conuentio*, a meeting of citizens called and presided over by a magistrate, who addressed the people, giving orders, rendering reports, introducing ambassadors, opening discussions, and in general informing public opinion, often before a more formal meeting of the Assemblies where voting could take place. In a *contio* there might be discussion, but no voting. The word is also used of a speech delivered before such a gathering. **rostra** was the orator's platform in the Forum, so called because it was decorated with the bronze prows (*rostra* = lit. ' beaks ') of some ships captured at Antium in 338 B.C.

5. **quin.** Lit. ' but that they signified,' &c. This is best translated, ' They could not contain their joy, but signified '. *quin* is only used in this way after a negative or implied negative. **quibusque aliis** = *aliisque quibus*.

6. Temples, which did not have regular priests, remained shut under the care of *aeditui*.

salutandi . . . agendique. These gerunds depend on *potestas*.

8. **esset regnaturus.** The so-called periphrastic subjunctive is

regularly used in cases such as this, where the imperfect subjunctive (*regnaret*) would be ambiguous, since being in indirect speech it would naturally represent *regnabat* in direct speech; *regnaturus esset = regnabit* in direct speech.

11. **amplum** 'futurum esse'. ' Would win him fame in the eyes of his fellow-countrymen.'

12. **rerum gestarum** depends on *gratulationem*. 'They had as much reason for congratulating the king as for receiving congratulations from him.' **cordi.** Locative = ' at heart'. Tr. ' was gratifying to '.

13. **sagula.** *Sagum* was a thick woollen cloak worn by all citizens except consulars when there was a war in Italy, as opposed to the toga or garb of peace (cf. *saga sumere*, Cic. Phil. viii, 11). The cloak worn by the general and superior officers is sometimes called *sagum*, but more often the diminutive *sagulum* is used, as here. **lato clauo.** The *latus clauus*, a broad purple band stretching from the neck to the centre of the tunic, was a distinctive badge of the senatorial order, while the *angustus clauus* was the decoration of the equestrian order. **phaleratos.** *Phalerae* were metal discs, used especially as ornaments attached to the harness of horses. They were often presented by Roman generals to horsemen as marks of bravery and merit.

14. **ne minus.** With the infinitive we should expect *non*. But the *ne* of direct speech (*dentur ne minus*) has been retained. The same peculiarity is found elsewhere in Livy—e.g., XXVIII, xxxix, 19, where a similar list of gifts occurs.

aeris. The early unit of Roman coinage was the copper *as*, carrying the nominal weight of the Roman pound (*libra* = 12 *unciae*); but it suffered continuous depreciation, so that in 209 B.C. it was reduced to about three ounces. It is on the basis of the *as* that we should calculate sums expressed as *quina, dena millia aeris*. **aedes liberae.** Foreign ambassadors in Rome, whose persons were regarded as inviolable, were treated as public guests ; cp. xxi, 12. **loca.** " Lodgings," or possibly " places at entertainments."

lautia. This word is explained by Plutarch (Quaestiones Romanae, 45) as the name given to the gifts bestowed on ambassadors sent from abroad to Rome. It is stated that the original form was *dautia* (Paul. Fest. 60, 6, L.).

XVIII. *Defeat of Mago in North Italy*

The military arrangements in North Italy have already been described (cf. on ii, 7). When Mago, who had landed in Liguria, moved his base to Savo, now Savona, the Romans had posted one legion under Sp. Lucretius at Genoa, while two more under Servilius Geminus guarded Etruria, and the main army of four legions, under Cornelius Cethegus and Varus, was based on Ariminum. When Mago crossed the Apennines into the northern plain of Italy, Servilius moved from Etruria into the valley of the Po to prevent the Boii joining him, while the main army abandoned the defensive and marched from Ariminum to meet him in battle. Once more, fifteen years after the defeat at Ticinus, a Roman army ventured into this district. Mago had some 30,000 men, many of whom were veterans from Africa and Spain. Livy's account of the battle is, however, of little value from the military point of view; it derives from a bad annalistic source, perhaps Valerius Antias. It is similar to Livy's description of a battle fought in Spain in 205 (Bk. XXIX, ii), and some details in both are so alike (cf. especially XXIX, ii, 9 and XXX, xviii, 8–9) that obviously one account is copied from the other, though it is impossible to say which of the two is the original. If, however, the details are uncertain, there is no reason to deny the historicity of the battle.

1. On **Varus** and **Cornelius** cf. I, 7 and 9.

Insubrum. The Insubres were a Gallic tribe living north of the Po in modern Lombardy. **Magone.** Mago, son of Hamilcar and brother of Hannibal, had accompanied Hannibal to Italy, fought at Trebia, and reported the victory of Cannae at Carthage. Sent to Spain, he had campaigned against, and finally defeated, the Scipios (211); at length defeated by Scipio Africanus at Ilipa, he had fled to Gades (Cadiz). Thence he made an abortive attempt to seize New Carthage, and on his return, finding Gades barred against him, he sailed off to the Balearic Islands, where he seized the capital of Minorca, which still preserves his name, Mahon. Then in 205 he had made his bold descent on the Ligurian coast, where he had sacked Genoa.

3. **nihil.** Adverbial, 'Not at all'. **commouebant.** Supply *hostem.* **induratur . . . timor.** 'Their fear is hardened'—i.e., is being turned into courage. **praeter spem** must be taken with *resistendo.* **uertat.** Intransitive.

5. **utram uellet.** 'Which of the two he preferred.' The subjunctive is due to the fact that it is in virtual Oratio Obliqua, since *accipiente* implies that the proconsul said he would accept whichever task the praetor preferred him to undertake.

6. **ad . . . motum.** 'At the first movement of the cavalry.'

7. **odorem.** Elephants had had a similar effect on the Roman cavalry at the Battle of Trebia (Livy XXI, lv, 7).

permixtus. 'In a mêlée at close quarters.' **roboris maioris.** Descriptive genitive. 'Was more effective.' **in ablatum.** Supply *equitem.* 'Against the cavalry when it withdrew.'

11. **nullo.** Supply *pilo.*

12. **donec.** 'So long as.'

13. **femine.** From *femen,* an old form of *femur* ('thigh').

14. **inde** = *ex ea legione.*

15. **equites illustres.** Under Augustus the *equites illustres* were a special class of knights who possessed the senatorial census and yet voluntarily remained knights. Here they are sons of nobles serving in the cavalry.

XIX. *Death of Mago. Events in Italy*

1. **quantum . . . extentis**—i.e., *itineribus tantum extentis quantum potuit pati :* ' by marches as long as he was able to endure '.

Ingaunos. A Ligurian tribe, living on the west side of the Gulf of Genoa and on the slopes of the Maritime Alps; their capital was Albingaunum (now Albenga), and they were allied with Mago.

2. **sinum Gallicum**, the Gulf of Genoa or of Lyons.

primo quoque tempore. ' At the earliest opportunity.'

4. **moranti** = *si moraretur*.

5. **superata.** ' Passed.' **moritur.** Another version of Mago's death in 193 B.C. is given by Nepos, *Hann.* 9; cf. Appian, *Lib.* 49, 59 and Zonaras IX, 13. **classe Romana.** Under the command of Cn. Octavius (ii, 4).

7. **patre . . . capti fuerant.** In 218 C. Lutatius Catulus (consul 220) and C. Servilius, who had been sent to found colonies at Placentia and Cremona, were driven to seek refuge in Mutina by an onslaught of the Boii, a Gallic tribe, who had doubtless been stimulated to prepare the way for Hannibal's arrival in North Italy. While parleying with the enemy these two Romans were treacherously captured (Livy XXI, xxv). A relieving army under a praetor was also defeated and shut up in Tannetum, some 20 miles from Mutina. **post sextum decimum annum.** As the rescue occurred in 203, we should reckon 15 years, but the Romans reckoned inclusively.

9. **fraudi.** Predicative dative. ' That it should not be to his prejudice.' Livy has not formulated the legal difficulty very accurately. It arose not from the fact that the father had held curule office, but because he was a patrician, and had not authorized at the right time his son to become plebeian. Thinking his father was dead, the son had changed the family into a plebeian gens (*transitio ad plebem*), in order to stand for the tribunate. When it was discovered that the father was alive, the son desired to regularize his position by legal action. An alternative explanation is that Livy is in fact correct and that a law existed which closed the plebeian offices of tribune and plebeian aedile to sons of curule magistrates while their fathers were still living.

10. **Consentia. . . . .** Except Consentia (Cosenza), none of these places is of much importance. Further, Livy has already recounted the defection of some of them from Hannibal in the preceding year, 204 (XXIX, xxxviii, 1). The earlier date is the more probable.

11. **in agro Crotoniensi.** Again Livy has recorded a battle here in 204 (XXIX, xxxvi, 4–9). This second battle, about which Livy himself has some doubts, may be dismissed. Croton was a Greek city in South Italy. On Valerius Antias see Introduction, § 5.

12. **nihil** must be taken with *rei* = *nulla res.*

XX. *Hannibal evacuates Italy*

4. **Hanno,** surnamed the Great, was the leader of the oligarchs and of the peace-party at Carthage. He is said by Appian (Lib. 34)

to have accompanied Hasdrubal on the embassy to Rome which Livy
describes below (ch. xlii), but it is not very probable that he was still
alive, as he had commanded Carthaginian armies half a century
before.

5. **inutili . . . turba . . . dimissa.** Abl. abs. **quae pauca.**
'A few of which.' **quod roboris** = *quod robur*.

6. This story is of very doubtful probability, and may be a mere
libel on Hannibal's reputation. Perhaps some Italian soldiers killed
themselves rather than face punishment for treachery to Rome. **secuturos.** *se* is omitted. 'Saying that they would not follow him.'
abnuentes = *negantes*, a not-infrequent usage.

Iunonis Laciniae delubrum. One solitary column of this temple
still stands on the cliff edge of the Lacinian promontory. It was on an
altar near this temple that Hannibal had set up a bilingual inscription
in Phoenician and Greek, recording details of his campaign, which
survived for Polybius to read.

7. **execratum.** 'Cursing himself and his own life.' The verb
is here followed, as elsewhere in Livy, by *in* with accusative, instead of
the more normal accusative.

8. **cruentum ab . . . uictoria.** 'Reeking with blood from the
victory of Cannae.'

Although his cavalry officer Maharbal urged Hannibal to march on
Rome after Cannae, saying that 'in five days we shall dine on the
Capitol ', Hannibal refused, and most modern military critics believe
that he judged the situation aright: he had no siege-train with which to
attempt to storm Rome.

qui . . . uidisset. This is scarcely true, as Scipio had slipped over
from Sicily during his consulship (205 B.C.) and had wrested Locri
from Hannibal: that a battle had not ensued was due to Hannibal's
decision to abandon Locri when threatened by the Roman armies.

9. **Trasumennum aut Cannas.** See Introduction, p. 13.

Casilinum Cumasque et Nolam. Three Campanian towns around
which campaigning centred from 216–214. **Italiae est detractus.**
It is uncertain whether the date of Hannibal's departure was autumn
203 or February–March 202: the former is the more probable. See
Appendix on Chronological Problems, p. 137.

XXI–XXIII. *The Carthaginian Envoys in Rome*

XXI. 1. minuit. The subject is the long clause with which the
sentence concludes (*quod . . . euasura esset res,* ' the fact that they seemed
. . . and were anxious '). **parum,** here a substantive, must be taken
with *aut animi aut uirium*: ' too little either of courage or of strength '.

2. **quo.** Lit. ' in what direction ': we should say ' how '.

3. Some modern historians reject this story of the Saguntine embassy
as deriving from a bad annalistic source.

traiecissent. Subjunctive because it gives what they said: ' who, they said, had crossed '. For Carthaginian attempts to hire mercenaries in Spain see the Celtiberians referred to in chs. vii, viii.

4. **pondo.** See on xvi, 12.

5. **carcerem.** ' The prison '—i.e., the Tullianum at the foot of the Capitol; the sole prison in Rome.

6. **mentio.** This must have taken place in the senate. **incidisse.** This is an exclamatory infinitive, like *fuisse* and *auditas* (*esse*) in section 8.

7. **uisa castra.** In 211 Hannibal had suddenly marched on Rome itself in the hope of drawing off the Roman armies which were besieging Capua. He camped four miles east of the city, and rode up to the Colline Gate, but the Romans remained undaunted and soon Hannibal withdrew.

8. **en umquam . . . essent.** These words represent the words (*uoces*) just mentioned. The question, though rhetorical—i.e., requiring no answer—is here expressed not by the infinitive, as it might have been, but by the subjunctive (*futurus esset*). **bona pace.** ' With the blessings of peace.'

9. **adeo . . . memores sint.** ' To such an extent do men fail to welcome blessings as they approach, not to mention the fact that they are unmindful of those that have been bestowed upon them in the past.'

10. **uti referret.** ' That he should put the matter before the house.' **puluinaria.** At the *lectisternia*, a symbolic feasting of the gods, figures of the gods were exhibited reclining on couches and seeming to partake of a meal set before them as they rested with their left arms on cushions (*puluinaria*). **immolarentur.** The word is derived from *mola* (' meal '), and strictly describes the sprinkling of meal on sacrificial victims; but it is frequently, as here, used in the more general sense of ' sacrifice '.

11. The following account of the delay at Rome, in confirming the peace terms arranged by Scipio in Africa, is confused, but Polybius makes it quite clear that the Senate did ultimately approve the peace. The Roman annalists, however, did not like the idea of the Senate thus calmly accepting the terms. Thus we find Livy's patriotic account of how the Punic embassy, as if knowing nothing of Scipio's terms, proposed a peace on the basis of that of 241 B.C. Rejecting this offer, the Senate sent back the ambassadors and ordered Scipio ' ne bellum remitteret ' (xxiii, 5). But if no peace was settled, why should there be any uneasiness in Rome at the later breaking of the truce (xxxviii, 6) ? Also in ch. xvii the Senate had determined to keep Laelius in Rome until the arrival of the Punic embassy, but now (xxi, 11) it does not appear to have heard of the embassy till it landed in Italy, and so has to recall Laelius, who had left Rome. It will thus be apparent that the historical value of this account is slight.

Puteolis. Puteoli (modern Pozzuoli), on the Bay of Naples, was one of the chief harbours of Italy. As the journey by sea thence to

Ostia, the port of Rome, was somewhat treacherous, it was common to land at Puteoli and finish the journey by land. This is what St. Paul did.

12. **uilla publica.** Envoys of states at war with Rome might not enter the city. The *uilla publica*, a building used for the reception of foreign envoys, and the temple of Bellona were both in the Campus Martius outside the walls. Fragments of a large temple have recently been discovered near the Flaminian Circus, which are probable remains of this temple of Bellona: see *Journ. Rom. Stud.* 1946, p. 7.

XXII. **consilio.** The senate of Carthage; cp. iv, 9. The envoy's speech is a piece of special pleading. Although it is true that Hannibal's plan of campaign was partly *priuatum consilium*, the Carthaginian Government, however, supported his general action. Hannibal's attack on Saguntum was the proximate cause of the war, and when he stormed it in 218, the Romans had demanded that the Carthaginian Government should surrender Hannibal and disavow his action: but this it refused to do.

2. **Hiberum.** The River Ebro in North Spain had formed the boundary between the Roman and Carthaginian spheres of interest in Spain in accordance with the treaty of 226 B.C. Cp. Introduction, p. 11.

4. **nihil aliud** is the object of *peterent.* **Lutatio.** C. Lutatius Catulus had brought the First Punic War to an end by his naval victory off the Aegates Insulae on 10 March 241. Cp. Introduction, p. 10.

5. **potestatem . . . fecisset.** 'Had given leave to the senate to ask any questions that any one among them might wish to ask.' **meminisse.** Supply *se.*

6. **conclamatum.** Supply *est.* **Punica fraude** : the stock charge of Punic ill faith. In fact, there is little reason to believe that the Carthaginians were any worse in this respect than their contemporaries.

XXIII. We here get a glimpse into the politics of the Roman Senate. There were no parties in the modern sense, but naturally senators tended to fall into different groups, and these were often determined by family connections. Just as a private Roman noble might be patron to a group of clients, so some of the lesser clans might seek the protection of the more powerful ones, and we find various groupings of the chief families which naturally changed from time to time. Thus it would be more correct to speak of family politics than party politics. By no means all the details which Livy records about the domestic affairs are to be accepted, but perhaps the main lines of his account go back to reliable sources. We need not concern ourselves with details here. The main point is that during Scipio's absence in Africa various noble families intrigued against him, while Metellus tried to protect Scipio's interests.

1. **M. Liuius Salinator,** as consul in 219, had defeated the Illyrians, but had withdrawn from public life after a scandal about the booty. He was later recalled, and held the consulship again in 207, when he shared in the glory of Hasdrubal's defeat at Metaurus; thereafter he served as proconsul in Etruria. The right of speaking first in the Senate

belonged to the *princeps senatus*. As Livius now spoke first, Fabius Maximus the *princeps* had either died already (cp. xxvi, 7) or was absent through illness. Nothing more is heard about Livius after this. **propior.** Gaius Servilius was in Etruria, the other, Gnaeus Servilius was in Bruttium.

2. **quam quanta.** A not uncommon idiom, though *quanta* is superfluous and need not be translated. **satis ex dignitate.** 'Sufficiently in accordance with the dignity of the Roman people.'

3. **Q. Metellus** had been consul in 206 and dictator in 205.

4. **qua mente.** 'With what intent.'

5. **M. Valerius Laeuinus** was only consul once, in 210, but he had served in Sicily as proconsul in 209 and 208. **iubendos** depends on the idea of speaking contained in *arguebat* ("sought to prove").

6. **et Scipionem.** Scipio as well as the senate. **in eo . . . si.** 'On the supposition that.'

7. **quamuis** goes with *recentium*. 'However recent.'

eo magis . . . discessum. Consequently there was a majority in favour of the proposal of Laevinus. When the motion was put, the Senate divided, those in favour passing to one side of the presiding magistrate, and those against to the other. *discedere* ('to go in different directions') is the technical term for this procedure. **pace infecta.** On the contrary, as Polybius implies, Scipio's terms were approved.

XXIV. *Incidents in Italy. The Carthaginians break the Truce*

1. It is difficult to say how much reliability is to be placed on this story of Cn. Servilius Caepio. **pacatae Italiae** depends on *gloria*.

3. It was necessary to appoint some one with greater authority (*maius imperium*) to check Servilius, who had arbitrarily left his province: the praetor was subordinate to the consul. **P. Sulpicius Galba,** consul in 211, had fought in Macedon until superseded by Sempronius Tuditanus in 205. According to the Fasti, the purpose of Sulpicius' dictatorship was to hold elections (dict. comit. habend. caussa). See also on xxvi, 12.

4. **M. Seruilio.** Sulpicius had appointed as his Master of the Horse M. Servilius Geminus, brother of the other consul, C. Servilius Geminus, who was elected consul for 202.

5. Livy's account of the following incidents derives probably from Polybius, although there are traces of another source (perhaps Coelius or the Greek historian Silenus who campaigned with Hannibal) less unfavourable to the Carthaginians. The chronology is not certain: see Appendix.

et. 'Also'—i.e., like the preceding events. **praesidio.** 'With an escort of twenty ships of war.' **ab hoste . . . ab tempestatibus** depends on *tuto*—i.e., 'the sea being safe both from the enemy and from storm'; tr. 'undisturbed either by the enemy or,' &c.

7. **Africum,** the south-west wind blowing from Africa.

8. Apollinis promunturium, probably the same as the cape called Pulchrum, where Scipio had landed, the western horn flanking the Gulf of Tunis; it is nearly due north of Carthage itself.

9. Aegimurum, now Zembra. **ab alto,** from the open sea. **urbem,** Carthage. **Calidas Aquas,** on the west of the peninsula of Cape Bon.

10. Carthage was no doubt overcrowded with refugees from the countryside. Further, Scipio was master of the open country, cutting off supplies from the interior, while he was also superior by sea. The ill-fed populace could scarcely let the opportunity slip when it saw great supplies within its grasp. Yet to seize them would mean breaking the truce. However, Hannibal had now returned, and the war-party was doubtless getting the upper hand once more.

11. concilio. The assembly, as opposed to the senate, which was a *consilium*. **Hasdrubal,** an admiral, not to be confused with any other Hasdrubal mentioned hitherto.

12. puppibus. ' By the stern.'

XXV. *Carthaginian attack on Roman ambassadors. Hannibal lands in Africa*

1. Nondum . . . legati. Livy here uses the fuller account of Polybius (XV, i, ii), although he makes two major alterations: (1) he states here that Senate's decision was not known to Scipio when he sent the embassy to Carthage, while Polybius XV, 1, 3–4 says that news had come from Rome (cf. note on xxiv, 5); and (2) he says (§ 5) that the attack on the Roman ship was due either to the Carthaginian Government or to Hasdrubal's private initiative, while Polybius states that the Carthaginians formed the plan: here presumably Livy was using another source beside Polybius, one more favourable to Carthage.

2. ab iis . . . uiolatam esse defines *iniuriam*. **L. Baebium. . . .** Little is known of these men. Baebius may be the same as L. Baebius Dives, praetor in 189. (Livy, XXXVII, xlvii, &c.). The praenomen Lucius is not found elsewhere among the patrician Fabii.

4. triremes. Warships might be quinqueremes, quadriremes, triremes, or biremes, words which are often translated ' with five, four, &c. banks of oars '. There is considerable doubt about the construction of ancient ships, but it is generally held that the trireme did not have three rows of oars, one above the other, but rather three oars to each rowlock port, the oars being thus grouped in threes, not superimposed. The quinquereme did not have five superimposed banks of oars, but probably teams of five men working a single large oar. It would contain 300–400 oarsmen, and was armed with a *rostrum* or trident-shaped beak for purposes of ramming.

Bagradam (modern Medjerdah), the chief river in Carthaginian territory, flowed into the Gulf of Tunis between Carthage and Castra

Cornelia. Near its mouth the modern river has slightly changed its course westwards, and now runs between Utica and Castra Cornelia. The modern coastline has advanced farther east than it was in Punic times, owing to the silt of the river, so that Utica is now a few miles from the sea. **ad Vticam,** ' near Utica,' perhaps at Rusucmon. They cannot have been ' at Utica,' which was still occupied by the Romans.

5. **tres quadriremes.** Polybius XVI, ii, 12 says they were triremes, but it is possible that the text is corrupt, and that in τρισὶ τριήρεσι the second τρι is an accidental repetition of the first and that the correct reading should be τετρήρεσι (i.e., quadriremes). **sine publica fraude.** ' Without any treachery on the part of the state.' As has been said (§ 1) Polybius's account is different, and expressly attributes the plot to the war-party in the Carthaginian Government, which had wished to renew the war now that Hannibal had returned.

6. **quinqueremem.** See on § 4. **promunturium,** that on which Castra Cornelia lay.

celeritate . . . subterlabentem. ' Slipping away from them by its speed.' *subter-* probably implies ' inshore ' as well.

10. **in legatis.** ' In respect of the envoys.' **tamen.** Despite the fact that he might have kept the Carthaginian envoys as prisoners by way of retaliation.

11. This anecdote probably derives from Coelius, while Hannibal's bad omen may be contrasted with the story of Scipio's good one (Livy XXIX, xxvii): when the Roman expeditionary force was nearing the African coast in 204 B.C. Scipio enquired the name of the nearest headland, and being told it was Pulchrum, he accepted it as a good omen, his Cape of Good Hope. Hannibal had, in fact, landed before the Carthaginian breach of good faith.

12. **abominatus.** ' After praying that the gods would avert the evil omen'—i.e. of the name.

Leptim. Leptis Minor lay on the bay of Hammamet, between Hadrumetum and Thapsus. From it Hannibal must have marched to Hadrumetum, for it is there that we next find him (xxix, 1). He wisely did not attempt to land at Carthage itself, where provisions were already short, and where he would be cut off from the hinterland by the Romans. Instead he chose a place far from the enemy, where he could receive reinforcements, get supplies, and prepare quietly for his campaign without the hampering control of the Carthaginian Government. The date of Hannibal's return is uncertain, probably late autumn 203 or less probably in the first three months of 202 : see Appendix.

XXVI. *Other events of the year* 203 B.C.

This and the next chapter are derived from annalistic accounts which are mainly trustworthy, although they contain some false interpolations.

1. **eo anno**—i.e., 203 B.C. Probably, however, the violation of the

armistice did not occur till the spring of 202. **M. Servilius.** See note on xxiv, 4. **Ti. Claudius Nero** had been praetor in Sardinia in 204. See also below xxvii, 1–5; xxxviii, 6, 7; xxxix, 1–3; xl, 9; xliv, 3.

2. The First Macedonian War between Rome and Hannibal's ally, Philip V, King of Macedon, had ended in 205 with the Peace of Phoenice. The incidents described in this and the next section are generally believed by most modern historians to be false. They are not recorded by the more reliable ancient historians. It is not possible to identify the Greek cities allied to Rome ; they are probably imaginary. Both Philip's aggression against these supposed allies and the force which he is said to have sent to Hannibal before Zama are inventions of Roman annalists, who wished to show that Rome's hostile attitude to Philip in 201 was justified on account of his earlier alleged misdeeds.

ad res repetendas. Lit. ' to demand restoration of the plundered goods ', but here used in the wider sense ' to demand redress '. **uastatos . . . admissos.** Supply *esse.*

3. **simul.** ' And at the same time.'

traiecta must be taken with *dici*; ' were said to have been sent across '.

4. **foedus.** The Peace of Phoenice. **C. Terentius.** Varro was the consul who had been defeated at Cannae (216). The usual tradition makes him a radical demagogue opposed to the Senate, but another tradition and his continued employment by the Senate show that he enjoyed its confidence. **C. Mamilius** Atellus had been praetor in Sicily in 207. **M. Aurelius** Cotta had not had a very distinguished career: he had been aedile in 216. Such a commission may have been sent to Greece, but the purpose which Livy assigns to it cannot be accepted.

5. **cliuus Publicius.** A street beginning by the Forum Boarium close to the Tiber and running south across the Aventine. **aquarum magnitudine.** Floods of the Tiber. **annonae uilitate.** The primary meaning of *annona*, which is derived from *annus*, is ' yearly produce '. Then it comes to mean ' price of corn ' or (as here) simply ' corn '. **praeterquam quod** = *non solum quod*, while *etiam quod* = *sed etiam quod* : cp. vi. 4, *praeterquam hostili odio etiam ne quis refugeret.* **aperta.** ' Opened up ' for commerce.

6. **M. Valerius Falto** and **M. Fabius Buteo** both held the praetorship in 201. **quaternis aeris.** ' At four *asses* (= 1 sesterce) the *modius* (= 2 gallons),' or a denarius a bushel. Unfortunately we have no references to normal prices at this time; in the second century wheat may have cost about 3 sesterces the modius (3 denarii or 2s. 6d. the bushel).

7. **exactae aetatis.** ' At a great old age.' Descriptive genitive instead of the more usual ablative, *exacta aetate*—' his active life being over '.

8. **cognomine.** Maximus. *Cognomen* is the term for the third name

which follows the family name (e.g., Fabius); such names generally indicate some moral or physical characteristic, when first given; but they frequently were transmitted from generation to generation. A man might have more than one *cognomen*. **inciperet.** 'Even if the name were a new title beginning with him.' As a matter of fact it had become hereditary in his family, having first been held by Quintus Fabius Maximus Rullus, his great-grandfather (five times consul from 322 to 295 B.C.), and his grandfather, Quintus Fabius Maximus Gurges (three times consul in 292, 275, and 265). He himself was called Q. Fabius Maximus Verrucosus Cunctator, and was five times consul. Nothing is known of his father. His great-grandfather, Rullus or Rullianus, had served Rome well during the Samnite Wars, his exploits culminating in victory at Sentinum in 295 B.C. **unus Hannibal.** 'The sole fact that he had Hannibal for his adversary.'

9. **Cautior quam promptior.** The comparative after *quam* where we should expect the positive (*promptus*) is a common, though not invariable idiom. **sicut . . . sic,** 'just as you might doubt . . . so nothing is more certain.' We should say, 'while it may be doubted . . . yet nothing is more certain'.

unum . . . restituisse. The line in Ennius runs *unus homo nobis cunctando restituit rem,* and is quoted by Cicero in the De Officiis, I, 34. Cp. Virgil, Aeneid, VI, 845. *quo fessum rapitis, Fabii? tu Maximus ille es,/unus qui nobis cunctando restituis rem.* Ennius of Rudiae in Calabria (239–169 B.C.) was famous as a writer of tragedy, satire, and above all for his epic the *Annales,* a poetic chronicle from the coming of Aeneas to Italy down to 177 B.C. He was the first poet to write hexameters on a large scale and in artistic form. Fabius was called Cunctator (the Delayer); the name was first applied in an abusive sense by the Romans and Italians, who were impatient with him for allowing Hannibal to ravage Italy virtually unchecked. But when the Battle of Cannae had shown with tragic clearness that a strategy of attrition was the only right policy in Italy (cf. Introduction, p. 14), the title came to be used as a mark of wisdom and honour. Fabius was also called the Shield of Rome.

10. **Augur . . . pontifex.** The two sacred Colleges at Rome each comprised nine members. The pontifices were responsible for the maintenance of many cults and for the development of religious jurisprudence. The augurs by means of divination (*auspicia* or *auguria*), observed and interpreted the signs of the goodwill or displeasure of the gods and reported all faults (*uitia*) which could nullify the effect of certain acts, such as business in the Comitia. **filius.** Livy is probably mistaken, as the Cunctator's son, Q. Fabius Maximus (consul in 213) had died before his father. The Q. Fabius elected augur in 203 was perhaps his son and a grandson of Cunctator; he died young in 196 B.C. **Seruius Sulpicius Galba** (aedile 209, died 199) was probably the brother of P. Sulpicius Galba (consul 211, dictator 203— see note on xxiv, 3).

11. Ludi Romani . . . plebeii. See on ii, 8. The Ludi Romani commenced on 4 September. The Ludi Plebeii were started some time in the third century B.C. and were celebrated on 4 November in the Circus Flaminius. At first they lasted for one day only, but were later prolonged for fourteen days. The religious nature of the Games was never forgotten. If there was the slightest omission or mishap, the proceedings had to be recommenced. Hence the Games were often prolonged by *instauratio*. **C. Liuius Salinator,** son of M. Livius (on whom see note on xxiii, 1), served in the Second Macedonian War, and is probably to be identified with the consul of 188 who reached this office for his services in the war against Antiochus. **C. Aurelius Cotta** reached the consulship in 200.

12. comitia. See note on xxiv, 3. According to the Fasti, Sulpicius was appointed dictator to hold the elections. **quaestiones . . . de coniurationibus.** In 204 one of the consuls had been commissioned by the Senate to hold a judicial investigation in Etruria in order to suppress local disaffection in favour of Mago (XXIX, xxxvi, 10–12). This inquiry was apparently still being prosecuted.

XXVII. *New Commands and Distribution of Forces.* 202 B.C.

The historicity of Ti. Claudius' attempt to supersede Scipio is doubtful: there are legal and factual difficulties in the way of its acceptance—e.g., if the People had in 203 prolonged Scipio's command *donec debellatum foret* (i, 10) further discussion was unnecessary. Some modern historians regard the incident as a garbled version of what really happened later in the year (see xxxviii–xxxix). On the other hand, since it is in fact doubtful whether Scipio's command had been prolonged indefinitely, it is possible that some political attack was made on him in Rome, where his interests were protected by Metellus, and that a solid fact underlies Livy's somewhat confused account.

1. M. Seruilius . . . Claudius, see on xxvi, 1. **rettulerunt,** see on i, 1.

2. Q. Metello, see on xxiii, 3.

3. iusserunt. Supply *bellum gerere*.

4. In fact the Senate had not the right to override a decision of the Sovereign People. But if the force of the pluperfect *decreuerat* is emphasized, it would be possible to argue that this refers to a decision taken before the Tribes were consulted. In which case the disregard of the People's will would be the responsibility of the consuls, rather than of the Senate, which might have turned a blind eye to the consuls' action in order to maintain its prestige with the People.

5. euenit. ' It fell to the lot of.' **ut.** ' With the instructions that.'

6. si. ' In case the Senate should decide.'

7. For the distribution of the commands in 203 see chs. i, ii. In 202 four commands remained unchanged: those in Liguria, Sardinia,

I

Spain, and Africa. The changes, which are recorded in this and the following sections, need not be discussed in detail, since they can easily be followed if once the disposition of the forces in 203 has been clearly grasped.

9. **urbana.** Supply *praetura*, or less probably *sors*. Cf. on 1, 9. **ita uti.** ' According to the provinces they already held.'

10. **sedecim.** Now that Hannibal had left Italy and Mago had been defeated, the number of the legions could be decreased. In 203 there had been twenty; these were now reduced to sixteen (the lowest number since 215) by disbanding the two in Gaul under M. Cornelius Cethegus and the two in Bruttium under Cn. Servilius.

11. **ludos.** See on ii, 8, where Livy implies they were celebrated in 203; perhaps they had been postponed till 202, or else Livy has reported the same event twice. **M. Claudio . . .** 208 B.C.

XXVIII. *Hopes and fears at Rome*

This chapter is designed as an artistic introduction to the last campaign, and Livy in all probability owes nothing here to earlier authorities, although he may have found a similar plan in Coelius (see on § 7).

2. **uatem.** ' The prophet of this great struggle ': an allusion to the speech of Fabius (at the close of Bk. XXVIII, ch. xlii, cp. esp. sections 18–19), in which Fabius criticizes Scipio's proposal to invade Africa. **canere.** ' To foretell.' This use of *cano* derives from the fact that oracles were often delivered in verse.

3. **barbariae.** A collective noun = *barbarorum.*
Statorius. A centurion who had served under the Scipios in Spain. He had been sent on an embassy to Africa to secure the alliance of Syphax. This done, he had remained there to help Syphax to train his army on Roman lines. **fugacissimo duce.** Hasdrubal, son of Gisgo, had fled from Scipio after three defeats, at Ilipa in Spain in 206, at the burning of his camp by night (above, ch. vi), and at Campi Magni (viii), after which he had been deprived of his command and condemned to death. **rem futuram.** The main verb of this long sentence which extends to *complesset.*

5. **senex.** Hannibal was actually only 44 at this date. **fretum.** The Straits of Messina. *fretum*, often used loosely for the ' sea ', is here used in its literal sense; cp. our ' frith '. **aequalem stipendiis suis.** ' Contemporary with his campaigns '—i.e., that had served under him in all his campaigns. *stipendium* (lit. ' pay ') comes to be used to describe each year of campaigning for which a soldier drew pay. **quas . . . passos.** ' Which it can scarce be believed that men should have endured'.

6. **imperatores,** here used for generals invested with imperium other than consuls and praetors—i.e., proconsuls, propraetors, dictators, magistri equitum. Three consuls had fallen in battle: Flaminius at Trasimene (217), Aemilius Paullus at Cannae (216), Marcellus in a

skirmish (208), and two proconsuls, Sempronius Gracchus in Lucania (212) and Cn. Fulvius in Apulia (210). The consul T. Quinctius Crispinus was mortally wounded in battle (208) and died soon after.

muralibus . . . coronis. In the Roman army these were decorations for valour in scaling city-walls or the palisaded ramparts of a camp. The crowns were of gold, the *muralis* representing the battlemented walls of a city, the *uallaris* the palisade of a camp.

captas urbes. After the battle of Cannae many towns revolted to Hannibal: Arpi and many Samnite strongholds, nearly the whole of Lucania and Bruttium, except the Greek cities, and above all Capua, the second city in Italy, and other Campanian towns. The chief town which he had actually captured was Tarentum in 213, and that was due largely to treachery within the city.

7. **fasces.** The bundles of rods, symbols of authority, carried by the lictors before magistrates who were invested with *imperium*. Livy says that the total number of *fasces* carried by lictors in attendance on the magistrates in Rome in one year was less than that which Hannibal had captured from Roman commanders-in-chief on the field of battle. That Livy may have been following Coelius here is suggested by a fragment of the latter: *duos et septuaginta lictoris domum deportauisse fascis qui ductoribus hostium ante soluerint ferri.* Presumably Coelius is thinking of the six consuls and proconsuls mentioned in the note on § 6, as each consul or proconsul had twelve *fasces*. It is scarcely profitable to attempt a mathematical calculation based on Livy's rhetorical statement, since the number of fasces carried by magistrates varied when they were in and outside Rome; the total also varied naturally in accordance with the number of proconsuls and propraetors appointed each year and with the existence or not of a dictator who had twenty-four fasces, while his *magister equitum* had six.

8. **etiam quod.** 'All the more because, having for a number of years been familiar with war waged under their very eyes in one part of Italy after another with faint hope and without any prospect of a speedy end to the struggle, now the minds of all were excited by the fact that Scipio and Hannibal were matched as it were face to face for the supreme conflict.' **lenta.** Their hope is 'sluggish' because it has been so long unfulfilled. **gerere** depends on *assuessent*; 'they had been accustomed to the waging of war'.

9. **quo magis . . . intentiores erant.** 'The more eager they were for the victory that was now so near, the more intense was their anxiety.'

11. **bis acie uictos.** In a cavalry engagement in 204 (Livy XXIX, xxxiv) and at Campi Magni.

XXIX. *The Advance to the Battlefield*

The Site of the Battle. The general military situation has been described in the introduction, p. 20. Zama, the conventional name of the battle, may be retained for convenience, although it certainly was not fought there. Some modern historians call it the Battle of Naraggara or Margaron, but that is to exchange one uncertainty for another. There was more than one town named Zama in North Africa in antiquity: one perhaps at Sidi Abd el Djedidi in the east (some 30 miles north-west of Kairouan), and one or two more at Jama and Seba Biar, some 25 miles to the west (possibly these last two, named Zama Major and Zama Regia, were one and the same place). It was to this western Zama, nearly 90 miles south-west of Carthage, that Hannibal marched (§ 1). Livy here follows Polybius very closely, though not always accurately—e.g., he wrongly states that Hannibal when seeking an interview with Scipio was aware that Masinissa had joined Scipio, but the chief difference is that he names the place where Scipio camped Naraggara (§ 9), (inferior MSS. give Narcara or Naggara), while Polybius calls it Margaron. Various explanations of this discrepancy have been offered. Naraggara is the modern village of Sidi Youssef farther west near the frontier of Tunisia and Algeria; Margaron is unknown. The question is further complicated by the fact that there is no site near Sidi Youssef which presents the features described by Polybius and Livy. Probably the situation was that Scipio was withdrawing south-west to meet Masinissa (at Naraggara?). Meantime Hannibal had marched to the western Zama and reconnoitred from there, seeking an interview with Scipio. Now that Scipio had been joined by Masinissa's cavalry he could move from the defensive to the offensive, and so he encamped on a well-watered hill opposite which was a waterless hill (this was at Margaron, or if it is thought that the text of Polybius is corrupt and should be emended to Naraggara, then the camp must have been some distance east of Naraggara). Then according to Polybius (Livy wrongly says it was before Scipio camped at Naraggara, §§ 8–9) Scipio said he was ready for an interview, and thus skilfully forced Hannibal to advance from Zama and camp on the ill-watered hill. The most probable site for these hills and the battle is the plain of Draa el Metnan about half-way between Naraggara and Zama (Seba Biar) some 8 miles from Sicca Veneria (El Kef).

1. **Hadrumetum** (modern Sousse). If Livy is correct in saying Hannibal landed at Leptis (see note on xxvi, 12), then his army had to recover from the fatigue of a march thence to Hadrumetum as well as of the sea voyage. **ex.** 'after'. **paucis diebus.** Hannibal may have rested his men for a few days, but there was a much longer interval than this between his arrival in Africa (probably late 203) and his march to Zama. See Appendix.

Zamam. For this and other topographical points in this chapter see the above note on the Site of the Battle.

2. The anecdote about the spies, which derives from Polybius, is rejected by some modern historians, because of a suspicious likeness to a story told by Herodotus (vii, 146) about a similar act of Xerxes. The incident may, however, be true; if so, it was less an act of magnanimity

on Scipio's part than a deliberate attempt to weaken the enemy's morale. And it is even possible that Scipio had read Herodotus.

3. satin = *satisne*. **per commodum** = *commode*. ' At their ease.'

4. nam et . . . As was said above, Livy is wrong, since Polybius (XV, v) says the spies were dismissed before Masinissa's arrival.

de nilo. ' Without good reason.'

5. turbauerat. It was Hannibal's arrival that had encouraged the war-party in Carthage to break the truce.

integer. ' With his strength still intact.'

6. neutrum . . . habeo. ' I have no ground for asserting either.' This is not strictly grammatical, though the sense is clear enough. The substitution of (e.g.) *nihil comperti* for neutrum would however give a perfectly normal construction.

7. Valerius Antias. See Introduction, p. 26. This alleged engagement is probably fictitious. The reference to Antias, however, shows that Livy was here adding a little from other sources than Polybius, who is his main authority in this part of the book.

9. cum . . . opportuno . . . consedit. = *loco consedit cum ad cetera opportuno tum quod*, &c.

10. a quattuor milibus. ' At a distance of four miles.'

XXX. *The Speech of Hannibal*

1. armatis—i.e., their escorts. **cum singulis.** ' Each with one.' **interpretibus.** Interpreters were, in fact, scarcely necessary, as both generals knew Greek, and Hannibal also probably spoke Latin. **congressi sunt.** This meeting, which is recorded by Polybius also, is rejected by some modern scholars on the basis of the supposed resemblance of a phrase of Polybius with one preserved in a fragment of the poet Ennius. This alleged objection may, however, be dismissed. It is unlikely that Polybius, with his intimate knowledge of the Scipionic house, would have recorded the incident if it were untrue : he was more than a Greek historiographer aiming at the dramatic. Scipio would not refuse to listen to terms, especially as by doing so he forced Hannibal to fight on ground he himself had chosen. Hannibal, faced by Scipio's army, which had been unexpectedly reinforced by Masinissa's cavalry, might well seek to avoid a battle by one last attempt at peace.

3. Tum Hannibal. Both Hannibal's speech and Scipio's reply are based upon the much shorter corresponding speeches in Polybius (XV, 6–8). Possibly Polybius may have heard something of the substance of the interview, but in the main both speeches must be regarded as an imaginary reconstruction of the arguments likely to be used on such an occasion. The arguments in themselves are natural, forcible, and moving. The eloquence with which they are expressed is Livy's own. Indeed, it is doubtful whether he ever rises to a greater height of oratory than here, although his history is full of noble rhetoric.

datum erat. The force of the pluperfect may be best expressed by translating ' if it was ordained by fate from the beginning '.

qui primus intuli. ' Who began the war.' The words have been taken to mean ' who was the first to attack the Roman people ', i.e., to wage a war of pure aggression. But it would be absurd to put such words in the mouth of Hannibal. The invasion of the Gauls and again of Pyrrhus make it so palpably untrue. **potissimum.** An adverb: ' above all others '.

4. **fuerit.** Fut. perfect. ' Will be found to have been,' i.e., in the judgement of after generations.

5. **hoc quoque . . . fortuna.** ' Moreover fortune will be found to have brought about this strange coincidence ' (lit. freak of chance).

cum . . . contulerim. ' Whereas I took up arms in your father's consulship and he was the first of Roman generals with whom I was engaged.' The first *cum* is the conjunction, the second the preposition. Scipio's father was Publius Cornelius Scipio, whom Hannibal defeated at the battles of Ticinus and Trebia in 218 B.C.

6. **fuerat.** Latin usually says ' it *was* better for such a thing to have been done ' even though it was not done, whereas we say ' it *would have been* better.' Hence the indicative *fuerat*, where English idiom might lead one to expect *fuisset*.

8. **appetiimus.** ' We have *both* sought to appropriate other men's possessions with the result that, &c.'

9. **quod.** ' A thing which.' **abominaremur.** The literal meaning of the imperfect is ' we should have been abhorring '; but English idiom forces us to translate ' we should have abhorred '. *Abominor* is here used in its metaphorical sense. For the primary sense cp. xxv. 12. **et qui quodcumque egerimus, ratum ciuitates nostrae habiturae sint.** The sense is clear, but the construction is incorrect. The logical construction would have been: *et quorum ciuitates, quodcunque egerimus, ratum habiturae sint.*

11. **ferociora utraque.** ' Both of them things more impetuous than quiet counsels need,' i.e., both are likely to breed intolerance of peaceful counsels. **non temere.** ' Not without good reason does he reflect on the uncertainties of fortune.'

12. **uixdum aetate.** A pardonable exaggeration. Scipio was twenty-five when he accepted the command in Spain (210 B.C.) and had seen his first fighting at the Ticinus in 218 B.C.

13. On the exploits of P. and Cn. Scipio in Spain, see Introduction, p. 14. **quattuor.** Presumably armies under Hasdrubal Barca at Baecula (208), Hanno in Celtiberia (207), and Hasdrubal Gisgo and Mago at Ilipa (206).

14. **animi.** depends on *parum.* **sextum decimum annum.** Acc. of duration after *haerentem.* ' While I still kept my grip on Italy for the sixteenth year.'

15. **Noui . . . utiles.** ' I know that pride which is great rather than useful.' (Cp. *Macbeth,* I. vii. 27: ' Vaulting ambition that o'erleaps itself ').

16. **Vt.** 'Although.' **satis ego . . . fortunae.** 'I am sufficient proof of the fickleness of fortune.' **documenti** depends on *satis*.

17. **castris . . . positis.** In 211 B.C. Hannibal made a daring feint on Rome in the hope that he might draw off the Roman armies that were besieging Capua. He came within three miles of the city, but did not venture to attack. He camped between Rome and the Anio, a tributary of the Tiber. **fratribus.** Hasdrubal, killed at Metaurus (207), and Mago, on whom see above xix.

18. **tibi . . . pax.** 'Peace, if you grant it, will bring you honour and renown.'

19. **haec** = *pax.* **in . . . discrimen.** 'To the hazard of a single hour.'

20. **Martem.** We should say 'fortune.' **communem.** I.e., that may favour either side. **respondent.** 'Answer your expectations.'

21. **adieceris . . . ademeris.** Conditional subjunctives. 'By victory in battle you would not add as much to the glory that you can win by peace as you would take from it, if you should fail.' **parta . . . sperata . . . decora.** Lit. 'Both the renown which you have already won and that for which you hope,' i.e., both the realities and the hopes of fame.

22. **potestatis.** A possessive genitive, 'In your power.' **tunc.** If you persist in war.

23. **M. Atilius.** A sinister and dramatic parallel. M. Atilius Regulus invaded Africa in 256 B.C. and after a victorious campaign occupied Tunis. Carthage sued for peace; the terms offered by Regulus were so hard that Carthage resolved to fight on. Not long after, with the aid of Greek mercenaries and a Greek general named Xanthippus, Carthage utterly defeated the Romans and took Regulus prisoner. He was in the end, according to the story generally believed at Rome, put to death by torture. Cp. Introduction, p. 10.

24. **est . . . eius.** 'It belongs to him'; i.e., 'It is for him'. **simus.** Subjunctive depending on *forsitan*.

25. The terms offered could scarcely have been accepted, as they were worse than those offered before the Punic violation of the truce; these had included the surrender of the Carthaginian fleet and prisoners, and the payment of an indemnity.

26. **externa etiam.** 'Foreign lands outside Italy as well as those which you possess in Italy.'

27. **non nimis sincere petitam.** See especially xvi, 14–15. **expectatam.** A reference to the breaking of the truce in xxiii. **Punicam fidem.** The general charge of treachery which the Romans customarily brought against the Carthaginians is scarcely justified, although on this occasion the Carthaginians had broken their pledge. **multum . . . pertinet.** 'The security (or 'the loyal observance') of peace depends largely on who they are that seek it': i.e., on the character of those by whom it is sought.

28. **quoque**, i.e., it is not only I that take this view. Your senate also took it when they refused to grant peace a short time ago. Cp. xxii. 6.

XXXI. *The Reply of Scipio*

1. **imperator Romanus . . . respondit.** The speech which Livy has placed in the mouth of Hannibal is long and persuasive, and is perhaps the finest example of that ' eloquence past all description ' with which Quintilian credits him (*Inst. Or.*, X. i. 101). The style of Scipio's reply is in sharp and dramatic contrast; its eloquence is of a sterner sort, terse, dignified, and severe, avoiding rhetorical ornament. **non me fallebat.** ' It did not escape my notice that.' **praesentem . . . fidem.** ' The existing truce to which you were pledged.'

2. **id**, i.e. the fact that the Carthaginians were gambling on the hope of his return: Scipio refers to sections 27–28 of Hannibal's speech. **qui . . . subtrahas.** The subjunctive is causal. ' Since you exclude from the former terms of peace everything save that which we have long since had in our power.' Scipio refers to the terms mentioned in xvi, 11–12.

3. **onere.** The burden of the terms excluded. **habeant.** ' May win.'

4. **indigni.** ' Though you are unworthy to receive the terms we then offered ': lit. ' unworthy to whom the same terms should be open.' **Sicilia.** It is true that the Romans had not fought the First Punic War to win Sicily, nor the Second for Spain. On the motives of Rome's policy and on the Mamertines and Saguntum see Introduction, § 2.

5. **secundum.** Preposition governing *ius fasque*. ' According to justice and the right.'

7. **ipsum.** ' Of your own accord.'

8. The language of this section is derived from the law-courts. In an action for possession of property the plaintiff summoned the defendant to join hands (*manum conserere*). *tergiuersor* is especially used of shiftiness in the law courts. Scipio has dragged Hannibal to Africa as a man might drag a ' reluctant and shifty ' defendant into court in an action for the possession of some property that is in dispute. The metaphor is ingenious and suggestive. For *manu prope conserta* can also be translated ' on the very verge of battle.'

uerecundia. ' Respect ': Tr. ' You have no claims on my consideration.'

9. **ad ea in quae pax conuentura uidebatur.** ' To those terms on which peace seemed likely to be agreed.' **quae sit** = *quod sit*. The relative is attracted into the gender of the predicate *multa* (' fine,' ' indemnity '). **nauium.** ' For the ships which were attacked &c.' **est quod . . . referam.** ' There is something that I can place before my council.'

XXXII. *Prelude to the Battle of Zama*

1. **arma expedirent.** Subjunctive of command in Or. Obl. **uictores** = *uictores futuri, si felicitas adesset.*

2. **iura gentibus daret.** 'Should rule the world.' Strictly speaking, as Polybius (XV, ix, 2) in the parallel passage points out, the immediate issue involved was the possibility of world dominion for Rome, and of preserving their African Empire for the Carthaginians. But he also envisaged the possibility that Carthage might ultimately achieve world dominion if she won the battle, for he says (§ 5), 'the conquerors would not be masters of Africa and Europe alone, but of all those parts of the world which now hold a place in history'.

par periculum. 'The danger to the defeated will be as great as the reward of the victors.'

3. **supremo auxilio effuso.** 'If her last resource was spent in vain.'

4. **cumulaturi.** 'Destined to crown.'

5. **anceps.** 'Wavering hopes and fears.' **contemplantibus . . . obuersabantur.** 'As they contemplated . . . joyful and sad reflections presented themselves to their minds.'

6. **decora.** 'Famous deeds.' **insignem . . . memoria.** 'Famous in the record of some battle.'

7. **Hispanias.** In 197 B.C. conquered Spain (Hispania) was divided into two provinces, Citerior and Ulterior; hence the frequent use of the plural *Hispaniae*, which strictly is anachronistic when applied to the year 202.

confessionem. 'Confession of weakness'. **quod . . . potuissent.** 'Since they had been able.' The verb is in the subjunctive, merely because it is in indirect speech.

8. **ad hoc.** 'In addition.' **liberum fingenti.** The colloquy had been secret, and therefore gave free scope to his invention. **qua uolt flectit.** 'Turned to suit his purpose.'

9. **ominatur.** 'He presaged.' **auspiciis.** Here in its primary sense of 'omens'. **Aegates insulas.** Islands a few miles off the west coast of Sicily, which gave their name to the sea battle which gave Rome the final victory in the First Punic War (241 B.C.). According to Zonaras, 8, 17, before the naval battle 'a meteor had appeared above the Romans, and after rising high to the left of the Carthaginians plunged into their ranks'. This reference to an omen suggests that Livy may have used Coelius as well as Polybius for this chapter, as it is likely that Coelius would have embroidered his account of the final battle of the Hannibalic war with some prodigies.

11. **celsus corpore.** We should say 'with head held high'. This reference to Scipio's inspired appearance probably derives from the popular tradition and does not come from Polybius or from Livy's own invention.

XXXIII. *The Battle Formations and the Elephant Charge*

For the battle of Zama Livy follows closely the account of Polybius, although he misunderstands and mistranslates here and there. That he did incorporate some references from other (annalistic) sources is seen from his reference to the quaestorship of Laelius (§ 2) and to the Macedonian legion (§ 5). Where Livy diverges from Polybius, the latter's account may unhesitatingly be accepted as the more authoritative. For a diagram of the battle see sketch opposite p. 33.

1. **primos hastatos.** This was the normal arrangement. See Introduction, § 4. **cohortes.** This is an anachronism. The cohort did not become the tactical unit till nearly a hundred years later; at this time the maniple (120 men) was the tactical unit. Livy's description of Scipio's arrangement is far from clear, but we can see from Polybius what he means. Instead of drawing up the maniples of the three lines in *quincunx* formation (Introduction p. 23), Scipio placed the maniples of the *principes* directly behind those of the *hastati*, instead of behind the intervals in the first line :—

Hastati	□	□	□	□			□	□	□	□
principes	□	□	□	□	instead of	□	□	□	□
triarii	□	□	□	□		□	□	□	□

The purpose of this was to counter the charge of Hannibal's elephants: clear lanes were to be left in the Roman lines, down which it was hoped to drive the beasts, who would thus be forced to the rear of the Roman army without damaging the Roman formation.

2. **quaestoris extra sortem.** 'Quaestor extraordinary,' i.e., specially designated for this service by the Senate, not selected by lot like the other quaestors. Presumably Laelius had received this appointment as a reward for his defeat of Syphax when he was reporting this in Rome.

3. **antesignanorum.** The *hastati* were sometimes called *antesignani*, the men stationed in front of the standards, in opposition to the *principes* and *triarii* taken together. **uelitibus.** The *uelites*, light-armed troops, were abolished in the time of Marius, about a hundred years later, and the name seems to have become obsolete in Livy's time: hence the explanation. But it is curious that Livy should give it, since he has mentioned the *uelites* frequently before, without thinking any explanation necessary. **directos.** 'Drawn up in line,' i.e., to the rear of the whole army. When the elephants charged, the *uelites* were to run before the beasts through the lanes to the back of the whole army, or else to turn right and left between the maniples of the *hastati* and *principes*, leaving the lanes clear for the elephants and incidentally preventing them running between the lines of the *hastati* and *principes*. **uiam . . . darent.** 'Might make a path through which the beasts might rush upon weapons cast from either side,' i.e., and expose themselves to volleys of weapons hurled from either side.

5. **Macedonum legionem.** These troops may be dismissed as an invention. See on xxvi, 2.

6. **modico . . . relicto.** A greater interval was left between the second and third lines than between the first and second. This was a vital element in Hannibal's plan: see below. **Italicorum.** Here Livy has blundered badly. In fact Hannibal's third line consisted of his best troops, the veteran Old Guard which he had brought back from Italy. Livy has mistranslated Polybius' phrase τοὺς ἐξ Ἰταλίας ἥκοντας μεθ' αὐτοῦ (XV. xi. 2), ('the troops which he had brought over from Italy ') as ' aciem Italicorum militum ', presumably because he found some reference to the Bruttian troops in his annalistic sources. With this is connected the ridiculous explanation that Hannibal placed them there because he did not trust them (xxxv, 9). Each of Hannibal's three lines numbered some 12,000 men, while he had perhaps 4,000 cavalry. Both the Romans and Carthaginians had between 35,000 and 40,000 men, the Carthaginians being slightly stronger in total although weaker in cavalry.

The Tactics. Polybius' account is much clearer than Livy's, but unfortunately it contains some difficulties and does not definitely state the tactical aims of either side. These may, however, be reconstructed with considerable probability on the following lines. Scipio hoped that his superior cavalry would quickly expose the enemy's wings, and then he could apply the outflanking movement which he had used with increasing skill and success at Baecula, Ilipa, and Campi Magni. Hannibal, realizing his weakness in cavalry, probably ordered it to simulate flight, and so draw the Roman cavalry off the field. He would then throw his elephants and all his infantry in successive waves against Scipio's numerically inferior infantry, while he would thwart an out-flanking movement by holding back his third line of veterans as a reserve: that is, if Scipio did encircle the enemy, he would find that he was only outflanking the two first lines of mercenaries and Cartha-ginians, while the third line would be left intact to fall on the attackers.

8. **tot homines.** The fact that Hannibal's army was such a motley host may have contributed to the formation of his plan to keep his lines separate, like waves which were to break one after the other on the enemy, the last being the strongest; it was not to be a con-tinuous swell, one line directly supporting the next. Thus it was not necessary to try to blend the varied elements in his army into one homogeneous whole.

quibus—' of such a kind that '. But in translation the subjunctive may be ignored, and we may say ' who had nothing in common, neither language, &c.'

esset. Consecutive subjunctive; we sould expect the plural, but as often the verb follows the number of the last of a quantity of subjects.

9. **praesens . . . ostentabatur.** ' Before the eyes of the auxiliaries was held the prospect of receiving their pay on the spot and multiplied many fold from the proceeds of the booty.'

Galli. The Gauls were the age-long enemies of Rome, which they had sacked in 387 B.C. A fresh Gallic invasion of Italy had been beaten back at the battle of Telamon in 225. Some Gauls had joined Hannibal in his campaign in Italy, while they renewed their attacks in North Italy in 200, after which they were finally repulsed. **Liguribus.** The Ligurians, who lived in the hard mountains above the Gulf of Genoa, would naturally covet the fertile plains of Italy where life was easier. **in spem uictoriae.** ' To fire them with hopes of victory.'

10. **Mauros.** The Moors who lived west of Numidia had not been under Masinissa's domination: in fact their king had helped Masinissa in his attempt to win back his kingdom. But they might fear for their independence if Masinissa became the most powerful king in North Africa, ruling with the support of Rome.

impotenti futuro dominatu. ' With prospect of Masinissa's tyranny.' **impotens** has two meanings: (1) ' powerless '; (2) ' having no self-control '. Here therefore it means ' uncontrollable,' ' savage '.

11. **Carthaginiensibus . . . ostentatur.** This sentence requires paraphrase. ' The Carthaginians were bidden to remember their native town . . . and their trembling wives, and were told that the choice lay between destruction and slavery on the one hand and the empire of the world on the other; between these extremes they had nothing either to hope or fear '. **nihil . . . medium.** Lit. ' nothing between either for fear or hope '.

12. **Cum maxime.** ' At the very moment when.' **inter immixtos alienigenis.** Lit. ' Among men intermingled with foreigners '. Tr. ' Interpreters being often employed owing to the admixture of foreigners'.

13. **elephanti.** A war-elephant carried on its back a driver and sometimes a tower or howdah containing four archers. On Hannibal's elephants, which were mainly African not Indian beasts, see H. H. Scullard, *Numismatic Chronicle*, 1948, pp. 158 ff. and 1950, pp. 271 ff. The elephants need not have greatly damaged their own ranks, since their drivers had the means of killing them if they got out of hand. Thus the first move in the battle was to Scipio's advantage. The elephant-charge miscarried, thanks partly to the lanes which he had left in his lines, while the Roman cavalry was pursuing the Carthaginian off the field, hoping to convert what was perhaps a deliberate flight into a decisive Roman victory: for it is more than likely that the Carthaginian horse had been commanded to retire in order to entice away the superior Roman cavalry.

14. **cum multis suis uulneribus.** ' Though they received many wounds in so doing.'

15. **ancipites ad ictum.** ' Exposed to their blows from both sides.'

XXXIV. *The Battle*

1. **nec . . . iam par.** ' No longer equal to the Romans.' **viribus.** If Livy means to imply that the Carthaginians were now outnumbered, he is probably wrong.

dictu parua . . . momenta. These words are the predicate to
clamor, uoces, pugna, &c. *erant* must be supplied. *momenta.* ' In-
fluences,' ' factors '. The sentence requires breaking up in translation.
' There were factors, seemingly trivial, which proved of great importance in the actual conflict. The war-cry of the Romans was in
unison and therefore the louder and the more terrible.' **discrepantibus linguis.** Ablative absolute. *ut* may be omitted in translation.

2. **pugna Romana . . . incumbentium.** 'The Roman attack was
given solidity by the weight of themselves and their weapons as they
pressed, &c.' The ablatives are ablatives of cause. *incumbentium* is a
genitive without any visible means of support; but *Romana* is the
equivalent of *Romanorum.* Cp. phrases such as *mea ipsius culpa.* **illinc.**
On the side of the Carthaginians.

3. **primo impetu.** The front lines on each side (i.e., *hastati* and
mercenaries) now engaged. Polybius says that at first the mercenaries
prevailed through their courage and skill, but gradually the Romans
advanced. In Livy the Romans sweep all before them.
ala. ' Shoulder.' A normal, but not very frequent use; the word
more often refers to the ' arm-pit '. **gradu inlato.** ' Advancing, as
they pushed them back ' (*in summotos*).

4. **et.** ' Also. '

5. **secunda acies.** The second line did not retreat, according to
Polybius. **ut contra etiam.** ' That, on the contrary, they even fell
back.' **resistentes . . . caedendo.** ' By cutting down such of the
first line as offered obstinate resistance.'

6. **refugere . . . caedere.** Historic infinitives. **non recipientes.**
' Those who refused to admit them.' **ut . . . non adiuti.** ' On the
ground that they had not been helped.'

8. **circa.** Adverb. **integram aciem.** Here Livy has parted
company with Polybius, who, after describing how the mercenaries
retreated and turned against the second line of Carthaginians, says that
this second line had to fight both the mercenaries and the Romans.
By their bravery they threw the *hastati* into confusion. Perhaps by this
time Scipio had seen Hannibal's third line of veterans stationed as a
reserve far behind the second line and had been forced to abandon
his plan of trying to outflank the enemy. At any rate the *principes* had
to support the *hastati* in the normal way till the Carthaginians were
driven back and a large number of them and of the till-then-surviving
mercenaries were killed. Scipio took the opportunity to break off the
battle (and here we may turn back to Livy: §§ 9–11), and both sides
re-formed. Scipio lengthened his front by bringing up the *principes*
and *triarii* on the flanks of the *hastati*, Hannibal probably (though
neither Livy nor Polybius makes this clear) by placing the surviving
Carthaginians and mercenaries on the flanks of his veterans. Hannibal
would need longer to prepare, while Scipio would give him as long as
he needed, hoping to delay until his cavalry might return from its

pursuit of the enemy's horsemen. Thus neither general had been able to use his favourite outflanking tactics : Hannibal because he was inferior in cavalry, Scipio because his attempt had been thwarted by Hannibal's use of a reserve. Thus it only remained for the two lengthened lines to join battle again and fight to a finish.

9. **difficilior,** i.e., for the Romans.

10. **tabem sanguinis.** 'Pools of blood.' *tabes* strictly means 'corruption '.

cernendo. The ablative of the gerund here is used practically as though it were an indeclinable present participle; cp. note on xiii. 2.

11. **receptui . . . canere.** 'The retreat to be sounded.' Dative of purpose. For *canere* cp. xxviii. 8. *gerere.* **hastatis.** Dative after *canere.* ' For the *hastati.*'

12. **ueros hostes.** Livy apparently is thinking of the Carthaginians themselves : actually the Romans were now fighting the surviving Carthaginians and the *ueros hostes,* i.e., the third line of veterans.

13. **secundam.** Really the third : see preceding note.

XXXV. *Victory*

1. **In tempore.** The return of the Roman cavalry was probably decisive, for until it came the issue was doubtful (Polybius, XV, xiv, 6 says, ' The contest was for long doubtful *until* Masinissa and Laelius— '). Livy more patriotically overlooks the extreme uncertainty of the final phase.

3. **supra uiginti milia.** These figures (with the exception of those of the military standards and elephants) are given by Polybius. Appian (*Lib.* 48), however, gives 25,000 killed and 8,500 prisoners for Carthage ; the Roman loss was 2,500 and that of Masinissa still more.

5. **singulari arte . . . instruxisse.** This clause explains *laudem.* ' For having drawn up his line.' *eum* must be supplied as a subject.

6. **elephantos.** This acc. together with those that follow down to *Italicos* (9) are in apposition to *aciem.*

7. **teneret.** The subjunctive is used because sections 6–9 represent what those who praised Hannibal said.

8. **simul.** ' And that at the same time.' *ut* must be supplied.

excipientes. Livy speaks as if Hannibal's dispositions had been defensive rather than offensive.

9. **Italicos.** In general, Livy followed Polybius in this chapter, but here he again introduces his own completely false conception of Hannibal's third line, which consisted of veterans, not Italians of doubtful loyalty. **incertos.** ' Of whom he could not say whether they were friends or foes.'

10. **sexto ac tricesimo.** Hannibal, aged nine, had left Carthage for Spain with his father Hamilcar in 237 **B.C.**

curia. i.e., of Carthage.

XXXVI. *Carthage sues for Peace*

1. **a.** ' After.' **ad mare.** i.e., to Castra Cornelia. At this point there is a break in the MSS. of Polybius, but doubtless Livy follows his account closely.

2. **quinquaginta rostris.** Livy makes a slip here. Lentulus had commanded only 20 the previous year (xxiv, 5) and we do not hear that he was given more ships when his command was prolonged (xxvii, 9). Livy's figure 50 probably represents the original 20 with the 30 of Octavius. Thus Scipio with his original fleet of 40 now had 90 warships, a considerable force with which he intended to make a demonstration against Carthage.

3. **admouendum.** 'To strike terror into.' **Cn. Octauium.** See xxiv, 6–9.

4. **uelata infulis ramisque oleae.** Boughs of olive with strips or fillets of wool wound round them were emblems of supplication. They were known as *uelamenta* (cp. next section). Here therefore *uelata*, though it may be translated ' hung with ', is really a technical term.

7. The story of the defeat of Vermina is not above suspicion : the enormous number of casualties, the lack of any reference to the site of the battle or to Masinissa, who would naturally be involved, and the fact that some other references to Vermina are of insecure foundation, tend to make the episode doubtful. There probably is a basis of fact behind the account, but details must be accepted with caution.

8. **Saturnalibus primis.** i.e., on the first day of the feast of the Saturnalia, or 17 December. Many editors consider these words corrupt, but no satisfactory emendation has been made. The use of this phrase shows that Livy was certainly not following Polybius, but a Roman annalist (? Valerius Antias).

9. **eodem . . . loco.** Cf. ix, 10 ; xvi, 1. **ab.** ' As a result of.'

10. **longi temporis.** Descriptive genitive.

11. **uenturi . . . famam.** ' Who was on the point of coming to appropriate the glory of ending the war for which another's toil and peril had paved the way.' On the alleged attempt of Ti. Claudius to succeed Scipio, see note on xxvii. Scipio did not refuse to undertake the siege of Carthage from fear of being superseded in his command and losing the glory of terminating the war, as Livy suggests. This charge has been rebutted even by Mommsen, not Scipio's most friendly critic. On military grounds Scipio might have faced the siege of an exhausted town, which was cut off by land and sea, with some prospect of success. But to destroy it would alienate the other African Powers to whom Scipio had appeared as a saviour, not an oppressor. Further, Italy desperately needed peace and rest and time for recovery ; fresh efforts could have been made, but Scipio would wish to avoid imposing a further burden, especially if he could get his terms accepted by

negotiation. He aimed at disarming but not destroying Carthage. Hannibal, too, was ready for peace. Though Carthage still had the strength of her walls and position and Hannibal's own military genius to direct her, she was nevertheless utterly exhausted in men, food, equipment, and money. Spain was lost, the hinterland of Africa cut off, and control of the sea had passed to Rome. Resistance might mean death, so peace was sought.

XXXVII. *The Terms of Peace*

1. This chapter mainly follows Polybius. **esse.** ' Really existed.'

4. **bellum . . . gererent.** Polybius (XV, xviii, 4) says the Carthaginians were not to make war (πόλεμον ἐπιφέρειν) on anyone outside Africa, and on none in Africa without consulting Rome: i.e., defensive wars in Africa were not forbidden, but Livy's version (*bellum gererent*) implies that they were. There are traces of another tradition (Livy, XLII, xxiii, 3 and Appian, *Lib.* 54), according to which Carthage was forbidden to fight any of Rome's allies. After the war Masinissa, Rome's ally, did in fact expand his kingdom at the expense of Carthaginian territory, and Carthage could get no redress from Rome when she complained and dared not attack an ally of Rome. If therefore the second version of this clause is more reliable than that given by Polybius, the treaty was much harsher than Polybius implied. In either case it was this clause which was the main burden added to the terms which Rome was willing to accept before Zama. Cf. xvi, 10-12.

res. i.e., all that had been taken from him. Polybius says, ' All which had belonged to him or his ancestors.' **foedus.** Livy adds this point which is incorrect: it would be contrary to Rome's procedure to allow her allies or protectorates to have separate treaties among themselves.

5. **decem milia.** This indemnity was double that proposed before Zama. The annual payment was perhaps less a concession to Carthage (she recovered so quickly that she offered to pay off the whole outstanding indemnity in 191 B.C.) than an attempt to keep her dependent on Rome for the fifty years.

7. **Gisgo.** Nothing is known of this man. Polybius does not even mention his name, but merely refers to ' one of the senators '.

eadem et. ' As well as.'

8. **superiore loco.** The platform from which he was addressing them. **species.** ' Manifestation.'

9. **nouem annorum.** ' When I was nine years old.' A descriptive genitive unsupported, such as Livy sometimes uses, leaving the reader to supply the missing word (e.g., *puer*).

fortuna priuata. While he was accompanying his father, Hamilcar Barca, in Spain as a boy, and later when as a young man he was serving under his brother-in-law Hasdrubal. **publica.** When he was himself commander-in-chief, i.e., from 221 B.C.

10. **quam nec iniqua et necessaria esset.** 'How far from being unfair and how necessary it was.'

11. **omnium.** 'Of all the terms imposed.' **qui arguerentur.** 'Since whoever was accused opposed the conclusion of peace.' The subjunctive is one of indefinite frequency; cp. note on iv, 1. *quos mitteret.* The accusation was that they had taken and held both prisoners and stores from the captured ships.

12. **utique.** 'At all costs.' **aestimanda . . . permitti.** 'That it should be left to Scipio to assess the value of whatever was not forthcoming.'

13. **Sunt qui.** Our text of Polybius breaks off here, and for the rest of this book Livy used annalistic sources, although he added a few details from Polybius' account, and even mentions him by name (xlv, 5). The story of Hannibal's flight to Antiochus, King of Syria, belongs to the year 195 B.C. When he was denounced by his political opponents at Carthage on the ground that he was plotting against Rome, the Romans demanded his surrender, and he fled to Antiochus. There is no reliable evidence that his surrender was demanded in 201 B.C.

XXXVIII. *The Armistice and Events in Italy*

1. **quae publica . . . iussi.** 'The quaestors were ordered to make an inventory from the public account showing what was public property, while the owners were ordered to declare what was private.' Quaestors were attached to every Roman army, and were responsible for the military chest, as the urban quaestors were for the Treasury in Rome (Aerarium); they also had to see to the collection and listing of booty, the selling of captives, &c.

2. **uiginti quinque.** This sum, which is equivalent to about 312 talents, seems excessive, since it has been estimated that the support of all Scipio's troops for six months would not cost more than 100 talents.

3. **quicunque . . . eos.** The relative clause is, as often, placed before the clause on which it depends; *eos* is grammatically the antecedent of *quicunque.*

4. **L. Veturius Philo,** praetor 209, had carried the news of the victory at Metaurus to Rome in 207 and had been consul in 206. **M. Marcius** as propraetor in 203 had guarded the coasts of Italy (ii, 5). **L. Scipio** had served with his brother in Spain, had commanded the right wing of the expeditionary force to Africa and later was to defeat King Antiochus at the battle of Magnesia (189), for which he was surnamed Asiaticus.

5. **pro uectura.** 'In lieu of freight-money'. The release of stores of corn caused a sharp drop in its price. Livy twice (xxvi, 6; XXXI, iv, 6) quotes the price of one denarius per bushel; finally the aediles disposed of the African stock at half this price (XXXI, l).

6. **rebellionis.** 'Renewal of hostilities'—a sense which it always bears. The allusion is to the breach of the truce described in ch. xxiv.

K

Tib. Claudius. The earlier story of Claudius' attempt to super-sede Scipio (xxvii) is somewhat doubtful, but he may well have been ordered to raise a fleet to support Scipio when news came of the breaking of the truce.

7. quod patres. . . . This vote of confidence in Scipio on the part of the Senate has not been mentioned before. The statement lends colour to the view that Claudius was not sent out with powers equal to Scipio's (xxvii, 5), but only to conduct a fleet to Africa. His preparations took some months (as had Scipio's own when he was preparing his African expedition), and he was not ready to start till late in 202. When he did, he never reached Africa. See xxxix, 1-3.

8. orbis minui. Possibly a partial eclipse. **lapideo imbri.** A volcanic phenomenon. Cumae lies on the edge of the volcanic region known as the campi Phlegraei, in which there has been at least one eruption in historic times (Monte Nuovo on the edge of the Lucrine Lake, A.D. 1538), while the Solfatara at Pozzuoli (Forum Vol-cani) still emits sulphur fumes, and is alleged to have erupted in 1198. But the centre of volcanic activity during the quiescence of Vesuvius (whose first known eruption was in A.D. 79) has always been Monte Epomeo, in the island of Ischia, not many miles away. There were special rites (see § 9) for averting this omen. See Warde Fowler, *Religious Experience of the Roman People*, pp. 316–17.

Veliterno. Supply *agro*. Velitrae was a small town on the S. slopes of the Alban hills. **terra consedit.** A subsidence.

9. Ariciae. Aricia is a town below the Alban Hills on the Via Appia. **Frusinone.** Ablative for locative. Cp. ii. 12. **de caelo tacta.** 'Struck by lightning.' *tacta* may be regarded as feminine, agreeing with the last subject (*porta*), or neuter plural representing all the subjects. **in Palatio . . . pluit.** Possibly wind-borne ashes from the eruption suggested in connexion with Cumae. The Alban Hills have been suggested as the cause of such showers at Rome. But there is strong reason to believe that they were never active in historic times. **nouemdiali.** "Lasting nine days."

10. religionem. See on ii. 9. **ludi Apollinares.** Games in honour of Apollo, established in 212 and made annual from 208; they were held in July and celebrated normally in the Circus Maximus. **circo.** The Circus Maximus in the low-lying valley between the Pala-tine and the Aventine Hills.

portam Collinam. The most northerly gate of Rome.

Veneris Erycinae. This temple was not founded till 184 B.C. Livy may have been ignorant of the fact or may merely have mentioned the temple to indicate the spot to his readers. The name *Erycina* is derived from Mt. Eryx, above Drepanum in the north-west of Sicily, on the lofty summit of which stood one of the most famous among the temples of Venus.

12. sedes . . . reddita. 'The restoration of its appropriate place.'

XXXIX. *The Adventures of Claudius and Events in Rome*

1. **Cosanum.** Cosa (now Ansedonia) on the coast of Etruria, much used as a starting-point for Sardinia. **Loretanum.** The exact site is uncertain. It probably lay north of Cosa, perhaps at the mouth of the Umbro.

2. **Populonium.** Still farther north, opposite the isle of Elba (Ilua). **superantem.** ' As he passed.' **Insanos Montes.** On the west coast of Sardinia; so called because of the squalls that swept down from them.

3. **quassatae.** ' Strained.' **Carales** (now Cagliari) in the south of Sardinia.

4. **M. Seruilius,** the other consul, who had obtained Etruria as his province (xxvii, 5).

dictatore. Beside the dictators appointed in times of national emergency, dictators with limited powers were appointed in the absence of the competent magistrate to carry out some special act, as holding elections, or celebrating games (*comitiorum habendorum, ludorum faciendorum*).

C. Seruilio, the consul of 203, cf. also xxvi, 12; xxvii, 6. **P. Aelium.** Cf. i, 9; xvii, 3–7; xxi, 10. He was consul in 201: xl, 5.

5. **tempestates.** During the night before a proposed meeting of the Comitia Centuriata (which elected the higher magistrates), the presiding magistrate took the auspices; if these were unfavourable the meeting was postponed. Further, if unfavourable omens appeared during the proceedings or the voting, the assembly was adjourned. Thunder or lightning could be interpreted as unfavourable signs. **pridie idus Martias.** The civil year began on 15 March. In 153 B.C. it was changed to 1 January. **curulibus magistratibus.** The right to the use of the curule chair (*sella curulis*) belonged to magistrates who had the imperium, i.e., those above quaestors. Strictly speaking there was still a curule magistrate in office, the dictator Servilius.

6. **T. Manlius,** consul in 235 and 224, had refused a third consulship in 210, but was dictator in 208. See on ii, 8; xxvii, 11. **C. Sulpicius** died in 198. **ludi Romani, see** ii, 8.

7. **scribae . . . uiatores.** Inferior paid officials, who were assigned to magistrates and from them received the titles of *scribae quaestorii, scribae aedilicii*, &c.

8. **aediles plebis.** There were two colleges of aediles, plebeian and curule. Although in origin the two offices were very different, at this time members of both colleges had essentially the same powers. **uitio creati.** If unfavourable omens accompanied the election of a magistrate, there existed a legal defect (*uitium*) which made it incumbent on the magistrate to lay down his office. **ludos,** i.e., *plebeios*, see on xxvi, 11. **epulum Ioui.** The Plebeian Games included an epulum Iouis on 13 November. **multaticio.** Fines imposed by magistrates were usually, and those imposed by the People were always, set apart for sacred purposes. **Cerialia.** Games in honour of Ceres, the protectress of the plebeians, held on 19 April. Presumably they were handed over to the dictator because the plebeian aediles had retired.

XL. *The Elections for* 201 B.C

1. **Bellonae.** See on xxi, 12.

2. **suprema** must be taken with *Carthaginiensibus*; 'in the last fight for the Carthaginians '.

4. **ut senatus sibi daretur.** ' That audience of the Senate should be granted them.'

5. **Cn. Cornelius :** quaestor in 212, aedile 205. **P. Aelius,** see xxxix, 4. The career of none of these four praetors was exceptional.

7. **Cn. Lentulus.** The truth of this story of his attempt to supersede Scipio, like that of Ti. Claudius the previous year, cannot be checked. Possibly it is true and a compromise was reached, as is described in § 13. At any rate Scipio's command was prolonged: xli, 1.

8. **negare.** Historic infinitive. **praeterquam . . . etiam ;** see on vi, 4. **quod . . . esset.** The subjunctive is used because it expresses his thought. ' He saw that the contest with Scipio would not only be unjust but would also be unequal '; i.e., would end in the discomfiture of Lentulus.

9. **Q. Minucius Thermus,** consul in 193, fought against the Ligurians. **Manius Acilius Glabrio,** a *nouus homo* who had a distinguished career; as consul in 191 he took a prominent part in the war against Antiochus.

temptatam. See xxvii, 2–3.

11. **ad populum.** ' Before the people.' *ut . . . permitterent.* ' That the tribunes left the matter for the Senate to decide.'

13–15. A series of commands in Oratio Obliqua. **M. Sextio:** see xxvii, 7.

XLI. *The Commands for* 201 B.C.

1. **haberet.** Subjunctive in virtual Oratio Obliqua as forming part of the orders given by the Senate. **duae legiones :** on the commands see xxvii, 7–8.

2. **P. Aelius . . . acciperet.** Oratio Obliqua. **habuisset.** See on *haberet* (1).

4–5. Oratio Obliqua.

4. **aliquot annos.** Since 205 B.C. **uti.** Merely serves to introduce a further command.

6. **esset.** See on *haberet* (1). **ut = *ita ut*.** ' With the proviso that.' **quas uellet naues.** He had not a very large choice, since Villius had twenty ships (xxvii, 8) and Octavius thirty (or fifty with those which Lentulus had had in 203: see on xxxvi, 1).

7–9. Oratio Obliqua to *non esset*.

9. **urbanas legiones.** See on ii, 6. **quattuordecim.** Two less than the previous year. The reduction was made by reducing the two legions in Spain to one (§ 5), by disbanding the three legions in Gaul and Liguria (under M. Sextius Sabinus and Sp. Lucretius) and transferring to Gaul the two legions stationed in Rome in 202, and by raising two new legions to replace the latter. As a result there was one less in North Italy and one less in Spain.

XLII. *Macedonian and Carthaginian Envoys in Rome*

1. **de legatis Philippi.** As has been said (see xxvi, 2), the situation about which this alleged embassy from King Philip of Macedon came to Rome is false. The allies of Rome whom Philip is said to have wronged (§ 2: *de populatione sociorum*) were non-existent. They have been sought in Illyria (cf. Polybius. XVIII, 1, 4), but wrongly. As Rome commenced the Second Macedonian War against Philip the next year (200), Roman annalists found various excuses to justify her interference. **Macedonas.** Greek acc. plural.

2. **quorum . . . Romani.** Break up this sentence in translating. 'Their speech was on various topics. Part was occupied with excuses of the conduct alleged against them by the envoys sent from Rome to the king, complaining that he had ravaged the territory of her allies; part with actual charges against the allies of the Roman people.'

3. **quem . . . pugnasse.** Oratio Obliqua giving a summary of their charges. **dilectu habito.** 'After levying troops among the allies of Rome.'

4. **postulantium** picks up the construction of section 2, the genitive agreeing with *quorum*. 'Part again took the form of demands that &c.

5. **M. Furius** may be the same man as M. Furius Crassipes, praetor in 187.

ad id ipsum. 'For this very purpose,' i.e., to justify the conduct of M. Aurelius. **ui atque iniuria.** Ablative of cause. 'Owing to the violence and injustice to which they were subjected.'

6. **purpuratis.** Magnates at the Macedonian court, entitled to wear crimson.

7. **tulerunt.** 'Received.'

8. Both these charges were false. There is no evidence that Philip had helped his erstwhile ally after the Peace of 205 B.C.

9. **quod . . . habeat.** 'In keeping.' **hostium numero.** 'As being enemies.'

10. **ex re publica.** 'In the interests of the State.'

11. **aetatibus conspectis.** cp. xxii, 6.

12. **Hasdrubal** known as *haedus* (the Kid). Not much is known about this man, who with Hanno was head of the party opposed to the Barcids. Appian (Lib. 34) says that he and Hanno the Great rescued from the Carthaginians the Roman ambassadors who had been sent to Carthage to complain of the breach of the truce (xxv).

13. **transferenti.** 'Since he sought to transfer.'

14. **purgando . . . fatendo.** Ablative of gerund used virtually as an indeclinable present participle. **negantibus.** Dative after **uenia esset,** 'lest if they shamelessly denied acknowledged facts, they might find pardon more difficult to obtain.'

15. **tempore.** 'A favourable opportunity.' **daturos fuisse.** i.e., after Cannae, when according to Livy XXIII, xii–xiii, Hanno had urged Carthage to make peace.

17. **mirandum fuisse.** 'It would be surprising.' The infinitive

fuisse corresponds to *erat* of the *oratio recta*, the indicative being used where a subjunctive might have been expected, as in ch. xxx. 6 (see note). **ex insolentia quibus** = *eos quibus ex insolentia* : ' those for whom good fortune is a new thing owing to its unfamiliarity, unable to control their joy, behave like madmen.' **auxisse.** Supply *eum* as subject.

parcendo. It is not by accident that two of the greatest writers of Augustus' reign echo the same thought. Cf. the well-known lines of Virgil, *Aeneid*. VI, 852 : *parcere subiectis et debellare superbos.*

18–19. **nihil iis . . . uelit.** Oratio Obliqua giving a summary of their sentiments.

19. **sui iuris.** Possessive genitive. ' Belonging to their jurisdiction.' **ita . . . si.** ' Only if the Roman people condescended not to vent their fury on those possessions as well, a fate than which there could be no worse.' **ea quoque.** i.e., *urbem et Penates* in addition to their empire.

21. **per quos deos . . . fefellissent.** Question in Oratio Obliqua.

XLIII. *The Granting of Peace*

1. **Cn. Lentulus.** On his obstructive tactics see ch. xl. Appian (Lib. 57–65) recounts a long debate in the Senate. **classis.** See xl, 12. **intercessit.** In the Senate the colleague of the presiding officer could interpose his veto (*intercessio*) by virtue of his *par potestas*. In fact, however, few officials other than tribunes exercised this right of veto. If no official vetoed an action of the Senate it was called a *senatus consultum*. A vetoed action, which still might represent the opinion of the majority of the Senate, was preserved in writing and called a *senatus auctoritas*.

3. **uti rogatae erant.** *uti rogas* (' As you propose,') was the regular formula by which the people expressed their assent.

4. **ex . . . sententia.** ' In accordance with the opinion expressed by.' The ten *legati* were to act as his council; this procedure was normal. **quibus legibus** = *eis legibus quibus*. On those terms on which it should seem good to him.'

7. **conuentis.** ' Having been agreed upon.'

9. **fetiales.** A college of priests in charge of the religious observances used in the making of peace or the declaration of war. They were of very ancient origin, as they used stone knives (*silices*) with which to kill the victims in the sacrifices necessary on such occasions. They also used *uerbenae* or *sagmina*, sacred herbs gathered from the *Arx*, one of the two summits of the Capitoline Hill; the object of these herbs was to avert the influence of hostile deities in the foreign land to which they were proceeding. The name *uerbena* is applied to all sacred herbs (e.g. laurel, olive, myrtle), and is not limited to the plant which we call verbena or vervain.

priuos. An archaic word = *singulos*. They were each to take their own stone knife; the *sagmina* were in charge of the *praetor*. **praetor**

here presumably alludes to the supreme magistrate (i.e., the proconsul Scipio). But in the early days of the Republic the consuls were called praetors: possibly the archaic use is preserved in this ancient rite.

11. **Q. Terentius.** How he showed his gratitude is told in xlv, 5.

12. **iussit.** i.e., Scipio. **quingentas.** Possibly exaggerated.

13. **grauis . . . consultum.** 'They took more severe measures with.'

XLIV. *Hannibal Rebukes the Carthaginian Senate*

1. **annis.** The dates are: close of first war 241 B.C.; outbreak of second 218; peace 201.

3. On the improbability of this view see on xxxvi, 11.

4. **Carthagini.** locative. **prima collatio.** Livy (XXXII, ii,1) says that this first instalment of the indemnity was not paid till 199 B.C., and that then the silver was of such poor quality that the Carthaginians had to make up the deficiency by borrowing money in Rome. How-ever, Carthage soon recovered with amazing rapidity, thanks partly to the financial reforms which Hannibal introduced, so that by 191 she could offer to pay off the whole of the outstanding debt in a lump sum. **exhaustis.** Dative.

5. **ipse.** Hannibal.

6. **laeti . . . amentis cordis.** Possessive genitive after *risum*. **absurdae.** The primary meaning is 'out of tune'. Tr. 'irrational'. **abhorrentes.** 'Out of place.'

9. **tantum . . . pertinet.** 'We feel public ills only in proportion as they affect our private interests.' **iis** = *publicis malis.* **stimulat.** 'Stings.'

10. **Carthagini.** Dative after *detrahebantur*. 'At the very moment when the spoils of victory were being torn away from Carthage.' This dative of the thing concerned is common after compound verbs.

11. **publico.** 'Of the commonwealth.'

12. **ad.** 'In addition to his own kingdom.' Cp. on xxxvii, 5. **uenissent.** Virtual Oratio Obliqua, as representing what Scipio said in making the gift.

13. **patrum . . . iussu.** Although Scipio had been given full powers and helped by the ten commissioners whom the Senate had appointed, the Peace had still to be approved by the Senate and People.

XLV. *Scipio's Triumph*

2. **ad habendos honores.** 'To do him honour.' **triumpho.** Scipio left Africa perhaps in the summer of 201 and celebrated his triumph at Rome. A fragment of Polybius, XVI, xxiii, describes the triumph. Livy refers to it as *omnium clarissimus*, but describes it briefly, although in later books there is more than one detailed description of a triumph. Perhaps he felt that such a description would be an artistic

error at the close of the great drama whose significance he has brought out so well, and whose hero, Scipio, he has sketched with such restraint and power. In any case we could hardly find anything more effective than the calm majesty of this ' quiet ending '.

3. **pondo** . . . cp. xvi, 12. 123,000 lb. of silver = a little over 11 million denarii. **quadringenos**, sc. *asses*. 400 asses = 25 denarii.

4. **spectaculo**. See on *Carthagini* (xliv, 10). **Tiburi**. Locative. Tibur, now Tivoli, is on the upper Anio at the point where it issues from the mountains into the Campagna. **conspecta** . . . **fuit**. ' Attracted public attention.' **elatus**. ' Was borne to the grave.' A regular use of *efferre*.

5. **Polybius**. See XVI, xxiii : no doubt his version is to be preferred (cf. Tacitus, *Annals*, xii, 38). For Livy's cavalier reference to Polybius see Introduction, p. 26.

pilleo. The cap of freedom worn by enfranchised slaves. Culleo regarded Scipio as a freed slave would regard his former master, now his *patronus*. He became praetor in 187 B.C., but stood in vain for the consulship in 185.

6. **Africani** . . . **habeo**. ' I have been unable to discover whether the name of Africanus derived its currency from the enthusiasm of the soldiers or from popular favour or whether . . . it originated in the flattering addresses of his friends.'

cognomen. The surname Scipio was a cognomen (cf. on i, 1). To this name there was sometimes added a second or even a third, which were in later times called *agnomina*; here, however, Livy uses the word *cognomen*. **popularis aura**. Lit. ' the popular breeze ', a metaphor for ' popular favour ' found elsewhere in Livy; Horace likewise uses it, while Cicero has *uentus popularis*. **Felicis**. Sulla solemnly adopted the name Felix, which flatterers had for some time applied to him, when he heard of the defeat of the younger Marius at Sacriportus in 82 B.C. **Magni**. In 80 B.C. Pompey returned to Italy after defeating the remaining Marians in Sicily and Africa: he was greeted by Sulla, perhaps half sarcastically as Gnaeus Pompeius Magnus. The title stuck. **compertum habeo**. This idiom spread and in due course *habeo* became a normal auxiliary verb.

7. **primus** . . . **nobilitatus**. Seneca, however, states (*De Vit. Brev.*, xiii, 5) that Valerius Corvinus, who captured Messana in 263, adopted the name *Messana*, which was afterwards changed to *Messala*. **nequaquam** . . . **pares**. ' Who were far less renowned for their victories.' **imaginum titulos**. Inscriptions placed beneath the family portraits, the wax masks of distinguished ancestors, that were hung in a wing of the *atrium*, the central hall of a Roman house. Tr. ' Portraits with honorific inscriptions '. **clara** . . . **familiarum**. ' Glorious names which have become hereditary in families '; as, for example, the name of Maximus had become in one branch of the *gens Fabia* (xxvi, 8); it may be noted that this title, which Fabius Cunctator had inherited, was passed on to his descendants.

APPENDIX

CHRONOLOGICAL PROBLEMS

THE dates of some events in this book are uncertain. Difficulties have arisen from two main causes: (1) The nature of the Roman Calendar. The Roman year of twelve lunar months was too short, and constantly got out of gear with the solar year. To counterbalance this, the pontifices used to intercalate some extra days every two years; but nevertheless before Julius Caesar's reforms the calendar did not always correspond with the seasons of the year. (2) Livy generally recounts the events of each year separately and describes the year by the names of the consuls in office. However, he took much of his subject-matter from Polybius, who naturally used a Greek method of reckoning time—*i.e.*, in periods of four years, called Olympiads, beginning from the year 776 B.C. But as each of the four years of every Olympiad began in the autumn, while the Roman official year started in March, it will be seen that there was plenty of opportunity for confusion on the part of a Roman writer who used both Greek and Roman sources.

Chronological Outline of the Campaign.

204. Scipio landed in Africa.

204–3 *winter*. Scipio wintered at Castra Cornelia.

203 *spring*. Scipio renewed the siege of Utica and destroyed the Carthaginian camps (? beginning of March).

   April. Hasdrubal collected his forces at Campi Magni, where Scipio defeated him towards the end of the month.

   June. Defeat of Syphax near Cirta (perhaps on the 22nd).

   June or *July*. Carthaginian naval attack at Utica.

   July (middle). Syphax sent to Scipio at Utica. Soon

after Laelius and Masinissa arrived and were sent to
Rome, while Scipio returned to Tunis.

August. Preliminary peace negotiations. Armistice.

September. Punic embassy sent to Rome to seek
ratification of terms.

Autumn.? Hannibal returned to Africa.

203–2 *winter.?* Hannibal wintered at Hadrumetum.

202. *March.* Senate ratified peace terms.

Spring. Punic violation of peace and renewal of war.

Summer. Claudius the consul left for Africa, but was
driven to Sardinia.

September.? Scipio marched to join Masinissa. Hannibal camped at Zama.

October.? Scipio and Hannibal advanced to site of
battle, which followed shortly.

December. Vermina defeated by the Romans.

202–1. Scipio at Tunis laid down terms of peace.

201. *Spring.* Peace with Carthage ratified at Rome.
Return of Scipio to Rome: his triumph.

The majority of these dates are reasonably certain; but
the following points need further discussion.

(1) *Hannibal's Recall and Return.*

The date of his return is uncertain. He was still in
Italy when the peace negotiations were opened; for one of
the clauses demanded his return (xvi, 10; cp. 14). It is
equally clear that he had returned when the Carthaginians
broke off the treaty (Polybius XV, i, 10–11; iii, 5). At
what point between these limits he returned is doubtful.
Livy (xxi, 1) assigns his departure to the consular year
203–2, *i.e.*, between 15 March 203 and 15 March 202.
In xix, 12 he implies that Hannibal left soon after the news
of his recall reached him, and about the same time as Mago.
If, as has been suggested, the year which terminated with
Hannibal's return was a Polybian year (*i.e.*, one of the
years of an Olympiad, which started in the autumn), and
if his next year (Olymp. 144, 2=203/2, and starting in
the autumn of 203) opened with Hannibal's rest at

Hadrumetum, then the autumn of 203 may be preferred to early 202 as the date of Hannibal's arrival in Africa.

(2) *Violation of the Armistice.*

Livy (xxiv) assigns the seizure of the Roman convoy to the consular year ending 14 March 202. But there is reason to believe that Scipio's terms of peace had been ratified in Rome after the entry into office of the magistrates of 202 (*i.e.*, after 15 March), a fact which was reported to Scipio about the same time as the seizure of the convoy. Livy therefore must be wrong, and the seizure must have occurred after and not before 15 March 202 (see Polybius XV, i, 3-4). Livy (xxv, 1) is wrong in saying that news of the ratification did not reach Africa until after the violation of the armistice. The references to Cn. Octavius and P. Lentulus (for whom see on i, 9 and ii, 4) do not help the chronological problem, as might be thought at first sight, because these men held the same commands both in 203 and 202.

(3) *The length of Hannibal's stay at Hadrumetum.*

The determining factors are obviously the dates of his arrival and his departure; but neither of them is certain. Livy says (xxv, 12) that Hannibal landed at Leptis, whence apparently he marched to Hadrumetum; for he is next described as being there (xxix, 1). Livy adds that he rested his men there for a few days (xxix, 1, *paucis diebus*); he then describes the march to Zama. But Livy's phrase (*paucis diebus*) is due to a careless reading of his source, Polybius. Between the disembarkation at Leptis, together with the march on to Hadrumetum, and the departure for Zama, come the events concerning the breach of the truce, as told by Polybius, who then says (XV, v, 3) that the alarmed Carthaginians urged Hannibal to move, which he did ' after a few days '. This phrase Livy has wrongly connected with the disembarkation and the rest. Thus we have no evidence for the length of Hannibal's stay at Hadrumetum other than the two uncertain terminal dates discussed in (1) and (4).

(4) *The Battle of Zama.*

There is no doubt that this battle was fought in 202, but every month from March to December has been suggested and supported by some scholar. Certainty is obviously impossible, but the evidence suggests a late date, about October. For instance, a late writer, Dio Cassius, records an eclipse of the sun before the battle, and a partial eclipse actually occurred on 19 October 202. Although Dio's account of the battle itself cannot be accepted, yet the fact of the eclipse may be true. Further, if the victory had been won in the spring of 202, why should peace not have been concluded before March 201 ? Probably, therefore, Scipio sent messages to recall Masinissa in the spring (202), and then marched slowly to meet him. Hannibal waited at Hadrumetum through the early summer, hoping for cavalry reinforcements from Vermina, son of Syphax (xxxvi, 7). At last he was joined by another Numidian prince named Tychaeus, who had the best cavalry in Africa (Polybius XV, iii, 5–7). Then, after the heat of summer was over, Hannibal moved to Zama in the early autumn.

INDEX OF PROPER NAMES

References are chiefly to the chapters of Livy; further explanations will generally be found in the relevant note. A few references to pages of the Introduction and Notes have been added. Roman personages are listed under the name of their *gens*—e.g., P. Cornelius Scipio s.v. Cornelius.

141

INDEX TO NOTES

(The numerals refer to pages.)

144

VOCABULARY

Numerals have been omitted

Diphthongs and final *i*, *o*, *u* are long, if unmarked. All other long vowels are marked, unless consonants make the syllable necessarily long. If an unmarked vowel precedes a mute followed by a liquid, the quantity of the syllable is doubtful.

Perfects and supines of all verbs of the third conjugation are given. Under other verbs they are not given, unless they are irregular. In words in which inflexion is indicated a hyphen denotes that all the letters which precede it are retained throughout, while those which follow it are replaced; it has no etymological significance.

a, ab (prep. c. abl.), *from, by, on the side of, in the direction of, consequent upon*

abdico, 1 (tr. with se), *abdicate*

ab-dūco, -duxi, -ductum, 3 (tr.), *lead away*

ab-eo, -ii, -itum, īre, *go away, depart*

abhorreo, 2 (intr.), *differ from, am inconsistent with, shrink from*

ab-nuo, -nui, -nuitum *or* -nūtum, 3 (tr. and intr.), *say no, refuse*

abrogo, 1 (tr.), *abrogate, annul*

ab-sisto, -stiti, —, 3 (intr.), *withdraw from, desist from*

absterreo, 2 (tr.), *frighten away*

abs-tinui, -tentum, 2 (tr. and intr.), *keep away, abstain from*

abs-traho, -traxi, -tractum, 3 (tr.), *drag away*

ab-sum, -fui, -esse, *am absent, away from, missing*

ab-sūmo, -sumpsi, -sumptum, 3 (tr.), *consume, carry off, destroy*

abundo, 1 (intr.), *abound, overflow*

ac-cēdo, -cessi, -cessum, 3 (intr.), *come to approach, am added*

ac-cendo, -cendi, -censum, 3 (tr.), *kindle, fire, inflame*

accessi-o, -ōnis (f.), *addition*

accid-o, -i, —, 3 (intr.), *happen, befall*

accio, 4 (tr.), *summon*

ac-cipio, -cēpi, -ceptum, 3 (tr.), *receive, welcome, hear*

āc-er, -ris, -re, *keen, energetic, fierce*

aciē-s, -i (f.), *line of battle, battle*

accūso, 1 (tr.), *accuse*

ad (prep. c. acc.), *to, towards, at, near, about* (with numerals), *with a view to, to serve as ;* ad hoc, haec, *in addition*

ad-do, -didi, -ditum, 3 (tr.), *add*

ad-dūco, -duxi, -ductum, 3 (tr.), *lead to, bring to*

adeo (adv.), *so, to, such an extent, indeed*

ad-eo, -ii, -itum, -īre, *go to, approach*

adfecto, 1 (tr.), *seek to gain, gain*

ad-fero, -tuli, -lātum, -ferre (tr.), *bring to, report*

ad-ficio, -fēci, -fectum, 3 (tr.), *affect*

ad-fīnitā-s, -tis (f.), *relationship*

ad-flīgo, -flīxi, -flīctum, 3 (tr.), *strike down, afflict*

adflo, 1 (tr.), *breathe upon, scathe*

ad-fluo, -fluxi, -fluxum, 3 (intr.), *flow to, flock to*

ad-fulgeo, -fulsi, -fulsum, 2 (intr.), *shine upon*

ad-gredior, -gressus sum, 3 (tr.), *attack*

adgrego, 1 (tr.), *bring up, together*

adhortāti-o, -ōnis (f.), *exhortation*

ad-icio, -iēci, -iectum, 3 (tr.), *add*

ad-imo, -ēmi, -emptum, 3 (tr.), *take away, take from* (c. dat.)

ad-ipiscor, -eptus sum, 3 (tr.), *obtain, overtake*

adit-us, -ūs (m.), *approach, entrance*

ad-iungo, -iunxi, -iunctum, 3 (tr.), *join to, add*

ad-iuuo, -iūui, -ūtum, 3 (tr.), *help, aid*

ad-loquor, -locūtus sum, 3 (tr.), *speak to, address* (c. acc.)

administro, 1 (tr.), *administer, govern*

admīrati-o, -ōnis (f.), *wonder, admiration*

ad-misceo, -miscui, -mistum *or* mixtum, 2 (tr.), *mingle with*

ad-mitto, -mīsi, -missum, 3 (tr.), *admit*

admodum (adv.), *quite, very*

admoneo, 2 (tr.), *admonish, warn, remind*

ad-moueo, -mōui, -mōtum, 2 (tr.), *move up to, bring up*

ad-nītor, -nīsus *or* nixus sum, 3 (intr.), *strive*

ad-orior, -ortus sum, 4 (tr.), *attack*

adpello, 1 (tr.), *call, address*

ad-pello, -puli, -pulsum, 3 (tr.), *drive to, up against* (with classem *or* nauem), *put in*

ad-peto, -petīui, -petītum, 3 (tr.), *seek*

adpropinquo, 1 (intr.), *approach*

adrōd-o, -si, -sum (tr.), *gnaw*

adsentāti-o, -ōnis (f.), *flattery*

ad-sentio, -sensi, -sensum, 4 (intr.), *agree to*

adsidu-us, -a, -um *continual, assiduous*

ad-suesco, -suēui, -sūetum, 3 (intr.), *become accustomed to* (contr. plpf. subj. adsuesset)

adsuēt-us, -a, -um, *accustomed to*

ad-traho, -traxi, -tractum, 3 (tr.), *carry to, drag to*

ad-tribuo, -tribui, -tribūtum, 3 (tr.), *assign, attribute*

ad-ueho, -uexi, -uectum, 3 (tr.), *carry to* (pass. *ride to, sail to*)

ad-uenio, -uēni, -uentum, 4 (intr.), *come to, approach*

aduent-us, -ūs (m.), *approach*

aduersor, 1 (intr. c. dat.), *oppose*

aduers-us, -a, -um, *opposing, opposite, adverse*

aduersus (adv.), *against, towards*

adulāt-or, -ōris (m.), *flatterer*

adulescen-s, -tis (m.), *youth, young man*

adulescenti-a, -ae (f.), *youth*

adūlor, 1 (tr. and intr.), *flatter*

aduoco, 1 (tr.), *summon*

aduol-uor, -ūtus sum, 3 (intr.), *grovel at*

aed-es, -is (f.), *temple*

aedilici-us, -a, -um, *serving under an aedile, ex-aedile*

aeditu-us, -i (m.), *temple guardian*

aeg-er, -ra, -rum, *sick, anxious ;* (adv.), *aegre, with difficulty, against one's will*

aemul-us, -i (m.), *rival*

aequāl-is, -e, *contemporary*

aequo, 1 (tr.), *equal, make equal*

aerari-um, -i (n.), *treasury*

aes, aeris (n.), *bronze ;* aeris (gen.) = asses aeris

aet-ās, -ātis (f.), *age, youth*

aeu-um, -i (n.), *time, age*

ag-er, -ri (m.), *field, land*

agg-er, -eris (m.), *mound, siege-mound*

agil-is, -e, *mobile, quick*

agito, I (tr.), *discuss, ponder, consider*

agm-en, -ins (n.), *column*

ago, ēgi, actum, 3 (tr. and intr.), *drive, do, discuss, deal with, plead, act, am stationed ;* gratias, grates agere, *thank*

agrest-is, -is, *peasant, rustic*

aio (defect. intr.), *say*

āl-a, -ae (f.), *wing, squadron, shoulder*

aliēnigen-a, -ae (c.), *alien-born*

aliēno, I (tr.), *alienate*

aliēn-us, -a, -um, *belonging to another, alien*

alioqui (adv.), *otherwise, else*

aliquando (adv.), *sometimes, at length*

aliquant-us, -a, -um, *of a certain amount, some*

aliqu-i, -a, -od (indef. adj.), *some*

aliquis (indef. subst. pron.), *someone, something*

aliquot (indecl. adj.), *some, a number of*

ali-us, -a, -ud, *other, rest of ;* alius . . . alius, *the one . . . the other ;* (adv.), aliter, *otherwise, else ;* aliā, *in one, in another place ;* alias, *at one, at another time (or place)*

alo, alui, alitum, 3 (tr.), *nourish, bring up*

alt-er, -era, -erum, *one of two, other second ;* alter . . . alter, *the one . . . the other (of two)*

altitūd-o, -inis (f.), *height, depth*

alt-us, -a, -um, *high, deep ;* altum, *deep sea*

ambigu-us, -a, -um, *doubtful, uncertain*

ambiti-o, -ōnis (f.), *ambition, popularity-hunting, display*

amb-o, -ae, *both*

ambust-us, -a, -um, *singed, half-burned*

amīciti-a, -ae (f.), *friendship*

amīc-us, -a, -um, *friendly ;* amicus, *friend*

ā-mitto, -mīsi, -missum, 3 (tr.), *lose*

amn-is, -is (m.), *river*

amo, I (tr.), *love*

am-or, -ōris (m.), *love*

ample-ctor, -xus sum, 3 (tr.), *embrace*

ampl-us, -a, -um, *ample, great, important*

an (conj.), *whether, or*

an-ceps, -cipitis, *twofold, doubtful, on two sides*

an-go, -xi, -ctum, 3 (tr.), *vex, distress*

angusti-ae, -arum (f.), *narrow places, straits*

animāt-us, -a, -um, *minded, disposed*

anim-us, -i (m.), *mind, disposition, courage, spirit*

annōn-a, -ae (f.), *corn-supply, price of corn*

ann-us, -i (m.), *year*

ante (prep. c. acc.), *before ;* (adv.), *before, earlier ;* (conj.), antequam (ante . . . quam), *before, before that . . . ;* antea (adv.), *before*

antemn-a, -ae (f.), *yard, yard-arm*

aper-io, -ui, -tum, 4 (tr.), *open, reveal, set forth*

apparāt-us, -ūs (m.), *preparation, equipment, gear*

appāreo, 2 (intr.), *appear ;* apparet, *it is clear, it appears*

applico, I (tr.), *attach*

apt-us, -a, -um, *fitted, apt, suitable*

apud (prep. c. acc.), *at, among, in*

aqu-a, -ae (f.), *water*

aquāti-o, -ōnis (f.), *place or facilities for drawing water*

arbit-er, -ri (m.), *witness*

arbitrat-us, -us (m.), *will, choice, pleasure*

arbitri-um, -i (n.), *free-will, choice, judgement, authority*

arbitror, 1 (tr.), *think*

arb-or, -oris (f.), *tree*

arcess-o, -īui, -ītum, 3 (tr.), *fetch, summon*

arc-us, -ūs (m.), *bow, halo*

ar-deo, -si, -sum, 2 (intr.), *burn, blaze*

ard-or, -ōris (m.), *blaze, burning, ardour, passion*

argent-um, -i (n.), *silver*

arg-uo, -ui, -ūtum, 3 (tr.), *prove, accuse*

armāment-um, -i (n.), *armament, equipment*

armatūra leuis, *light-armed troops*

arm-um, -i (n.), *arm, weapon*

ar-s, -tis (f.), *art, skill, quality*

art-us, -a, -um, *narrow*

ascens-us, -ūs (m.), *ascent, way up*

asp-er, -era, -erum, *rough, rugged, harsh*

aspernor, 1 (tr.), *despise*

ass-er, -eris (m.), *pole*

atque (*or*) ac (conj.), *and ;* after idem, etc., *as ;* after alius, etc., *than*

atqui (conj.), *and yet*

atrōcit-ās, -ātis (f.), *cruelty*

atr-ox, -ōcis, *cruel, fierce*

attinet, 2 (impers.), *it pertains to, concerns*

at-tingo, -tigi, -tactum, 3 (tr.), *touch*

attonit-us, -a, -um, *astounded, dumbstruck*

auāriti-a, -ae (f.), *avarice*

auct-or, -ōris (m.), *author, authority, messenger ;* auctor sum, *assert*

auctōrit-as, -atis (f.), *authority, influence*

auct-us, -ūs (m.), *increase*

audāci-a, -ae (f.), *daring*

aud-ax, -ācis, *bold, daring*

audeo, ausus sum, 2 (tr.), *dare, venture*

audio, 4 (tr.), *hear*

auer-to, -ti, -sum, 3, *turn away, divert*

aufero, abstuli, ablātum, auferre (tr.), *carry off, away*

augeo, auxi, auctum, 2 (tr.), *increase*

auit-us, -a, -um, *of a grandfather, ancestral*

aur-a, -ae (f.), *breeze, favour*

aure-us, -a, -um, *golden*

aur-is, -is (f.), *ear*

aur-um, -i (n.), *ear*

auspici-um, -i (n.), *auspice, command, leadership*

aut (conj.), *or ;* aut . . . aut, *either . . . or*

autem (conj.), *but, however*

au-us, -i, (m.), *grandfather, ancestor*

auxiliar-is, -e, *auxiliary, helping*

auxili-um, -i (n.), *help, support ;* auxilia, *auxiliaries*

barbari-a, -ae (f. collective for), *barbarians*

barbar-us, -a, -um, *barbarian, barbarous*

bellic-us, -a, -um, *warlike, of war*

bello, 1 (intr.), *make war*

bell-um, -i (n.), *war*

bēlu-a, -ae (f.), *beast, monster*

bene (adv.), *well*

benefici-um, -i (n.), *benefit, service*

benign-us, -a, -um, *kindly*

besti-a, -ae (f.), *beast*

bidu-um, -i (n.), *two days*

blanditi-ae, -ārum (f.), *blandishments, flattery*

bon-us, -a, -um, *good ;* bona, *goods, property*

breu-is, -e, *short ;* (abl.), breui, *in a short time*

cado, cecidi, cāsum, 3 (intr.), *fall*

caed-es, -is (f.), *slaughter*

caedo, cecīdi, caesum, 3 (tr.), *cut, cut to pieces, beat, kill*

cael-um, -i (n.), *heaven*

calamit-ās, -ātis (f.), *calamity*

calīg-o, -inis (f.), *mist, darkness*

cal-o (m.), *soldier's servant*

campestr-is, -e, *level*

camp-us, -i (m.), *plain*

cano, cecini, —, 3 (tr. and intr.), *sing, sound, prophesy*

capio, cēpi, captum, 3 (tr.), *take, have room for, hold*

captīu-us, -a, -um, *captive, captured*

cap-ut, -itis (n.), *head, capital*

carc-er, -eris (m.), *prison*

cas-a, -ae (f.), *hut*

castīgāti-o, -onis (f.), *chastisement, rebuke*

castīgo, 1 (tr.), *chastise, reprimand, rebuke*

castr-a, -orum (n.), *camp*

cās-us, -ūs (m.), *chance, misfortune, fall*

catēn-a, -ae (f.), *chain*

caueo, cāui, cautum, 2 (tr. and intr.), *beware, take precautions*

cauern-a, -ae (f.), *hollow, cavern*

caus-a, -ae (f.), *cause, case, question*

caut-us, -a, -um, *cautious*

cēdo, cessi, cessum, 3 (tr. and intr.), *yield, withdraw, retire, go*

celebrit-ās, -ātis (f.), *fame, celebrity*

celebro, 1 (tr.), *celebrate, make famous*

cel-er, -eris, -ere, *swift, quick*

celerit-ās, -ātis (f.), *speed, quickness*

cels-us, -a, -um, *lofty*

cens-eo, -ui, -um, 2 (intr.), *vote, propose*

cerno, crēui, crētum, 3 (tr.), *see, distinguish*

certām-en, -inis (n.), *struggle, contest*

certo, 1 (intr.), *vie, contend, fight, display zeal*

cert-us, -a, -um, *certain, sure ;* (adv.), certe, *certainly at all events*

cesso, 1 (intr.), *am slack, remiss*

cēter-us, -a, -um, *the other, the rest ;* (adv.), cēterum, *for the rest, but, however*

circā, circum (adv. and prep. c. acc.), *around, about*

circul-us, -i (m.), *circle*

circum-ago, -ēgi, -actum, 3 (tr.), *bring round*

circum-do, -dedi, -datum, 1 (tr.), *place round, surround, flank*

circum-dūco, -duxi, -ductum, 3 (tr.), *lead round*

circum-eo, -ii, -itum, -īre (intr.), *go round*

circum-fundo, -fūdi, -fūsum, 3 (tr.), *pour round*

circum-sedeo, -sēdi, -sessum, 2 (intr.), *encamp around, beset, besiege*

circum-sto, -steti, —, 1 (intr.), *stand round, beset*

circum-uenio, -uēni, -uentum, 4 (tr. and intr.), *come round, surround, entrap*

cito, 1 (tr.), *drive at speed*

citro, *see* ultro

cīu-is, -is (m.), *citizen*

cīuit-ās, -ātis (f.), *state, town*

clad-es, -is (f.), *disaster*

clam (adv.), *secretly*

clām-or, -ōris (m.), *clamour, shout, warcry*

clār-us, -a, -um, *clear, famous*

class-is, -is (f.), *fleet*

claudo, clausi, clausum, 3 (tr.), *shut, shut in*

clāu-us, -i (m.), *stripe*

co-eo, -ii, -itum, -īre (intr.), *meet*

coep-i, -tum, -isse (tr. and intr.), *begin*

cōgitāti-o, -ōnis (f.), *thought, reflection*

cognōm-en, -inis (n.), *last name, nickname*

cog-nosco, -nōui, -nitum, 3 (tr.), *know, learn, enquire*

cōgo, coēgi, coactum, 3 (tr.), *force, collect*

colo, colui, cultum, 3 (tr.), *cultivate, honour, worship*

cōmiter, *courteously, kindly*

comiti-a, -orum, *assembly, elections*

commeāt-us, -ūs (m.), *supplies, provisions*

commemoro, 1 (tr.), *call to memory, record, relate*

commeo, 1 (intr.), *go to and fro*

commīlit-ō, -ōnis (m.), *fellow-soldier*

comminus (adv.), *at close quarters*

com-mitto, -mīsi, -missum, 3 (tr.), *join, entrust*

commod-us, -a, -um, *convenient*

com-moueo, -mōui, -mōtum, 3 (tr.), *move, stir*

commūn-is, -e, *common*

commūnio, 4 (tr.), *fortify*

compāreo, 2 (intr.), *appear*

comparo, 1 (tr.), *get ready, get, compare, match together*

com-pello, -puli, -pulsum, 3 (tr.), *drive, compel*

comper-io, -i, -tum, 4 (tr.), *ascertain*

com-pleo, -plēui, -plētum, 2 (tr.), *fill, man*

complōrāti-o, -ōnis (f.), *lamentation*

complōro, 1 (tr. and intr.), *lament*

com-pōno, -posui, -positum, 3 (tr.), *put together, arrange, compose;* ex composito, *in accordance with plan*

comp-os, -otis (c. gen.), *in possession of*

comprehen-do (comprendo), -di, -sum, 3 (tr.), *grasp, comprehend, seize, link together*

comprobo, 1 (tr.), *approve*

conāt-us, -ūs (m.), *attempt, effort*

con-cēdo, -cessi, -cessum, 3 (tr. and intr.), *yield, grant, go*

con-cido, -cidi, -cāsum, 3 (intr.), *fall*

concilio, 1 (tr.), *win over, win*

concili-um, -i (n.), *assembly*

con-cino, -cinui, —, 3 (tr. and intr.), *sing, sound together*

con-cipio, -cēpi, -ceptum, 3 (tr.), *conceive*

concito, 1 (tr.), *drive at speed, hurry on*

conclāmo, 1 (intr.), *shout, raise a cry together*

con-curro, -curri, -cursum, 3 (intr.), *run together, charge, close*

concursāti-o, -ōnis (f.), *running together*

concurs-us, -ūs (m.), *assembly, throng, running together*

condici-o, -ōnis (f.), *terms, lot, condition*

con-do, -didi, -ditum, 3 (tr.), *store, put together, put away*

con-dūco, -duxi, -ductum, 3 (tr.), *lead, lead together, hire*

con-fero, -tuli, -lātum, -ferre (tr.), *bring together, compare, contribute, join* (battle), *betake* (with se)

confert-us, -a, -um, *dense, serried, crowded*

confessi-o, -ōnis (f.), *confession, admission*

confestim (adv.), *hastily*

confirmo, 1 (tr.), *strengthen, confirm, affirm*

conflāgro, 1 (intr.), *blaze*

con-flīgo, -flixi, -flictum, 3 (tr. and intr.), *strike together, contend, fight*

con-fugio, -fūgi, —, 3 (intr.), *fly, take refuge*

con-fundo, -fūdi, -fūsum, 3 (tr.), *confound, confuse, rout*

con-gero, -gessi, -gestum, 3 (tr.), *put together, accumulate*

conglobo, 1 (tr.), *mass together*

congruo, 3 (intr.), *agree, am in unison*

coniect-us, -ūs (m.), *cast*

con-icio, -iēci, -iectum, 3 (tr.), *throw, throw together;* (in sortem) *put to the lot*

coniūrāt-or, -ōris (m.), *conspirator*

con-iunx, -iugis (c.), *husband, wife*

con-lābor, -lapsus sum, 3 (intr.), *fall*

conlāti-o, -ōnis (f.), *contribution*

conlaudo, 1 (tr.), *praise*

conlēgi-um, -i (n.), *college, body*

con-ligo, -lēgi, -lectum, 3 (tr.), *collect, gather*

conloqui-um, -i (n.), *conversation, parley*

con-loquor, -locūtus sum, 3 (intr.), *talk with, converse, parley*

conluui-o, -ōnis (f.), *medley, dregs*

con-queror, -questus sum, 3 (intr.), *complain*

conqui-esco, -ēui, -ētum, 3 (intr.), *rest, remain quiet*

con-quiro, -quīsīui, -quīsītum, 3 (tr.), *seek, collect*

conquīsīt-or, -ōris (m.), *recruiting officer*

con-senesco, -senui, —, 3 (intr.), *grow old, become enfeebled*

consens-us, -ūs (m.), *agreement*

con-sīdo, -sēdi, -sessum, 3 (intr.), *sit down, encamp, sink*

consili-um, -i (n.), *plan, strategy, prudence, counsel, council*

conspect-us, -ūs (m.), *sight*

con-spicio, -spexi, -spectum, 3 (tr.), *see*

constanti-a, -ae (f.), *constancy, courage*

consternāti-o, -ōnis (f.), *consternation, alarm*

con-sto, -stiti, -statum, 1 (intr.), *stand firm; constant;* (impers.), *it is agreed*

constrāt-um, -i (n.), *deck*

consulār-is, -is, *consular* (as noun), *ex-consul*

consulāt-us, -ūs (m.), *consulate*

consul-o, -ui, -tum, 3 (tr. and intr.), *consult, deliberate, take counsel, resolve;* (c. dat.), *consult for the interest of*

consultāti-o, ōnis (f.) *consultation*

consulto, 1 (tr. and intr.), *consult*

consult-um, -i (n.), *decree*

consummo, 1 (tr.), *complete, accomplish*

contemplor, 1 (tr.), *contemplate*

con-tendo, -tendi, -tentum, 3 (intr.), *go, hasten, struggle*

content-us, -a, -um, *content*

conticeo, 2 (intr.), *am silent*

continenti-a, -ae (f.), *restraint, self-control*

con-tineo, -tenui, -tentum, 2 (tr.), *hold, contain, restrain*

continu-us, -a, -um, *continuous, unbroken*

conti-o, -ōnis (f.), *assembly, speech to an assembly*

contrā (prep. c. acc.), *against, contrary to;* (adv.), *on the other hand*

con-ueho, -uexi, -uectum, 3 (tr.), *carry together*

con-uenio, -uēni, -uentum, 4 (tr. and intr.), *meet, come together;* (in 3rd person), *is agreed, is fitting*

con-uerto, -uerti, -uersum, 3 (tr.), *turn*

cōpi-a, -ae (f.), *plenty, resources, opportunity, access;* (plur.), *forces*

cōr, cordis (n.), *heart;* cordi, *at heart, dear, desired*

cōram (prep. c. abl.), *in the presence of;* (adv.), *face to face*

corn-u, -ūs (n.), *horn, wing*

corōn-a, -ae (f.), *crown*

corp-us, -oris (n.), *body*

cor-rigo, -rexi, -rectum, 3 (tr.), *set right, correct, reform*

cor-rumpo, -rūpi, -ruptum, 3 (tr.), *corrupt, spoil*

corruo, 3 (intr.), *fall*

coru-us, -i (m.), *crow*

cotīdie (adv.), *daily*

crastin-us, -a, -um, *on the morrow*

crĕb-er, -ra, -rum, *frequent, numerous*

crĕd-o, -idi, -itum, 3 (tr. c. dat. and intr.), *believe, trust, entrust*

cresco, crĕui, crētum, 3 (intr.), *grow, increase*

crīm-en, -inis (n.), *charge, accusation, guilt*

crudēl-is, -e, *cruel*

crudēlit-ās, -ātis (f.), *cruelty*

cruent-us, -a, -um, *bloodstained*

cru-or, ōris (m.), *blood*

crux, crucis (f.), *cross*

cubīl-e, -is (n.), *bed*

cum (prep. c. abl.), *with*

cum (conj.), *when, although ;* cum . . . tum, *both . . . and*

cumulo, 1 (tr.), *heap up, accumulate, complete, crown*

cunctanter (adv.), *tardily, slowly*

cunctāt-or, -ōris (m.), *delayer*

cunctor, 1 (intr.), *delay*

cupidit-ās, -ātis (f.), *greed, desire*

cupid-us, -a, -um, *greedy, eager*

cup-io, -īui, -ītum, 3 (tr.), *desire*

cur (adv.), *why*

cūr-a, -ae (f.), *care, anxiety, charge*

cūro, 1 (tr.), *care for, attend to, treat*

cūrāti-o, -ōnis (f.), *treatment, care*

cusp-is, -idis (f.), *spear*

custōdi-a, -ae (f.), *watch, guard*

cust-ōs, -ōdis (m.), *guard, watchman*

damn-um, -i (m.), *loss, damage*

dē (prep. c. abl.), *down from, from, concerning ;* (victory) *over*

de-a, -ae (f.), *goddess*

dēbello, 1 (tr.), *war down, finish a war*

dēbeo, 2 (tr. and intr.), *owe, ought*

dē-cēdo, -cessi, -cessum, 3 (intr.), *go away, go down*

dē-cerno, -crēui, -crētum, 3 (tr. and intr.), *decree, decide, resolve, judge, propose*

decet, 2 (impers.), *it is proper, fitting*

dē-cipio, -cēpi, -ceptum, 3 (tr.), *deceive*

decoro, 1 (tr.), *decorate, adorn, honour*

dē-curro, -curri, -cursum, 3 (intr.), *manoeuvre, run down ;* (naut.) *run in*

dec-us, -oris (n.), *honour, glory*

dē-do, -didi, -ditum, 3 (tr.), *surrender*

dē-dūco, -duxi, -ductum, 3 (tr.), *lead away, down, escort, launch*

dēfecti-ō, -ōnis (f.), *revolt*

dēfen-do, -di, -sum, 3 (tr.), *defend*

dē-fero, -tuli, -lātum, -ferre (tr.), *carry down, carry to, bring, report*

dē-ficio, -fēci, -fectum, 3 (intr.), *fail, give out, revolt*

dēformit-ās -ātis (f.), *disfigurement, hideousness, disgrace*

dēformo, 1 (tr.), *disfigure, mar*

dē-gredior, -gressus sum, 3 (intr.), *go down*

dē-icio, -iēci, -iectum, 3 (tr.), *cast down*

dein, deinde (adv.), *then, next, after that*

deinceps (adv.), *next, successively*

delēniment-um, -i (n.), *blandishment, charm*

dēleo, 2 (tr.), *destroy, blot out*

dē-ligo, -lēgi, -lectum, 3 (tr.), *choose*

delūbr-um, -i (n.), *shrine, temple*

de-mitto, -mīsi, -missum, 3, *let down, send down*

dēm-o, -psi, -ptum, 3 (tr.), *take away*

dēmum (adv.), *not till* (*the time being indicated by the preceding word*)

denso, 1 (tr.), *thicken, close up*

dēplōro, 1 (tr.), *lament*

dēporto, 1 (tr.), *carry down, carry away, bring away*

dēprecor, 1 (tr.), *pray to be spared*

dēpr-imo, -essi, -essum, 3 (tr.), *depress*

dēscen-do, -di, -sum, 3 (intr.),
  descend, disembark
dē-scisco, -scīui, -scītum, 3 (intr.),
  desert, revolt from
dē-scribo, -scripsi, -scriptum, 3
  (tr.), write down, describe
dē-sero, -serui, -sertum, 3 (tr.),
  desert, abandon
dēsīderi-um, -i (n.), longing, sense of
  want
dēsīdero, 1 (tr.), long for, miss
dēstit-uo, -ui, -utum, 3 (tr.),
  desert, forsake
dē-traho, -traxi, -tractum, 3 (tr.),
  drag away, draw off
dē-uinco, -uīci, -uīctum, 3 (tr.),
  conquer utterly
de-us, -i (m.), god
dext-er, -ra or -era, -rum or -erum,
  right; dextra (sc., manus),
  right hand; dextrā, on the right
dici-o, -ōnis (f.), sway, dominion
dī-co, -xi, ctum, 3 (tr.), say, tell,
  speak of, appoint
di-es, -ēi (m. or f. in sing.: m. in
  plur.), day, daylight
differo, distuli, dilātum, differre
  (tr.), postpone, put off
difficil-is, -e, difficult
dignit-ās, -ātis (f.), worth, rank,
  dignity
dign-us, -a, -um, worthy
dīlect-us, -ūs (m.), choice, levy
dī-luo, -lui, -lutum, 3 (tr.), clear
dīmicāti-o, ōnis (f.), struggle
dīmico, 1 (intr.), contend, fight
dīmidi-um, -i (n.), half
dī-mitto, -mīsī, -missum, 3 (tr.),
  send off, dismiss, distribute
dī-rigo, -rexi, -rectum, 3 (tr.),
  draw up, direct
dīr-imo, -ēmi, -emptum, 3 (tr.),
  separate
dī-ripio, -ripui, -reptum, 3 (tr.,
  plunder
dīrut-us, -a, -um, overthrown,
  ruined

dis-cēdo, -cessi, -cessum, 3 (intr.),
  depart, divide to vote
disciplīn-a, -ae (f.), discipline,
  training
discrep-o, -ui, -itum, 1, differ, dis-
  agree
discrīm-en, -inis (n.), distinction,
  difference, crisis, danger, hazard
discr-ībo, -psi, -ptum, 3 (tr.),
  distribute, divide
discurs-us, -ūs (m.), running in
  different directions
dis-cutio, -cussi, -cussum, 3 (tr.),
  dash to pieces, scatter
dis-icio, -iēci, -iectum, 3 (tr.),
  scatter
dispa-r, -is, unlike, unequal
disper-go, -si, -sum, 3 (tr.),
  scatter, disperse
dispertio, 4 (tr.), distribute, divide
dis-pōno, -posui, -positum, 3 (tr.),
  arrange, dispose
disse-ro, -rui, -rtum, 3 (tr. and
  intr.), discuss, discourse
dissimulo, 1, conceal, pretend not to
dissipo, 1 (tr.), scatter
disson-us, -a, -um, discordant
dis-suādeo, -suāsi, -suāsum, 2 (tr.),
  advise against, dissuade
distan-s, -tis, distant, separated from
diu, (adv.), long, for long
diuers-us, -a, -um, different
dīu-es, -itis, rich
dīu-ido, -īsi, -īsum, 3, divide, distribute
dīuiti-ae, -arum (f.), riches
diūtin-us, -a, -um, long, lengthy
do, dedi, datum, dare (tr.), give,
  create, occasion
doc-eo, -ui, -tum, 2 (tr.), teach,
  inform, instruct
document-um, -i (n.), proof, lesson
domināt-us, -ūs (m.), sway,
  tyranny
domin-us, -i (m.) master, lord
dom-o, -ui, -itum, 1 (tr.), subdue
dom-us, -ūs (f.), house, home

dōnec (adv.), *until, so long as, while*

dōno, 1 (tr.), *give, present*

dubito, 1 (intr.), *doubt, hesitate*

dubi-us, -a, -um, *doubtful, hesitant*

dūco, duxi, ductum, 3 (tr.), *lead, guide, think, marry*

dum (conj.), *while, until, so long as ;* (c. subj.), *provided that*

dupl-ex, -icis, *double ;* (adv.), dupliciter

dupl-us, -a, -um, *double*

dūro, 1 (tr.), *harden*

dūr-us, -a, -um, *hard, harsh*

dux, ducis (m.), *leader, guide*

e, ex (prep. c. abl.), *out of, from, in accordance with, as a result of*

eburne-us, -a, -um, *ivory*

ecūle-us, -i (m.), *foal*

e-dīco, -dixi, -dictum, 3 (tr.), *proclaim*

edictu-m, -i (n.), *proclamation*

ē-do, -didi, -ditum, 3 (tr.), *put forth, give out, publish, manifest*

ĕdo, ēdi, esum, 3 (tr.), *eat*

e-doceo, -docui, -doctum, 2 (tr.), *teach, set forth*

ē-dŭco, 1 (tr.), *bring up, educate*

effect-us, -ūs (m.), *effect, result, performance, success*

effero, extuli, elātum, efferre (tr.), *carry out, bury, bear up, laud, exalt, elate*

ef-fugio, -fūgi, —, 3 (tr. and intr.), *escape*

effugi-um, -i (n.), *escape*

ēf-fundo, -fūdi, -fūsum, 3 (tr.), *pour out, spend ;* effus-us, -a, -um, *scattered, disorderly, uncurbed, thrown from ;* effuse (adv.), *in disorder, far and wide*

ē-gero, -gessi, -gestum, 3 (tr.), *remove*

ē-gredior, -gressus sum, 3 (intr.), *go out, come out*

ēgregi-us, -a, -um, *excellent, outstanding, remarkable*

ē-icio, -iēci, -iectum, 3 (tr.), *cast out*

elephant-us, -i (m.), *elephant*

ē-lic-io, -licui, -licitum, 3 (tr.), *lure out*

ē-ligo, -lēgi, -lectum, 3 (tr.), *choose, pick out*

ēmer-go, -si, -sum, 3 (tr.), *emerge*

ē-mitto, -mīsi, -missum, 3 (tr.), *send out, launch*

ē-moueo, -mōui, -mōtum, 2 (tr.), *remove*

ēn (interj.), *behold !*

enim (conj.), *for ;* neque enim, *for . . . not*

ē-nītor, -nīsus or nixus sum, 3 (intr.), *struggle, struggle on*

ēnixius (comp. adv.), *more strenuously*

eo (adv.), *thither, therefore, by so much*

eōdem (adv.), *to the same place*

epul-um, -i (n.), *banquet*

equ-es, -itis (m.), *horseman, knight ;* (collective sing.) *cavalry*

equest-er, -ris, -e, *cavalry, equestrian*

equidem (adv.), *indeed* (generally with first pers.)

equitāt-us, -ūs (m.), *cavalry*

equ-us, -i (m.), *horse*

ergo (conj.), *therefore*

e-rigo, -rexi, -rectum, 3 (tr.), *raise, erect, excite, cheer*

e-ripio, -ripui, -reptum, 3 (tr.), *snatch away*

err-or, -ōris (m.), *error, mistake, wandering*

ērudio, 4 (tr.), *educate, train*

ērupti-o, -ōnis (f.), *sally, sortie*

ēscen-do, -di, -sum, 3 (tr. and intr.), *ascend, mount*

et (conj. and adv.), *and, also, even ;* et . . . et, *both . . . and*

etiam (adv.), *also, even*

etiamsi (conj.), *although, even if*

etsi (conj.), *although*

ēuād-o, -si, -sum, 3 (intr.), *go out, escape*

ēue-ho, -xi, -ctum, 3 (tr.), *carry out*

ē-uenio, -uēni, -uentum, 4 (intr.), *happen, result, fall*

ēuent-us, -ūs (m.), *event, result*

ē-uerto, -uerti, -uersum, 3 (tr.), *overthrow*

ēuoco, 1 (tr.), *summon, call*

exacerbo, 1 (tr.), *embitter*

exact-us, -a, -um, *past, spent*

exaedifico, 1 (tr.), *build*

exaudio, 4, *hear, hear with favour*

ex-cēdo, -cessi, -cessum, 3 (tr. and intr.), *depart from, overlap*

ex-cello, -cellui, -celsum, 3 (tr. and intr.), *excel*

excidi-um, -i (n.), *destruction*

ex-cido, -cidi, —, 3 (intr.), *fall out, am forgotten*

excio, 4 (tr.), *summon*

excito, 1 (tr.), *summon, stir up, rouse*

ex-clūdo, -si, -sum, 3 (tr.), *shut out, exclude*

ex-curro, -rri, -cursum, 3 (intr.), *run out*

excursi-o, -ōnis (f.), *sally*

execror, 1 (tr.), *curse*

exempl-um, -i (n.), *example, precedent*

ex-eo, -ii, -itum, -īre, *go out*

exerceo, 2 (tr.), *train*

exercit-us, -us (m.), *army*

ex-igo, -ēgi, -actum, 3 (tr.), *drive out, exact*

exigu-us, -a, -um, *small*

exili-um, -i (n.), *exile*

eximi-us, -a, -um, *outstanding, picked, excellent*

existimo, 1 (tr.), *think*

exitiābil-is, -e, *destructive*

exit-us, -ūs (m.), *end, exit, way out, result*

expecto, 1 (tr.), *wait for*

expedio, 4, *disentangle, get ready, provide, find means ;* expedit-us, *light-armed*

expediti-o, -ōnis (f.), *expedition*

exper-ior, -tus sum, 4 (tr.), *try, experience*

exper-s, -tis (c. abl. or gen.), *free from, devoid of*

expio, 1 (tr.), *expiate, atone for*

ex-pleo, -plēui, -plētum, 2 (tr.), *fill, make good*

ex-pli-co, -cui, -citum, 1, *form, deploy*

explōrat-or, -ōris (m.), *scout, spy*

explōrō, 1 (tr.), *explore, reconnoitre*

ex-pōno, -posui, -positum, 3 (tr.) *put out, disembark, set forth, explain*

expo-sco, -posci, —, 3 (tr.), *demand*

expugno, 1 (tr.), *take by storm*

exsaeuio, 4 (intr.), *rage to a close*

exsangu-is, -e, *bloodless, fainting*

ex-sequor, -secūtus sum, 3 (tr.), *follow up, execute, perform*

ex-sto, -stiti, -stitum, 1 (intr.), *arise, come forward*

extemplo (adv.), *immediately, forthwith*

ex-tendo, -tendi, -tentum, 3 (tr.), *extend*

extern-us, -a, -um, *foreign, external*

extollo, —, —, 3 (tr.), *extol, exalt*

extra (prep. c. acc. and adv.), *outside*

extrinsecus (adv.), *outside*

exu-l, -lis (m.), *exile*

exulto, 1 (intr.), *exult*

ex-ūro, -ussi, -ustum, 3 (tr.), *burn completely*

exuui-ae, -arum (f.), *spoils*

facil-is, -e, *easy ;* (adv.), *facile*

facin-us, -oris (n.), *crime*

facio, fēci, factum, 3 (tr.), *make produce, do cause ;* factum, *deed*

facult-ās, -ātis (f.), *chance, opportunity, power*

fācund-us, -a, -um, *eloquent*

fallo, fefelli, falsum, 3 (tr.), *deceive, escape the notice of*

fām-a, -ae (f.), *rumour, report, fame*

famili-a, -ae (f.), *family, household*

familiār-is, -e, *intimate, belong to the household*

fās (indecl. subst.), *right, divine law*

fātal-is, -e, *destined, fatal, ordained by fate*

fateor, fassus sum, 2 (tr.), *confess, acknowledge*

fatīgo, 1 (tr.), *weary, trouble*

fāt-um, -i (n.), *fate, doom*

fau-or, -ōris (m.), *favour, popularity*

faut-or, -ōris (m.), *favourer, supporter*

fāx, facis (f.), *torch, meteor*

felīcit-ās, -ātis (f.), *good fortune*

fēl-ix, -īcis, *happy, fortunate*

fem-en, -inis (n.), *thigh*

fēmin-a, -ae (f.), *woman*

fer-a, -ae (f.), *wild beast*

ferio, 4 (tr.), *strike*

ferme (adv.), *nearly, about, generally*

fero, tuli, lātum, ferre (tr.), *bear, carry, carry off, propose, celebrate, say ;* with se, *move, advance*

fer-ox, -ōcis, *bold, confident, passionate, courageous*

ferre-us, -a, -um, *iron*

ferr-um, -i (n.), *iron, the sword*

fess-us, -a, -um, *weary*

festinati-ō, -ōnis (f.), *hurry, haste*

fībul-a, -ae (f.), *broach*

fidēl-is, -e, *faithful, loyal*

fid-ēs, -ēi (f.), *good faith, belief, allegiance, obligation, pledge, protection*

fīdo, fīsus sum, 3 (c. dat.), *trust, confide*

fīdūci-a, -ae (f.), *confidence*

fīd-us, -a, -um, *faithful, loyal*

figūr-a, -ae (f.), *figure, shape*

fīli-a, -ae (f.), *daughter*

fīli-us, -i (m.), *son*

fingo, finxi, fictum, 3 (tr.), *feign, invent, imagine*

fīnio, 4 (tr.), *finish, end*

fīn-is, -is (m. or f.), *end ;* (plur.), *territory*

fīnitim-us, -a, -um, *neighbouring, near*

fīo, factus sum, fieri (pass. of facio), *am made, become, happen*

firm-us, -a, -um, *firm, strong*

flāgro, 1 (intr.), *burn*

flamm-a, -ae (f.), *flame*

flēbil-is, -e, *tearful, sad*

flecto, flexi, flexum, 3 (tr.), *bend, turn, wheel*

fleo, flēui, flētum, 2 (tr. and intr.), *weep, bewail*

flex-us, -ūs (m.), *bend, winding*

flōreo, 2 (intr.), *flourish, am at the prime*

fluct-ūs, -ūs (m.), *wave*

foed-us, -eris (n.), *treaty*

foed-us, -a, -um, *foul, horrible, ghastly, evil*

foris (adv.), *outside, abroad*

form-a, -ae (f.), *shape, plan, beauty*

formīd-o, -inis (f.), *fear*

forsitan, *perhaps*

forte, *perhaps, by chance*

fort-is, -e, *brave*

fortūn-a, -ae (f.), *fortune, hazard, chance*

fortuit-us, -a, -um, *chance, fortuitous*

for-um, -i (n.), *market-place, Forum*

frango, frēgi, fractum, 3 (tr.), *break*

frāt-er, -ris (m.), *brother*

frau-s, -dis (f.), *treachery, hurt, damage*

fremit-us, -ūs (m.), *murmur, noise*

frem-o, -ui, -itum, 3 (intr.), *murmur, make a noise*

frendo, frendui, fresum, 3 (intr.), *gnash*

frēno, 1 (tr.), *curb.*

frequen-s, -tis, *frequent, crowded*

fron-s, -tis (f.), *forehead, front*

frūment-um, -i (n.), *corn*

frustrā (adv.), *in vain*

fug-a, -ae (f.), *flight*

fugā-x, -cis, *fugitive, prone to fly*

fugio, fūgi, -fugitum (tr. and intr.), *fly, flee*

fugitīu-us, -i (m.), *runaway slave*

fugo, 1 (tr.), *put to flight*

fundo, fūdi, fūsum, 3 (tr.), *pour, rout, spread*

fūn-is, -is (m.), *rope*

fūn-us, -eris (n.), *funeral, death*

furi-a, -ae (f.), *fury*

fur-or, -ōris (m.), *madness*

gaudeo, gāuisus sum, 2 (intr.), *rejoice*

gaudi-um, -i (n.), *joy, rejoicing*

gemit-us, -ūs (m.), *groan*

geniāl-is, -e, *nuptial*

gen-s, -tis (f.), *race, nation, family*

gen-ū, -ūs (n.), *knee*

gen-us, -eris (n.), *race, kind*

gero, gessi, gestum, 3 (tr.), *carry, carry on, wage, administer*

gigno, genui, genitum, 3 (tr.), *beget, produce*

gladi-us, -i (m.), *sword*

glōri-a, -ae (f.), *glory*

glōrior, 3 (intr.), *boast, glory in*

grad-us, -ūs (m.), *step, pace*

grātes (f.), *thanks*

grāti-a, -ae (f.), *favour, credit, influence, gratitude, thanks* (pl.); gratiā (c. gen.), *on account of*

grātificor, 1 (tr.), *do a favour to, gratify*

grātulāti-ō, -ōnis (f.), *congratulation, thanks*

grātulor, 1 (intr. c. dat.), *congratulate, thank*

grāt-us, -a, -um, *pleasing, grateful*

grau-is, -e, *heavy, weighed down, serious, powerful;* (adv.), grauiter

grauo, 1 (tr.), *weigh down*

grex, gregis (m.), *herd*

gubernāt-or, -ōris (m.), *pilot, helmsman*

gurges, gurgitis (m.), *eddy, deep water*

habeo, 2 (tr.), *have, keep, hold, consider, deliver (a speech)*; habere honores, *to do honour to*

habito, 1 (tr.), *inhabit*

habit-us, -ūs (m.), *condition, garb, appearance, mien, temper*

hae-reo, -si, -sum, 2 (intr.), *stick fast, remain, am held fast*

harund-o, -inis (f.), *reed*

hast-a, -ae (f.), *spear*

haud, *not;* haudquāquam, *by no means*

hau-rio, -si, -stum, 4 (tr.), *drain, engulf, swallow*

hebeto, 1 (tr.), *blunt*

herb-a, -ae (f.), *grass, herb*

hibernācul-um, -i (n.), *winter quarters*

hiem-s, -is (f.), *winter*

hinc (adv.), *hence, on this side*

homo, hominis (c.), *man, human being*

honest-us, -a, -um, *honourable, good*

hon-or, -ōris (m.), *glory, distinction, office*

hor-a, -ae (f.), *hour*

horde-um, -i (n.), *barley*

horreo, 2 (intr. and tr.), *shudder, dread*

horre-um, -i (n.), *barn, granary*

hortor, 1 (tr.), *exhort*

hospiti-um, -i (n.), *hospitality, ties of hospitality*

hosti-a, -ae (f.), *victim*

hostīl-is, -e, *hostile*

host-is, -is (m.), *enemy*

humānit-ās, -ātis (f.), *humanity, kindness*

humil-is, -e, *low, humble, grovelling*

iaceo, 2 (intr.), *lie, lie low*

iacio, iēci, iactum, 3 (tr.), *throw*

iactāti-o, -ōnis (f.), *shaking, tossing*

iacto, 1 (tr.), *throw, spread abroad, boast*

iactūr-a, -ae (f.), *loss*

iacul-um, -i (n.), *javelin*

iam (adv.), *now, already, further-more ;* iam tum, *even then*

ibi (adv.), *there, then*

īco, īci, ictum, 3 (tr.), *strike, con-clude*

ict-us, -ūs (m.), *blow, stroke*

īdem, eadem, idem, *the same*

īdōne-us, -a, -um, *suitable, fitting*

īdus, -uum (f.), *Ides*

iecur, iecinoris (n.), *liver*

igitur (adv.), *therefore*

ignār-us, -a, -um, *ignorant, unaware*

ignōbil-is, -e, *undistinguished, in-significant*

ignōro, 1 (tr.), *am ignorant of*

ignōt-us, -a, -um, *unknown*

ille-, -a, -ud, *that ;* *he, she, it ;* *the former*

illinc (adv.), *thence, on that side*

illū-cesco, -xi, —, 3 (intr.), *dawn, grow light*

illustr-is, -e, *famous, distinguished*

imāg-o, -inis (f.), *image, portrait*

imbell-is, -e, *unwarlike, non-com-batant*

imb-er, -ris (m.), *rain, shower*

immān-is, -e, *monstrous, cruel*

immineo, 2 (intr.), *overhang, am intent on*

immisceo, -miscui, -mistum or mixtum, 2 (tr.), *intermingle*

im-mitto, -mīsi, -missum, 3 (tr.), *send into, launch into, drive against*

immodic-us, -a, -um, *unrestrained, excessive*

immolo, 1 (tr.), *sacrifice*

immortālit-ās, -ātis (f.), *immor-tality*

impauid-us, -a, -um, *fearless*

impens-a, -ae (f.), *expense*

imperāt-or, -ōris (m.), *commander-in-chief*

imperi-um, -i (n.), *command, authority, empire*

impero, 1 (tr. and intr.), *command, order, rule*

impetrābil-is, -e, *easy to obtain, attainable*

impetro, 1 (tr.), *gain (a request)*

impertio, 4 (tr.), *impart*

impet-us, -ūs (m.), *attack, charge, speed*

impig-er, -ra, -rum, *active, energetic*

implōro, 1 (tr.), *implore*

im-pōno, -posui, -positum, 3 (tr.), *place upon, embark,* (with finem), *put an end to*

impoten-s, -tis, *powerless, uncon-trollable, violent ;* (c. gen.), *unable to control*

improbit-ās, -ātis (f.), *wickedness, unscrupulousness*

improbo, 1 (tr.), *disapprove*

imprōuīso (adv.), *unexpectedly*

imprūdenti-a, -ae (f.), *imprudence, lack of foresight*

impuden-s, -tis, *shameless ;* (adv.), impudenter

impūne (adv.), *with impunity*

impūnit-ās, -ātis (f.), *impunity*

in (prep. c. abl.), *in, on, in the case of ;* (c. acc.), *into, to, towards. against, with a view to, for*

inambulo, 1 (intr.), *walk*

incaute (adv.), *incautiously*

in-cēdo, -cessi, -cessum, 3 (intr.), *go, proceed*

incendi-um, -i (n.), *fire, conflagra-tion*

incen-do, -di, -sum, 3 (tr.), *fire, kindle*

incept-um, -i (n.), *enterprise, under-taking*

in-cido, -cidi, -cāsum, 3, *fall upon, befall*

in-cīdo, -cīdi, -cīsum, 3 (tr.), *cut*

incito, 1 (tr.), *incite, urge on*

inclīno, 1 (tr. and intr.), *incline, bend, give way*

in-clūdo, clūsi, -clūsum, 3 (tr.), shut in

incoho, 1 (tr.), begin

incolum-is, -e, safe, scatheless

incommod-us, -a, -um, inconvenient, disadvantageous

incondit-us, -a, -um, disorderly

incrēment-um, -i (n.), increase

in-crepo, -crepui, -creptium, 1 (tr.), chide, rebuke

in-cruent-us, -a, -um, bloodless

in-cumbo, -cubui, -cubitum, 3 (tr. c. dat.), press on

incūriōse (adv.), carelessly

in-curro, -curri, -cursum, 3 (tr. and intr.), run into, charge

in-cutio, -cussi, -cussum, 3, strike into, inspire (with dat. of indir. obj.)

inde (adv.), thence, thereupon, from that point, therefore

ind-ex, -icis (m.), informer

indico, 1 (tr.), declare, indicate, reveal

indīco, 3, -dixi, -dictum, announce, fix

indigeo, 2 (intr. c. gen.), am in need of

indignāti-o, -ōnis (f.), indignation, anger

indignor, 1 (tr.), resent, am indignant at

indign-us, -a, -um, unworthy, undeserved

in-dūco, -duxi, -ductum, 3 (tr.), lead against, lead into

indul-geo, -si, -tum, 3 (tr. and intr. (c. dat.)), indulge, concede

in-duo, -dui, -dūtum, 3 (tr.), put on, assume

indūro, 1 (tr.), harden

industri-a, -ae (f.), industry, energy; de industria, on purpose

indūti-ae, -arum (f.), truce

inerm-is, -e, unarmed

infāmi-a, -ae (f.), infamy, disgrace

infect-us, -a, -um, undone

in-fero, -tuli, -lātum, -ferre (tr.), carry against, into, wage (war) against

infest-us, -a, -um, hostile, dangerous

infim-us, -a, -um, lowest, grovelling

infirmit-ās, -ātis (f.), weakness

infirm-us, -a, -um, weak

inful-a, -ae (f.), fillet, band

ingem-o, -ui, -itum, 3 (intr.), groan over, lament

ingeni-um, -i, (n.) mind, character, talent

ingen-s, -tis, great, huge

ingrāt-us, -a, -um, unpleasing

in-gredior, -gressus sum (tr. and intr.), go into, enter

inhibeo, 2 (tr.), keep back, back

in-icio, -iēci, -iectum, 3 (tr.), throw on

inimīc-us, -a, -um, hostile, unfriendly ; as a noun, enemy

inīqu-us, -a, -um, unfair, unjust

initi-um, -i (n.), beginning

iniūri-a, -ae (f.), wrong, injury

iniussū (abl. only), without orders

inligo, 1 (tr.), lash, tie

in-necto, -nexui, -nexum, 3 (tr.), bind, fasten

inquam (defect. intr.), say

inquiēt-us, -a, -um, restless, unquiet

inquīsiti-o, -ōnis (f.), inquiry

inrītāment-um, -i (n.), incitement, incentive

inrīto, 1 (tr.), stir up, incite

inrogo, 1 (tr.), impose

in-ruo, -rui, -rutum, 3 (intr.), rush into, upon

insāni-a, -ae (f.), madness

insānio, 4 (intr.), am mad

insepult-us, -a, -um, unburied

in-sequor, -secūtus sum, 3 (tr.), follow

insidi-ae, -ārum (f.), ambush

insidior, 1 (intr.), lay an ambush for, make a surprise attack (c. dat.)

insign-is, -e, conspicuous, marked, distinguished ; insigne (as a noun) badge

in-sisto, -stiti, —, 3 (intr.), proceed, enter upon, begin

insit-us, -a, -um, *implanted, in-grained*

insolenti-a, -ae (f.), *unfamiliarity*

inspērāt-us, -a, -um, *unhoped for, unexpected*

instauro, 1 (tr.), *renew*

instit-uo, -ui, -ūtum, 3 (tr.), *instruct, institute*

institūt-um, -i (n.), *institution*

in-sto, -stiti, —, 1 (intr.), *press upon, pursue*

instrūment-um, -i (n.), *instrument, equipment, gear*

in-struo, -struxi, -structum, 3 (tr.), *draw up, equip*

insuēt-us, -a, -um, *unaccustomed*

insul-a, -ae (f.), *island*

intact-us, -a, -um, *untouched, entire*

integ-er, -ra, -rum, *untouched, intact, fresh*

intemperan-s, -tis, *intemperate, un-restrained*

intempestīu-us, -a, -um, *untimely*

inten-do, -di, -tum, 3 (tr. and intr.), *direct, go ;* intent-us, -a, -um, *alert, intent, strict*

inter (prep. c. acc.), *between, among*

inter-cēdo, -cessi, -cessum, 3, *intervene, veto*

inter-cipio, -cēpi, -ceptum, 3 (tr.), *intercept, cut off, seize*

inter-clūdo, -clūsi, -clūsum, 3 (tr.), *shut off*

intercurs-us, -ūs (m.), *running between*

inter-dīco, -dixi, -dictum, 3 (tr. c. dat.), *forbid*

interdiu (adv.), *by day*

inter-est, -fuit, -esse (impers. c. gen.) (mea, tua, &c., with pronouns of 1st and 2nd persons), *it is to the interest of, concerns ;* (used absolutely) *it makes a difference*

inter-ficio, -fēci, -fectum, 3 (tr.), *kill*

interim (adv.), *meanwhile*

interpr-es, -etis (m.), *interpreter*

interrogo, 1 (tr.), *question*

interuall-um, -i (n.), *interval, gap*

inter-uenio, -uēni, -uentum, 4 (intr. c. dat.), *come upon, interrupt*

intolerābil-is, -e, *unendurable*

intrā (prep. c. acc. and adv.), *inside, within*

intrepid-us, -a, -um, *fearless*

intro, 1 (intr. and tr.), *enter*

intro-dūco, -duxi, -ductum, 3 (tr.), *lead in, introduce*

intro-eo, -ii, -itum, īre, *go in, enter*

intueor, 2 (tr.), *gaze at, see*

intus (adv.), *within*

inuā-do, -si, -sum, 3 (tr.), *invade, assail*

in-ueho, -uexi, -uectum, 3 (tr.), *carry against, to ;* with se pass., *ride against, into*

in-uenio, -uēni, -uentum, 4 (tr.), *find*

in-uideo, -uīdi, -uīsum, 2 (tr.), *envy, grudge, hate*

inuidi-a, -ae (f.), *envy, jealousy, hatred*

inuid-us, -a, -um, *envious, jealous*

inuiolāt-us, -a, -um, *unbroken, inviolate*

inuīs-o, -i, -um, 3 (tr.), *go to see, visit*

inuīt-us, -a, -um, *unwilling*

inundo, 1 (tr.), *flood*

inūtil-is, -e, *useless, unprofitable*

ips-e, -a, -um, *self*

īr-a, -ae (f.), *anger*

īrascor, irātus sum, 3 (intr.), *am angry with* (c. dat.)

is, ea, id, *this, that, he,* &c.

ita (adv.), *thus, so, as follows ;* itaque, *and so, therefore*

it-er, -ineris (n.), *journey, road, march*

iubeo, iussi, iussum, 2 (tr.), *command, order ;* iussum, *a command*

iūdici-um, -i (n.), *judgement, trial, law-court*

iūdıco, 1 (tr.), *judge*

iug-um, -i (n.), *ridge, crest, hill*

iun-go, -xi, -ctum, 3 (tr.), *join, unite*

iurgi-um, -i (n.), *recrimination, dispute*

iūro, 1 (intr.), *swear;* iūrātus, *sworn, on oath*

iūs, iūris (n.), *right authority, justice, law;* iūris dictio, *jurisdiction*

iūsiūrandum, iūrisiūrandi (n.), *oath*

iussu (abl. only), *by order*

iust-us, -a, -um, *just, regular*

iuuen-is, -is, *young, of military age*

iuuent-ūs, -ūtis (f.), *youth*

iuuo, iūui, iūtum, 1 (tr.), *help*

lab-or, -ōris (m.), *labour, hardship*

labōro, 1 (intr.), *labour, be in trouble, in pain*

lacero, 1 (tr.), *tear, wound, shatter*

lacess-o, -īui, -ītum, 3 (tr.), *provoke, harass, challenge*

lacrim-a, -ae (f.), *tear*

laetiti-a, -ae (f.), *joy*

laetor, 1 (intr.), *rejoice, am glad*

laet-us, -a, -um, *glad, rejoicing*

laeu-us, -a, -um, *left*

lapide-us, -a, -um, *of stone*

lapi-s, -dis (m.), *stone*

latebr-a, -ae (f.), *hiding-place*

latrōcini-um, -i (n.), *robbery, brigandage*

lat-us, -eris (n.), *side*

lāt-us, -a, -um, *broad, wide*

lau-s, -dis (f.), *praise, glory*

lēgāti-o, -ōnis (f.), *embassy, deputation*

lēgāt-us, -i (m.), *envoy, deputy, commissioner, general*

legi-o, -ōnis (f.), *legion*

lego, -lēgi, -lectum, 3 (tr.), *choose, gather, read*

lēn-is, -e, *gentle*

lent-us, -a, -um, *slow*

M

leu-is, -e, *light, fickle, easy, insignificant*

leuo, 1 (tr.), *lighten, relieve*

lex, lēgis (f.), *law, term*

libenter (adv.), *gladly*

lībe-r, -ra, -um, *free*

līber-i, -ōrum (m.), *children*

lībero, 1 (tr.), *free*

libīd-o, -inis (f.), *lust, desire, caprice*

lībrāt-us, -a, -um, *forcible, heavy*

licenti-a, -ae (f.), *licence, leave*

lic-et, -uit, -itum, 2 (impers.), *it is allowed*

ligne-us, -a, -um, *wooden*

līm-en, -inis (n.), *threshold*

līne-a, -ae (f.), *line*

lingu-a, -ae (f.), *tongue, language*

litter-ae, -ārum (f.), *letter*

līt-us, -oris (n.), *shore*

lo-cus, -i (m.), *place, station, position*

locust-a, -ae (f.), *locust*

longinqu-us, -a, -um, *far, distant*

long-us, -a, —, -um, *long;* longa nauis, *warship;* (adv.), longe, *far*

loquor, locūtus sum, 3 (tr. and intr.), *speak*

lōrīc-a, -ae (f.), *breastplate*

luct-us, -ūs (m.), *grief, mourning*

lūdibri-um, -i (n.), *mockery*

lūd-us, -i (m.), *game, sport*

lūgubr-is, -e, *mournful, woeful*

luo, lui, lutum, 3 (tr.), *pay, atone for, wipe out*

māchin-a, -ae (f.), *engine*

macto, 1 (tr.), *sacrifice*

maestiti-a, -ae (f.), *sadness*

maest-us, -a, -um, *sad*

magis (adv.), *more, rather*

magist-er, -ri (m.), *master*

magistrāt-us, -ūs (m.), *magistrate, magistracy*

magnific-us, -a, -um, *magnificent*

magnitūd-o, -inis (f.) *greatness, size*

magn-us, -a, -um, *great ;* mai-or,
-us, *greater ;* (plur.), maior-es,
-um, *ancestors ;* maxim-us, -a,
-um, *greatest*

maiest-ās, -ātis (f.), *majesty, dignity*

mālo, mālui, malle, 3 (tr. and
intr.), *prefer*

mal-us, -a, -um, *bad, evil ;* malum
(n.), *evil, disaster*

māl-us, -i (m.), *mast*

mandāt-um, -i (n.), *message,
instruction*

mando, 1 (tr.), *charge, command*
(c. dat. indir. obj.)

man-eo, -si, -sum, 2 (tr. and intr.),
wait, await, remain

manipul-us, -i (m.), *maniple*

man-us, -ūs (f.), *hand, handful, band*

mar-e, -is (n.), *sea*

māteri-a, -ae (f.), *material, timber*

mātrimōnium, -i (n.), *marriage*

mātrōn-a, -ae (f.), *married woman*

mātūro, 1 (tr. and intr,), *hasten,
make haste*

medi-us, -a, -um, *middle, midst of,
in the middle, intervening*

meli-or, -us, *better*

memin-i, -isse (tr. c. gen.), *remember*

mem-or, -oris, *mindful*

memorābil-is, -e, *worthy of mention*

memori-a, -ae (f.), *memory, record,
history, mention*

men-s, -tis (f.), *mind, thought, purpose ;* mens bona, *good sense*

menti-o, -ōnis (f.), *mention*

mercennari-us, -i (m.), *mercenary
soldier*

merc-ēs, -ēdis (f.), *reward, pay*

mereor, 2 (tr.), *deserve, serve in army*

merit-um, -i (n.), *merit, desert*

met-uo, -ui, -ūtum, 3 (tr.), *fear*

met-us, -ūs (m.), *fear*

mīl-es, -itis (m.), *soldier*

mīlitār-is, -e, *military*

mīliti-a, -ae (f.), *military service*

mīlito, 1 (intr.), *serve as a soldier*

min-ae, -ārum (f.), *threats*

minist-er, -ri (m.), *servant*

minor, 1 (tr. and intr. c. dat.
indir. obj.), *threaten*

min-or, -us, *less, smaller ;* minim-
us, -a, -um, *least ;* minus (adv.),
less ; minime, *least, very little,
not at all*

mīror, 1 (tr. and intr.), *wonder,
wonder at*

mīr-us, -a, -um, *wonderful, strange*

misceo, miscui, mixtum, 2 (tr.),
mix, confuse, disturb

miserābil-is, -e, *pitiable*

miseri-a, -ae (f.), *misery*

misericordi-a, -ae (f.), *pity*

missil-is, -e, *missile*

mītis, -e, *gentle*

mitto, mīsi, missum, 3 (tr.), *send,
let go, dismiss*

moderāt-us, -a, -um, *moderate, re-
strained*

modic-us, -a, -um, *moderate, humble,
insignificant*

modi-us, -i (m.), *peck*

modo (adv.), *only, but now, lately ;*
modo . . . modo, *now . . . now*

mod-us, -i (m.), *manner, way,
proper limit, bounds ;* modo (c.
gen.), *like*

moeni-a, -um (n.), *walls, ramparts*

mōl-es, -is (f.), *bulk, weight, difficulty*

molest-us, -a, -um, *troublesome,
vexatious*

mōlior, 4 (intr.), *struggle, exert myself ;* (tr.), *plot, contrive*

mollio, 4 (tr,), *soften, mollify*

moll-is, -e, *soft, gentle*

mōment-um, -i (n.), *movement of
the scale, deciding factor, importance, moment*

moneo, 2 (tr.), *warn, admonish*

mon-s, -tis (m.), *mountain, hill*

mor-a, -ae (f.), *delay ;* in mora esse,
to prevent

mor-ior, -tuus sum, mori, 3 (intr.),
mortuus, *dead*

moror, 1 (tr.), *delay*

mor-s, -tis (f.), *death*

mōs, mōris (m.), *custom, manner ;* mōres, *character, manners ;* more (c. gen.), *after the fashion of*

mōt-us, -ūs (m.), *movement, disturbance, emotion*

moueo, mōui, mōtum, 2 (tr.), *move, remove*

muli-er, -eris (f.), *woman*

mult-a, ae (f.), *fine, indemnity ;* (adj.), multātici-us, -a, -um, *resulting from a fine*

multi-plex, -plicis, *manifold*

multiplico, 1 (tr.), *multiply*

multitūd-o, -inis (f.), *multitude*

mūnio, 4 (tr.), *fortify*

mūn-us, -eris (n.), *gift, duty, task*

mūr-us, -i (m.), *wall*

mū-s, -ris (m.), *mouse*

mūtilo, 1 (tr.), *mutilate*

mūtuor, 1 (tr.), *borrow*

mūtu-us, -a, -um, *mutual, borrowed*

nāt-us, -a, -um, *born*

nātu (abl. only), *by birth*

nātūr-a, -ae (f.), *nature*

naufragi-um, -i (n.), *shipwreck*

naut-a, -ae (m.), *sailor*

nautic-us, -a, -um, *naval ;* nauticus, *seaman*

nāuāl-is, -e, *naval*

nāuigāti-o, -ōnis (f.), *navigation, voyage*

nāuigo, 1 (intr.), *navigate, sail*

nāu-is, -is (f.), *ship*

nāuiter (adv.), *strenuously, actively*

nāuo, 1, (tr.), *perform actively*

nē (conj.), *that not, lest ;* nē . . . quidem, *not even*

necessāri-us, -a, -um, *necessary*

neco, 1 (tr.), *kill*

nēdum (adv.), *not to speak of, much more, much less*

nefāri-us, -a, -um, *wicked, criminal*

neglegenti-a, -ae (f.), *negligence, carelessness*

neg-lego, -lexi, -lectum, 3 (tr.), *neglect*

nego, 1 (tr.), *deny*

nēmo (gen., nullius), *no one*

nēquāquam (adv.), *not at all*

nēquīquam (adv.), *in vain*

neque (nec), *and not, nor ;* nec . . . nec, *neither . . . nor*

ne-queo, -quīui, -quītum, -quīre (intr.), *am unable*

neu-ter, -tra, -trum, *neither*

neutiquam (adv.), *by no means*

nex, necis (f.), *death*

nihil (indecl. n.), *nothing ;* (adv.), *not at all*

nīmīrum (adv.), *no wonder, without doubt, assuredly*

nimis (adv.), *too much, excessively*

nimi-us, -a, -um, *too much, excessive*

nisi, ni (conj.), *unless, if not*

nōbil-is, -e, *famous, well known, noble*

nōbilito, 1 (tr.), *render famous*

noctu (abl. only), *by night*

nocturn-us, -a, -um, *nightly, during the night*

nōlo, nōlui, nolle (tr. and intr.), *am unwilling, do not wish, refuse*

nōm-en, -inis (n.), *name, fame, race*

non (adv.), *not*

nondum (adv.), *not yet*

nōs, *we*

nosco, nōui, nōtum, 3 (tr.), *know, enquire into ;* nōt-us, -a, -um, *known*

nost-er, -ra, -rum, *our*

nōtiti-a, -ae (f.), *knowledge*

nou-us, -a, -um, *new, strange ;* nouissim-us, -a, -um, *last*

nox, noctis (f.), *night*

nox-a, -ae (f.), *guilt, crime, harm*

nūbil-is, -e, *marriageable*

nū-bo, -psi, -ptum, 3 (tr. and intr. (c. dat.)), *marry*

nūdo, 1 (tr.), *lay bare, strip*

null-us, -a, -um, *no*

numer-us, -i (m.), *number, class, category*

nunc (adv.), *now, as matters stand*

nunquam (adv.), *never*

nuntio, 1 (tr.), *announce, report*

nunti-us, -i (m.), *messenger, news*

nupti-ae, -ārum (f.), *wedding*

nuptiāl-is, -e, *nuptial*

nusquam (adv.), *nowhere*

ob (prep. c. acc.), *on account of*

obequito, 1 (intr.), *ride up to, against*

ob-icio, -iēci, -iectum, 3 (tr.), *throw in the way, expose*

obligo, 1 (tr.), *bind, pledge*

obliquu-us, -a, -um, *slanting*

obliuiscor, oblītus sum, 3 (tr.), *forget*

oboedienter (adv.), *obediently*

oboedio, 4 (intr. c. dat.), *obey*

ob-orior, -ortus sum, 4 (intr.), *rise*

ob-ruo, -rui, -rutum, 3 (tr.), *overwhelm*

obscūr-us, -a, -um, *obscure*

obseruo, 1 (tr.), *observe*

ob-sideo, -sēdi, -sessum, 2 (tr.), *besiege, blockade*

obsidi-o, -ōnis (f.), *siege*

ob-sisto, -stiti, -stitum, 3 (intr. c. dat.), *withstand, stand in the way of*

obsit-us, -a, -um, *covered with*

obsolēt-us, -a, -um, *obsolete, outworn*

obstīnāt-us, -a, -um, *obstinate*

ob-stringo, -strinxi, -strictum, 3 (tr.), *bind, pledge*

ob-struo, -struxi, -structum, 3 (tr.), *block, obstruct*

ob-tero, -trīui, -trītum, 3, (tr.), *crush*

obtestor, 1 (tr.), *implore*

ob-tineo, -tenui, -tentum, 2 (tr. and intr.), *hold, keep, gain currency*

obtrectāti-o, -ōnis (f.), *disparagement*

ob-uenio, -uēni, -uentum, 4 (intr.), *come into, meet, befall, fall to the lot of*

obuersor, 1 (intr.), *move before, present itself to*

obui-us, -a, -um, *in the way of meeting*

occāsi-o, -ōnis (f.), *occasion, opportunity*

occās-us, -ūs (m.), *setting*

occidi-o, -ōnis (f.), *destruction*

occī-do, -di, -sum, 3 (tr.), *kill*

occul-o, -ui, -tum, 3 (tr.), *hide*

occupo, 1 (tr.), *occupy, seize*

oc-curro, -curri, -cursum, 3 (intr. c. dat.), *meet*

ocul-us, -i (m.), *eye*

od-or, -ōris (m.), *smell*

offero, obtuli, oblātum, offerre (tr.), *offer*

offici-um, -i (n.), *kindness, attention, good office, duty*

ole-a, -ae (f.), *olive*

ōm-en, -inis (n.), *omen*

ōminor, 1 (tr.), *divine, presage*

om-itto, -īsi, -issum, 3 (tr.), *let go, abandon*

omn-is, -e, *all, every*

onerāri-a, -ae (f.), *transport, cargo vessel*

onero, 1 (tr.), *load*

on-us, -eris (n.), *load, burden*

onust-us, -a, -um, *laden, burdened*

oper-a, -ae (f.), *work, service;* operam dare, *pay attention;* operam nauare, *to act vigorously*

oportet, 2 (impers.), *it behoves*

opper-ior, -tus sum, 4 (tr.), *wait for*

oppid-um, -i (n.), *town*

op-pōno, -posui, -positum, 3 (tr.), *place opposite, oppose, expose*

opportūn-us, -a, -um, *opportune, suitable*

op-primo, -pressi, -pressum, 3 (tr.), *crush, surprise, overwhelm* oppugno, 1 (tr.), *attack*

(ops), opis (f.), *help ;* opes, *wealth, resources*

opulent-us, -a, -um, *wealthy, powerful*

orāti-o, -ōnis (f.), *speech ;* orationem habere, *to deliver a speech*

orāt-or, -ōris (m.), *orator, envoy*

orb-is, -is (m.), *circle, orb ;* orbis terrarum, *world*

orbo, 1 (tr.) (c. acc. of pers., abl. of thing of which deprived), *deprive, bereave*

ordino, 1 (tr.), *draw up, organise*

ord-o, -inis (m.), *order, rank, line, centurion*

or-ior, -tus sum, 4 (intr.), *rise, begin, dawn ;* oriundus, *sprung from*

ornāt-us, -ūs (m.), *ornament, decoration*

orno, 1 (tr.), *adorn, equip*

ōro, 1 (tr.), *entreat, plead*

ort-us, -ūs (m.), *rising*

osten-do, -di, -sum *or* -tum, 3 (tr.), *display, show, set forth*

ostento, 1 (tr.), *display, show*

ōti-um, -i (n.), *leisure, peace*

pāco, 1 (tr.), *appease, pacify*

paenitet, 2 (impers.), *it repents*

palam (adv.), *openly*

palmāt-us, -a, -um, *embroidered with palms*

pālor, 1 (tr.), *straggle, stray*

pango, pepigi, pactum, 3 (tr.), *strike, plight*

par, paris, *equal, like ;* pariter (adv.), *equally, at once*

paren-s, -tis (c.), *parent*

pario, peperi, partum, 3 (tr.), *bring forth, get, acquire*

paro, 1 (tr.), *prepare, get ;* parāt-us, -a, -um, *ready*

par-s, -tis (f.), *part, side, direction ;* partim, *partly*

parum (indecl. noun and adv.), *little, too little*

paru-us, -a, -um, *small*

passim (adv.), *in every direction, far and wide*

pass-us, -ūs (m.), *pace*

pate-facio, -fēci, -factum, 3 (tr.), *open*

pateo, 2 (intr.), *lie open*

pat-er, -ris (m.), *father ;* patres, *the senate*

pater-a, -ae (f.), *cup, bowl*

patern-us, -a, -um, *paternal*

patienti-a, -ae (f.), *patience, endurance*

patior, passus sum, 3 (tr.), *suffer, endure, permit*

patri-a, -ae (f.), *native land*

patri-us, -a, -um, *of one's father, of one's country*

patru-us, -i (m.), *uncle*

pauc-us, -a, -um, *few*

paueo, pāui, 2, (intr.), *am afraid*

pauid-us, -a, -um, *afraid*

paulātim (adv.), *little by little*

paulisper (adv.), *a little while*

paulo (adv.), *by a little*

pau-or, -ōris (m.), *fear*

pax, pācis (f.), *peace*

pecco, 1, (intr.), *sin, err*

pecūni-a, -ae (f.), *money*

ped-es, -itis (m.), *foot-soldier*

pello, pepuli, pulsum, 3 (tr.), *drive back, away ; strike, move*

penāt-es, -ium (m.), *household gods*

penes (prep. c. acc.), *in power of, in possession of*

pensi-o, ōnis (f.), *payment, instalment*

penso, 1 (tr.), *weigh, compensate*

per (prep. c. acc.), *through, along, over, during, by, among*

peragro, 1 (tr.), *overrun*

per-cello, -culi, -culsum, 3 (tr.), *strike (with dismay)*

percunctor, 1 (tr. and intr.), *ask, inquire*

per-do, -didi, -ditum, 3 (tr.), *ruin, destroy, lose*

per-domo, -ui, -itum, 1 (tr.), *subdue utterly*

per-dūco, -duxi, -ductum, 3 (tr.), *lead through*

per-eo, -ii, -itum, -īre (intr.), *perish, am wasted*

perfidi-a, -ae (f.), *faithlessness, treachery*

perfug-a, -ae (m.), *deserter*

per-fugio, -fūgi, —, 3 (intr.), *take refuge*

per-fundo, -fūdi, -fūsum, 3 (tr.), *steep, drench*

per-go, -rexi, -rectum, 3 (intr.), *go, proceed* (oft. c. acc.)

pergrand-is, -e, *very large*

perīcul-um, -i (n.), *danger*

perīt-us, -a, -um, *skilful, skilled in* (c. gen.)

per-misceo, -miscui, -mixtum, 2 (tr.), *mix, confuse*

per-mitto, -mīsi, -missum, 3 (tr.), *entrust, permit* (c. dat. of indir. obj.), with equos, *gallop*

permūnio, 4 (tr.), *fortify thoroughly*

pernici-es', -ēi (f.), *destruction*

peropportūn-us, -a, -um, *most opportune*

perperam (adv.), *wrongly*

perplexe (adv.), *obscurely*

per-sequor, -secūtus sum, 3 (tr.), *follow up, avenge*

pertin-ax, -ācis, *obstinate*

pertinet, 2 (impers.), *belongs to, concerns*

per-traho, -traxi, -tractum, 3 (tr.), *draw right on*

perturbo, 1 (tr.), *disturb, throw into disorder*

peruagor, 1 (intr.), *roam about*

per-uenio, -uēni, -uentum, 4 (intr.), *arrive, come*

perui-um, -i (n.,) *a way through, passage*

pest-is, -is (f.), *plague, curse*

pet-o, -īui, -ītum, 3 (tr.), *seek, aim at, attack*

phalerāt-us, -a, -um, *adorned with trappings, caparisoned*

piācular-is, -e, *expiatory*

pict-us, -a, -um, *painted, embroidered*

pīle-us, -i (m.), *cap (of liberty).*

pīl-um, -i (n.), *heavy javelin*

pi-us, -a, -um, *dutiful, pious, loving*

placeo, 2 (intr.), *please*

plāco, 1 (tr.), *appease*

plēr-ique, -aeque, -aque, *many, most ;* plērumque (adv.), *for the most part*

plōrāt-us, -ūs (m.), *lamentation*

pluo, plui,—,3 (intr.), *rain*

plūrim-us, -a, -um, *most, very much, very many*

plū-s, -ris (n.) (noun or adv. in sing. adj. in plur.), *more, many, several*

pōcul-um, -i (n.), *cup*

poen-a, -ae (f.), *penalty, punishment*

pomp-a, -ae (f.), *procession*

pondo (abl. only), *by weight*

pond-us, -eris (n.), *weight*

pon-s, -tis (m.), *bridge, gangway*

pontif-ex,-icis (m.),*pontiff ;* (adj.), pontificius

populār-is, -e, *popular ;* populares, *people, countrymen*

pōpulāti-o, -ōnis (f.), *devastation*

pōpulāt-or, -ōris (m.), *devastator*

pōpulor, 1 (tr.), *ravage, devastate*

popul-us, -i (m.), *people*

porrigo (porgo), porrexi, porrectum, 3 (tr.), *stretch out*

porro (adv.), *further*

port-a, -ae (f.), *gate*

porten-do, -di, -tum, 3 (tr.), *portend*

porto, 1 (tr.), *carry*

port-us, -ūs (m.), *port, harbour*

possessi-o, -ōnis (f.), *possession*

possum, potui, posse, *am able, am powerful*

post (adv. and prep. c. acc.), *after, behind*

posteā (adv.), *afterwards*

poster-us, -a, -um, *following, next ;* (superl.), postrem-us, -a, -um, *last ;* (adv.) postremo, *lastly ;* ad postremum, *at last*

postmodo (adv.), *afterwards*

postquam (conj.), *after that, after*

postulo, 1 (tr.), *demand*

poten-s, -tis, *powerful ;* (superl.), potentissimus

potenti-a, -ae (f.), *power*

potest-ās, -ātis (f.), *power, opportunity*

potior, 4 (tr.), *get possession of* (c. gen. or abl.)

potissimum (adv.), *preferably, especially*

prae (prep. c. abl.), *before, by reason of, through ;* prae se ferre, *display*

praebeo, 2 (tr.), *show, provide, present, render*

prae-cēdo, -cessi, -cessum, 3 (intr.), *go before, precede*

prae-ceps, -cipitis, *headlong, precipitate*

praecept-um, -i (n.), *precept, instruction, order*

prae-cipio, -cēpi, -ceptum, 3 (tr.), *secure in advance, instruct*

praecipu-us, -a, -um, *special*

praec-o, -ōnis (m.), *herald*

praed-a, -ae (f.), *booty, spoil*

praedor, 1 (tr.), *plunder*

praefect-us, -i (m.), *commander*

prae-ficio, -fēci, -fectum, 3 (tr.), *place in command of*

prae-figo, fixi, -fixum, 3 (tr.), *fix, fit in front*

prae-gredior, 3 (tr. and intr.), *precede, go in front*

prae-mitto, -mīsi, -missum, 3 (tr.), *send ahead*

praemi-um, -i (n.), *reward*

praenom-en, -inis (n.), *first name*

praeparo, 1 (tr.), *prepare in advance*

prae-pōno, -posui, -positum, 3 (tr.), *place in command of*

praerapid-us, -a, -um, *very swift*

praesāgio, 4 (tr.), *presage*

praesen-s, -tis, *present, ready (money)*

praesenti-a (f.), *presence, present time*

praesidi-um, -i (n.), *garrison, guard, post, protection*

prae-sto, -stiti, -itum *or* -atum, 1 (tr. and intr.), *show, make good, guarantee, excel*

prae-sum, -fui, -esse, *am in command* (c. dat.)

praeter (prep. c. acc.), *past, along, besides, except, contrary to*

praeterēa (adv.), *besides*

praeterit-us, -a, -um, *past*

praeter-mitto, -mīsi, -missum, 3 (tr.), *omit, neglect*

praeterquam (adv.), *besides, except*

praeter-uehor, -uectus sum, 3 (intr.), *am carried by, sail by*

praetōria nāuis, *flagship*

praetōri-um, -i (n.), *headquarters council of war*

praeualid-us, -a, -um, *very strong*

preces, precum (f.), *prayers*

preti-um, -i (n.), *price, reward, payment*

pridie, *on the day before*

prīm-us, -a, -um, *first ;* (adv.), primo, *at first ;* primum, *first*

prin-ceps, -cipis (m.), *leader, head ;* (adj.), *first, chief*

principi-um, -i, (n.), *beginning*

pri-or, -us, *former, previous ;* (adv.), prius, *before*

prīuāt-us, -a, -um, *private ;* (adv.) priuatim

priusquam (conj.), *before that, before*

pro (prep. c. abl.), *for, in front of, on behalf of, instead of, in proportion to, in conformity with, in the light of*

probr-um, ĭ (n.), *insult*

prob-us, -a, -um, *honest ;* (adv.), probē, *rightly, quite*

pro-cēdo, -cessi, -cessum, 3 (intr.), *advance, proceed, go forward*

procell-a, -ae, (f.), *storm, combat*

procul (adv.), *at or from a distance*

prō-cumbo, -cubui, -cubitum, 3 (intr.), *fall prostrate*

prō-curro, -curri, -cursum, 3 (intr.), *run forward*

prōd-eo, -ii, -īre, *go forth*

prōdigi-um, -i (n.), *prodigy*

prōdit-or, -oris (m.), *traitor*

prō-do, -didi, -ditum, 3 (tr.), *betray, publish*

prō-dūco, -duxi, -ductum, 3 (tr.), *lead forward*

proeli-um, -i (n.), *battle*

profecti-o, -ōnis (f.), *setting forth, departure*

prō-fero, -tuli, -lātum, -ferre (tr.), *carry forward*

proficiscor, profectus sum, 3 (intr.), *set out, depart*

prō-fiteor, fessus sum, 2 (tr.), *declare*

profund-us, -a, -um, *deep*

prohibeo, 2 (tr.), *prevent, ward off*

prō-icio, -iēci, -iectum, 3 (tr.), *throw, abandon*

prō-lābor, -lapsus sum, 3 (intr.), *fall*

prōmiss-um, -i (n.), *promise*

prōm-o, -psi, -ptum, 3 (tr.), *produce, bring out*

prompt-us, -a, -um, *prompt, ready*

prōmunturi-um, -i (n.), *promontory, cape*

prōnuntio, 1 (tr.), *proclaim, order*

prope (prep. c. acc.), *near ;* (adv.), *near, nearly ;* (comp.), propi-or, -us ; (superl.), proxim-us, -a, -um

propediem (adv.), *at a near date, shortly*

propinquit-ās, -ātis (f.), *nearness*

propinqu-us, -a, -um, *near, related ;* (as a noun.), *relative*

prō-pōnō, -posui, -positum, 3 (tr.), *put before, propose*

propri-us, -a, -um, *one's own, special, proper ;* proprie, *peculiarly*

prōpugnacul-um, -i (n.), *defence, bulwark*

prōpugnāt-or, -ōris (m.), *defender*

prōr-a, -ae (f.), *prow*

prō-ripio, -ripui, -raptum, 3 (tr.), *snatch forth ;* (with) se, *rush forth*

prōrogo, 1 (tr.), *prolong*

prorsus (adv.), *straightway, absolutely*

prō-sequor, -secūtus sum, 3 (tr.), *escort*

prōspecto, 1 (tr.), *gaze forth on, view*

prōspect-us, -ūs (m.), *view, prospect*

prosper-us, -a, -um, *prosperous*

prō-spicio, -spexi, -spectum, 3 (tr. and intr.), *look forward at, look forward*

prō-sum, -fui, -desse, *profit, be of advantage*

prō-uehor, -uectus sum, 3 (intr.), *advance, sail out*

prōuidenti-a, -ae (f.), *foresight, seeing ahead*

prōuinci-a, -ae (f.), *province, sphere of operations*

prout (conj.), *according as*

prūdenti-a, -ae (f.), *prudence, skill*

public-us, -a, -um, *public, national, belonging to the State*

pud-or, -ōris (m.), *shame, modesty, honour*

pue-r, -ri (m.), *boy*

pugn-a, -ae (f.) *fight*

puluīnā-r, -ris (n.), *couch*

pupp-is, -is (f.), *stern*

purgo, 1 (tr.), *excuse, clear*

purpure-us, -a, -um, *crimson*

quā (adv.), *where, by which way ;* (after ne), *anywhere*

quācunque (adv.), *wherever*

quadru-plex, -plicis, *fourfold*

quae-ro, -siui, -situm, 3 (tr.), *seek, seek out, enquire*

quaeso, quaesumus, *I seek, I pray you*

quaesti-o, -ōnis (f.), *enquiry*

quāl-is, -e, *of what kind*

quāl-iscunque, -ecunque, *such as it is, of whatever quality*

quam (adv.), *than, as, how ;* also used to strengthen superlatives

quamquam (adv.), *although, and yet*

quamuis (adv.), *although, however*

quant-us, -a, -um, *how great, how much ;* (adv.), quantum, *as far as*

quantuscunque, *how great soever, of whatever size*

quasso, 1 (tr.), *shake, strain*

quemadmodum (adv.), *how, as*

querell-a, -ae (f.), *complaint*

que-ror, -stus sum, 3 (intr.), *complain*

qui (adv.), *how ? how*

quia (conj.), *because*

quidam, quaedam, quoddam, *a certain*

quidem, *indeed ;* ne . . . quidem, *not even*

quiesco, quiēui, quiētum, 3 (intr.), *am quiet, rest*

quiēt-us, -a, -um, *quiet*

quin (conj.), *but that, but*

quippe (adv.), *assuredly, for*

quis, quid, 1 (indef. pron.), *any one, any thing ;* 2 (interrog. pron.), *who ? what ?*

quisquam, quicquam, *any one, anything*

quisque, quaeque, quidque, quodque (pron. and adj.), *each, each one*

quo (adv.), *whither*

quoad (conj.), *as long as, until*

quod (conj.), *that, because*

quodsi (conj.), *but if, and if*

quomodo, *how, as*

quondam (adv.), *formerly*

quoniam (conj.), *since*

quoque (adv.), *also*

quot (indecl. adj.), *as many as, how many*

rām-us, -i (m.), *bough*

rap-io, -ui, -tum, 3 (tr.), *snatch, carry off, hurry on, sweep away, plunder ;* rapto uiuere, *to live by plunder*

raptim (adv.), *hastily, rapidly*

rāro (adv.), *rarely*

rati-o, -ōnis (f.), *reason, system, method, accounts*

rat-us, -a, -um, *ratified*

recen-s, -tis, *fresh, recent*

recept-us, -ūs (m.), *retreat, retirement*

re-cido, -ccidi, -cāsum, 3 (intr.), *fall back*

recipero, 1 (tr.), *recover*

re-cipio, -cēpi, -ceptum, 3 (tr.), *take, recover, receive back, withdraw*

reconcilio, 1 (tr.), *reconcile, win back*

recordāti-o, -ōnis (f.), *remembrance*

recte (adv.), *rightly*

re-curro, -curri, -cursum, 3 (intr.), *run back*

recūso, 1 (tr.), *refuse*

red-do, -didi, -ditum, 3 (tr.), *restore, render*

red-eo, -ii, -itum, -īre, *return, go back*

red-igo, -ēgi, -actum, 3 (tr.), *bring back, reduce, collect*

red-imo, -ēmi, -emptum, 3 (tr.), *purchase, ransom, buy back* redintegro, 1 (tr.), *renew*

redit-us, -ūs (m.), *return*

re-dūco, -duxi, -ductum, 3 (tr.) *lead back, bring back*

redu-x, -cis, *returning*

re-fero, -ttuli, -lātum, -ferre (tr.), *carry back, refer, relate, report, bring forward a proposal*

refert-us, -a, -um, *full, crammed*

re-ficio, -fēci, -fectum, 3 (tr.), *refresh, repair*

re-fringo, -frēgi, -fractum, 3 (tr.), *break open*

re-fugio, -fūgi, —, 3 (intr.), *flee back*

rēgi-a, -ae (f.), *palace*

regi-o, -ōnis (f.), *district, region, direction*

rēgi-us, -a, -um, *royal*

regno, 1 (intr.), *reign*

regn-um, -i (n.), *kingdom, kingship*

rego, rexi, rectum, 3 (tr.), *rule, direct, guide*

rēgul-us, -i, (m.), *prince, petty king*

rē-icio, -iēci, -iectum, 3 (tr.), *throw back, refer*

religi-o, -ōnis (f.) *scruple, punctiliousness, religious fear, religious observance*

re-linquo, -līqui, -lictum, 3 (tr.), *leave, abandon*

reliqui-ae, -arum (f.), *remnants*

reliqu-us, -a, -um, *left over, remaining*

re-lūceo, -luxi, —, 2 (intr.), *shine back, am reflected*

rēm-ex, -igis (m.), *rower, oarsman*

re-mitto, -mīsi, -missum, 3 (tr.), *send back, slacken*

re-moueo, -mōui, -motum, 2 (tr.), *remove*

renouo, 1 (tr.), *renew*

renuntio, 1 (tr.), *bring back news, report*

reor, ratus sum, 2 (tr.), *think*

reparo, 1 (tr.), *renew, revive, reinforce*

repente (adv.), *suddenly*

repentīn-us, -a, -um, *sudden ;* (adv.), repentīno

repet-o, -īui, -ītum, 3 (tr.), *seek again, recover, reclaim*

re-pleo, -plēui, -plētum, 2 (tr.), *fill*

re-pōno, -posui, -positum, 3 (tr.), *place, replace, put aside*

reporto, 1 (tr.), *bring back*

reprehen-do, -di, -sum, 3 (tr.), *blame, criticise, rebuke*

repugno, 1 (intr.), *resist*

reputo, 1 (tr. and intr.), *reflect, consider*

res, rei (f.), *thing, affair, circumstance, deed, action, property ;* in rem, *to the point ;* res publica (respublica), *state, commonweal, public affairs*

re-sisto, -stiti, —, 3 (intr.), *halt, stand fast, resist* (c. dat.)

respect-us, -ūs (m.), *looking back, regard*

re-spicio, -spexi, -spectum, 3 (tr. and intr.), *look back at, consider*

re-spondeo, -spondi, -sponsum, 2 (intr.), *reply, answer expectations*

respons-um, -i (n.), *reply*

restin-guo, -xi, -ctum, 3 (tr.), *extinguish*

restito, 1 (intr.), *hang back*

restit-uo, -ui, -ūtum, 3 (tr.), *restore*

re-sto, -stiti, —, (intr.), *stand fast, remain*

re-tineo, -tinui, -tentum, 2 (tr.), *hold back, keep back, retain*

re-traho, -traxi, -tractum, 3 (tr.), *drag back*

retro (adv.), *backward, behind*

re-uerto, -uerti, -uersum, 3 (tr. and intr.), *turn back, return ;* (pass.), *turn back, return*

reuoco, 1 (tr.), *call back*

rex, rēgis (m.), *king*

rī-deo, -si, -sum, 2 (intr.), *laugh, smile*

rīs-us, -ūs (m.), *laughter, smile*

rīt-us, -ūs (m.), *rite, custom*

rŏb-ur, -oris (n.), *strength, solidity, main body, pick*

rogati-ō, -ōnis (f.), *proposal brought before the popular assembly*

rostrāt-a, -ae (f.), *beaked ship, warship*

rostr-um, -i (n.), *beak, ram;* (plur.), rostra, *platform from which speeches were made in the forum*

rub-or, -ōris (m.), *blush*

ruīn-a, -ae (f.), *ruin*

rumpo, rūpi, ruptum, 3 (tr.), *break*

ruo, rui, rutum, 3 (intr.), *rush, fall*

rursus (adv.), *again, on the other hand*

sac-er, -ra, -rum, *sacred;* sacrum, sacra, *rites, sacrifice*

sacrifico, 1 (tr. and intr.), *sacrifice*

saepe (adv.), *often*

saeuio, 4 (intr.), *rage, am infuriated, act cruelly*

saeu-us, -a, -um, *fierce, cruel*

sagul-um, -i (n.), *cloak*

sal-ūs, ūtis (f.), *safety, health*

salūtār-is, -e, *salutary*

salūto, 1 (tr.), *salute, greet*

san-cio, -xi, -ctum, 4 (tr.), *decree, ordain;* sanct-us, -a, -um, *venerable, good, holy*

sangu-is, -inis (m.), *blood*

sapio, 3 (intr.), *am wise*

sati-ās, -ātis (f.), *satiety*

satiet-ās, -ātis (f.), *satiety*

satio, 1 (tr.), *satiate, glut*

satis (adv.), *enough;* with adj. *tolerably, fairly, quite;* satin= satisne?

sauci-us, -a, -um, *wounded, crippled*

scan-do, -di, -sum, 3 (tr.), *climb, scale*

scel-us, -eris (n.), *crime*

scindo, scidi, scissum, 3 (tr.), *tear, cut*

scio, 4 (tr.), *know*

scipi-o, -onis (m.), *staff, sceptre*

scrīb-a, -ae (m.), *scribe*

scrībo, scripsi, scriptum, 3 (tr.), *write, enrol, inscribe*

se-clūdo, -clūsi, -sum, 3 (tr.), *shut off*

sēcrēt-um, -i (n.), *secret place*

secundum (prep. c. acc.), *after, next, according to*

secund-us, -a, -um, *second, favourable*

secūr-is, -is (f.), *axe*

sed, *but*

sedeo, sēdi, sessum, 2 (intr.), *sit*

sēd-ēs, -is (f.), *seat, dwelling*

sēditi-o, -ōnis (f.), *mutiny, sedition*

segn-is, -e, *slow, sluggish*

sell-a, -ae (f.), *chair*

sēmerm-is, -e, *half-armed*

sēmilix-a, -ae (m.), *half a camp follower*

sēmisomn-us, -a, -um, *half asleep*

senāt-us, -us (m.), *senate*

senesco, senui, 3 (intr.), *grow old, decay, weaken*

sen-ex, -is, *old man, senior, older*

sensim (adv.), *gradually*

sententi-a, -ae (f.), *opinion, proposal, decision*

sen-tio, -si, -sum, 4 (tr.), *feel, perceive, hold an opinion*

sēparātim (adv.), *separately*

sepulcr-um, -i (n.), *tomb*

sequor, secūtus sum, 3 (tr.), *follow*

serēnit-ās, -ātis (f.), *fair, bright weather*

seri-ēs, -ēi (f.), *succession, row*

serm-o, -ōnis (m.), *talk, speech*

ser-po, -psi, -ptum, 3 (intr.), *creep*

seruīl-is, -e, *of a slave, slavish*

seruio, 4 (intr.), *am a slave, serve*

seruiti-um, -i (n.), *slavery, slave*

seru-us, -ī (m.), *slave*

si (conj.), *if*

sic (conj.), *so, thus*

sicc-us, -a, -um, *dry;* siccum, *dry land*

sīcut, sīcuti (conj.), *just as*

significo, 1 (tr.), *signify, indicate*

sign-um, -i (n.), *sign, signal, standard;* signa conferre, *join battle;* signa ferre, *advance*

silenti-um, -i (n.), *silence*

simil-is, -e, *like*

simul (adv.), *at the same time, at the same time as*

simulācr-um, -i (n.), *semblance, likeness*

simulāti-o, -ōnis (f.), *pretence*

simulo, 1 (tr.), *pretend, feign*

sincēr-us, -a, -um, *sincere, intact, unshaken*

sine (prep. c. abl.), *without*

singulār-is, -e, *unique, peculiar*

singul-i, -ōrum, *one each, individuals*

sinist-er, -ra, -rum, *left*

sino, sīui, situm, 3 (tr.), *allow*

sin-us, -ūs (m.), *hollow, gulf, bay*

sisto, —, —, 3 (tr.), *stop, place*

sit-us, -ūs (m.), *site, position*

sit-us, -a, -um, *placed, situated*

soc-er, eri (m.), *father-in-law*

societā-s, -tis (f.), *alliance*

soci-us, -a, -um, *allied, associated;* socius, *ally, comrade*

sōl, sōlis (m.), *sun*

solāci-um, -i (n.), *solace, consolation*

soleo, solitus sum, 2 (intr.), *am wont;* solit-us, -a, -um, *usual, wonted*

sollicito, 1 (tr.), *trouble, vex, disturb*

sollicit-us, -a, -um, *anxious, troubled*

sōlor, 1 (tr.), *console*

sol-um, -i (n.), *ground, soil*

sol-uo, -ui, -utum, 3 (tr.), *loose, pay;* soluere classem (nauem), *set sail*

sōl-us, -a, -um, *alone, only;* (adv.), solum

somn-us, -i (m.), *sleep*

son-s, -tis, *guilty*

sōpīt-us, -a, -um, *asleep*

sord-ēs, -ium (f.), *squalor, filth*

sor-s, -tis (f.), *lot*

sortior, 4 (tr. and intr.), *draw lots, secure by lot*

spar-go, -si, -sum, 3 (tr.), *scatter*

spati-um (n.), *space, distance*

speci-ēs, -ēi (f.), *appearance, sight, show, semblance, pretext*

speciōs-us, -a, -um, *beautiful, plausible*

spectācul-um, -i (n.), *sight, show*

specto, 1 (tr.), *look at, view;* (intr.), *look on, point to;* spectāt-us, -a, -um, *proved*

specul-a, -ae (f.), *look-out*

speculāt-or, -ōris (m.), *spy, scout;* (adj.), speculatori-us, -a, -um

speculor, 1 (tr.), *watch, observe, spy out*

sperno, sprēui, sprētum, 3 (tr.), *despise*

spēro, 1 (tr.), *hope, expect*

spēs, spēi (f.), *hope, expectation*

spīrit-us, -ūs (m.), *breath, spirit, pride*

spoliāti-o, -ōnis (f.), *spoliation, plundering*

spolio, 1 (tr.), *despoil*

spoli-um, -i (n.), *spoil*

spondeo, spopondi, sponsum, 2 (tr.), *pledge, promise*

sponte (abl. only), *of my own accord, voluntarily, spontaneously*

stabil-is, -e, *stable, steady, firm*

stati-o, -ōnis (f.), *post, outpost, station*

stat-uo, -ui, utum, 3 (tr.), *place, appoint, decide*

stat-us, -ūs (m.), *condition, position*

stimulo, 1 (tr.), *goad on, urge, spur*

stīpendi-um, -i (n.), *pay, campaign*

stirp-s, -is (f.), *stock, race*

sto, steti, statum, 1 (intr.), *stand, am settled, fixed*

store-a, -ae (f.), *straw*

strāg-ēs, -is (f.), *heap (of slain), carnage*

strēnue (adv.), *strenuously*

strīd-or, -ōris (m.), *squealing, trumpeting (of elephants)*

studi-um, -i (n.), *zeal, enthusiasm, party spirit*

stult-us, -a, -um, *foolish, stupid*

sub (prep. c. abl.), *under ;* (c. acc.) *under, close to (in time or place)*

sub-dūco, -duxi, -ductum, 3 (tr.), *draw up, beach*

sub-icio, -iēci, -iectum, 3 (tr.), *throw, place beneath, subject, suggest*

subiect-us, -a, -um, *subject, underneath, below*

sub-igo, -ēgi, -actum, 3 (tr.), *subdue*

subinde (adv.), *subsequently, from time to time*

subit-us, -a, -um, *sudden ;* (adv.), subito

subsidiāri-us -a, -um, *reserve, in reserve*

subsidi-um, -i (n.), *reserve, support, reinforcement*

sub-sisto, -stiti, —, 3 (intr.), *halt, remain*

sub-stituo, -stitui, -stitutum, 3 (tr.), *substitute*

subter-lābor, -lapsus sum, 3 (intr.), *slip past*

sub-traho, -traxi, -tractum, 3 (tr.), *withdraw, remove*

sub-uenio, -uēni, -uentum, 3 (intr. c. dat.), *come to the help of*

suc-cēdo, -cessi, -cessum, 3 (intr.), *succeed, come up*

success-or, -ōris (m.), *successor*

succlāmo, 1 (intr.), *cry out, interrupt*

suc-curro, -curri, -cursum, 3 (intr.), *run up, help, occur*

suf-ficio, -fēci, -fectum, 3 (tr.), *appoint in place of ;* (intr.), *suffice*

suf-fundo, -fūdi, -fūsum, 3 (tr.), *suffuse ;* (pass.) *suffuse itself*

summ-a, -ae (f.), *supreme issue*

sum-moueo, -mōui, -motum, 2 (tr.), *remove, drive off*

summ-us, -a, -um, *highest, greatest*

sumo, sumpsi, sumptum, 3 (tr.), *take, spend*

supell-ex, -ectilis (f.), *furniture, equipment*

super (prep. c. acc. and adv.), *over, above, in addition to*

superbi-a, -ae (f.), *pride*

superb-us, -a, -um, *proud*

superin-sterno, -strāui, -strātum, 3 (tr.), *lay over*

superi-or, -us, *higher, superior, previous*

superne (adv.), *from above*

supero, 1 (tr. and intr.), *overcome, surpass, pass, am superior*

super-sum, -fui, -esse, *survive, am left over*

super-uenio, -uēni, -uentum, 4 (intr. c. dat.), *come upon, arrive*

supīn-us, *lying face upwards, aimed upwards*

suppl-ex, -icis, *suppliant*

supplicāti-o, -ōnis (f.), *supplication, thanksgiving*

supplici-um, -i (n.), *penalty, punishment*

supplico, 1 (tr.), *supplicate*

suprēm-us, -a, -um, *highest, last*

sus-cipio, -cēpi, -ceptum, 3 (tr.), *undertake*

suspect-us, -a, -um, *suspect*

sus-pendo, -pendi, -pensum, 3 (tr.), *suspend, hang*

sus-tineo, -tenui, -tentum, 2 (tr. and intr.), *keep up, maintain, support, bear up against, hold my own*

su-us, -a, -um, *one's own ;* (strong form of abl.), suapte

tabern-a, -ae (f.), *shop*

tāb-es, is (f.), *corruption*

tabernāculum, -i (n.), *tent*

tabul-a, -ae (f.), *plank*

tacit-us, -a, -um, *silent*

tāl-is, -e, *such*

tam (adv.), *so, so much*

tamen (adv.), *yet, nevertheless*

tango, tetigi, tactum, 3 (tr.), *touch, strike*

tanquam (conj.), *as though, as*

tantum, tantummodo (adv.), *only*

tant-us, -a, -um, *so great, so much*

tard-us, -a, -um, *slow, sluggish*

tect-um, -i (n.), *proof, house*

te-go, -xi, -ctum, 3 (tr.), *cover, mask, protect*

tēl-um, -i (n.), *missile, weapon, spear, javelin*

temerāri-us, -a, -um, *blind, hasty*

temere (adv.), *blindly, hastily, at random*

temerit-ās, -ātis (f.), *blindness, rashness, rash act*

temperanti-a, -ae (f.), *self-control, temperance*

tempero, 1 (tr.), *moderate, control ;* (intr. c. dat. or abl.), *refrain from, restrain*

tempest-ās, -ātis (f.), *time, storm, weather*

templ-um, -i (n.), *temple, precinct*

tempto, 1 (tr.), *try, attempt*

temp-us, -oris (n.), *time, period*

tendo, tetendi, tensum, 3 (tr. and intr.), *stretch, strive, go*

ten-eo, -ui, -tentum, 2 (tr.), *hold, keep, reach*

ten-or, -ōris (m.), *course*

tenu-is, -e, *thin*

tergiuersor, 1 (intr.), *shift, shuffle*

terg-um, -i (n.), *back*

tero, trīui, trītum, 3 (tr.), *crush, spend, pass, waste (time)*

terr-a, -ae (f.), *land, earth*

terreo, 2 (tr.), *terrify*

terrestr-is, -e, *land*

terribil-is, -e, *terrible, alarming*

terr-or, -ōris (m.), *terror*

test-is, -is (m.), *witness*

tex-o, -ui, -tum, 3 (tr.), *weave, contrive*

timeo, 2 (tr.), *fear*

tim-or, -ōris (m.), *fear*

titul-us, -i (m.), *title, inscription*

tolero, 1 (tr.), *endure*

tollo, sustuli, sublatum, 3 (tr.), *raise, take up, take away*

torment-um, -i (n.), *siege-engines, catapult*

tot (indecl. adj.), *so many*

totidem (indecl. adj.), *just so many, just as many*

toties (adv.), *so many times, as often*

tōt-us, -a, -um, *whole, all*

trā-do, -didi, -ditum, 3 (tr.), *hand over, surrender, hand down, relate*

trā-dūco, -duxi, -ductum, 3 (tr.), *lead over, transfer*

traho, traxi, tractum, 3 (tr.), *drag, draw, tow, draw out*

trā-icio, -iēci, -iectum, 3 (tr. and intr.), *take across, cross*

tranquill-us, -a, -um, *quiet, calm*

trans (prep. c. acc.), *across, on the other side of*

transcen-do, -di, -sum, 3 (tr. and intr.), *cross*

trans-eo, -ii, -itum, -īre (tr. and intr.), *go over, cross*

trans-fero, -tuli, -lātum, -ferre (tr.), *carry across, transfer*

trans-fīgo, -fixi, -fixum, 3 (tr.), *transfix; pierce*

transil-io, -ui, —, 4 (tr. and intr.), *leap across*

trans-itus, -ūs (m.), *passage, crossing*

transporto, 1 (tr.), *carry across, transport*

trā-ueho, -uexi, -uectum, 3 (tr.), *carry across*

trepidāti-o, -ōnis (f.), *agitation, hurry, alarm*

trepido, 1 (intr.), *hurry, betray alarm or excitement*

trepid-us, -a, -um, *hurried, excited, alarmed*

tribūn-āl, -ālis (n.), *platform, dais, seat of judgement*

trib-uo, -ui, ūtum, 3 (tr.), *pay tribute, grant ;* tribut-um, -i (n.), *tribute*

trib-us, -ūs (f.), *tribe*

tridu-um, -i (n.), *three days*

trienni-um, -i (n.), *three years*

trist-is, -e, *sad, stern, gloomy*

tritic-um, -i (n.), *wheat*

triumpho, 1 (intr.), *triumph, hold a triumph*

triumph-us, -i (m.), *triumph*

trux, trucis, *fierce*

tub-a, -ae (f.), *trumpet*

tu-eor, -itus sum, 2 (tr.), *keep, guard*

tum (adv.), *then, next*

tumultuāri-us, -a, -um, *hastily raised*

tumultuōs-us, -a, -um, *disorderly, promiscuous*

tumult-us, -ūs (m.), *tumult, uproar, disturbance*

tumul-us, -i (m.), *hill, mound*

tunic-a, -ae (f.), *tunic*

turb-a, -ae (f.), *throng, crowd, confusion*

turm-a, -ae (f.), *troop of cavalry*

tūtor, 1 (tr.), *guard, protect*

tūt-us, -a, -um, *safe ;* (adv.), tūto

uacu-us, -a, -um, *empty*

uag-us, -a, -um, *wandering, reeling*

ualeo, 2 (intr.), *am strong, prevail*

ualid-us, -a, -um, *strong*

uall-is, -is (f.), *valley*

uall-um, -i (n.), *rampart*

uān-us, -a, -um, *empty, vain, false*

uari-us, -a, -um, *various, changeable, chequered*

uasto, 1 (tr.), *waste, lay waste*

uast-us, -a, -um, *huge, waste, wild*

uāt-ēs, -is (m.), *prophet*

ūb-er, -eris, *fertile*

ubi (conj.), *where, when*

uectūr-a, -ae (f.), *carrying, freight-money*

ueho, uexi, uectum, 3 (tr.), *carry ;* (pass.), *ride*

uel (adv. and conj.), *even, or*

uēl-ĕs, -ĭtis (m.), *light-armed soldier*

uēlōcit-ās, -ātis (f.), *speed*

uelut, ueluti (conj.), *just as, as if*

uenēn-um, -i (n.), *poison*

ueni-a, -ae (f.), *leave, pardon*

uenio, uēni, uentum, 4 (intr.), *come*

uent-us, -i (m.), *wind*

uen-us, -eris (f.), *love, passion*

uēr, uēris (n.), *spring*

uerbero, 1 (tr.), *beat, scourge*

uerb-um, -i (n.), *word*

uerecund-us, -a, -um, *respectful, modest*

uereor, 2 (tr. and intr.), *fear*

uert-ex, -icis (m.), *top*

uerto, uerti, uersum, 3 (tr.), *turn ;* (pass.), *turn*

uēr-us, -a, -um, *true ;* (adv.) uero, *assuredly, indeed, however ;* uerum, *but indeed ;* uere, *truly*

uestibul-um, -i (n.), *fore-court*

uestīgi-um, -i (n.), *footprint, track*

uestīment-um, -i (n.) ; uest-is, -is (f.) ; uestīt-us, -ūs (m.), *clothing*

uet-us, -eris ; uetust-us, -a, -um, *old*

ui-a, -ae (f.), *road, way*

uiāt-or, -ōris (m.), *apparitor, usher*

uicāri-us, -i (m.), *substitute*

uīcātim (adv.), *street by street*

uicem, in, *in turn*

uict-or, -ōris (m.) ; uictr-ix, icis (f.), *victor, victorious*

uictōri-a, -ae (f.), *victory*

uictum-a, -ae, (f.), *victim*

uideo, uīdi, uīsum, 2 (tr.), *see ;* (pass.), *seem, am thought, seem good*

uigi-l, -lis (m.), *guard, watchman ;* (adj.), *watchful*

uigili-a, -ae (f.), *wakefulness, watch, guard ;* measure of time = *a fourth part of the night* uīlit-ās, -ātis (f.), *cheapness*

uincio, uinxi, uinctum, 4 (tr.), bind, chain

uinco, ūīci, uictum, 3 (tr.), *conquer*

uincul-um, -i (n.), *chain*

uindico, 1 (tr.), *save, free*

uīn-um, -i (n.), *wine*

uiolāti-o, -ōnis (f.), *violation*

uiolāt-or, -ōris (m.), *violator*

uiolenter (adv.), *violently*

uiolo, 1 (tr.), *violate, wrong*

ui-r, -ri (m.), *man*

uirt-ūs, -ūtis (f.), *virtue, courage, excellence*

uīs, uīm, ui (f.), *force, vigour, power, violence, quantity ;* (plur.) uīr-es, -ium, *strength*

uīs-o, -i, -um, 3 (tr.), *examine, view, go to see*

uīt-a, -ae (f.), *life*

uiti-um, -i (n.), *fault, blemish*

uīto, 1 (tr.), *avoid*

uīu-us, -a, -um, *living*

uix (adv.), *scarcely ;* uixdum, *scarcely yet*

ulciscor, ultus sum, 3 (tr.), *take vengeance on, punish, avenge*

ulteri-or, -us, *further ;* ultim-us, -a, -um, *last, least*

ultrā (adv. and prep. c. acc.), *beyond*

ultrō (adv.), *actually, spontaneously ;* ultro citroque, *this way and that*

unc-us, -i (m.), *hook*

unde, *whence, from which, on the side of whom, wherefore*

ūniuers-us, -a, -um, *all, all together*

unquam (adv.), *ever*

uōciferati-ō, -ōnis (f.), *outcry*

uoco, 1 (tr.), *call, summon*

uolo, uolui, uelle (tr.), *wish*

uolunt-ās, -ātis (f.), *wish, will*

uolupt-ās, -ātis (f.), *pleasure*

uolūto, 1 (tr.), *ponder*

uōtīu-us, -a, -um, *votive*

uōt-um, -i (n.), *vow, prayer*

uoueo, uōui, uotum, 2 (tr.), *vow*

uōx, uōcis (f.), *voice, utterance, sound*

urbān-us, -a, -um, *city*

urb-s, -is (f.), *city*

ur-geo, -si, —, 2 (tr.), *push, press, urge*

ūsitāt-us, -a, -um, *usual*

ūs-us, -ūs (m.), *use, profit, experience*

ut, uti (adv. and conj.), *how, as, when ;* (c. subj.), *in order that, so that, that, how, though*

ut-er, -ra, -rum, *which (of two)? whichever (of two)*

ut-erque, -raque,-rumque, *each (of two), both*

ūtil-is, -e, *useful, profitable*

utique (adv.), *especially*

ūtor, ūsus sum, 3 (tr. c. abl.), *use, enjoy*

utpote (adv.), *seeing that, inasmuch as*

utrimque (adv.), *on both sides*

utrum (adv.), *whether*

uulgo, 1 (tr.), *spread abroad, publish*

uulg-us, -i (n.), *crowd, multitude*

uulnero, 1 (tr.), *wound*

uuln-us, -eris (n.), *wound*

uult-us, -ūs (m.), *countenance, expression, mien*

ux-or, -ōris (f.), *wife*